DCOM Explained

DCOM Explained

Rosemary Rock-Evans

Digital Press

Boston • Oxford • Johannesburg • Melbourne • New Delhi • Singapore

Library of Congress Cataloging-in-Publication Data

Rock-Evans, R. (Rosemary)
    DCOM explained / by Rosemary Rock-Evans.
      p.   cm.
    Includes index.
    ISBN 1–55558–216–8 (alk. paper)
    1. Electronic data processing—Distributed processing. 2. Object-
Oriented programming (Computer science) 3. DCOM (Computer architecture)
I. Title.
QA76.9.D5R63 1998
005.2'76—dc21
                                        98-16648
                                           CIP

British Library Cataloguing-in-Publication Data

A catalogue record for this book is available from the British Library.

The publisher offers special discounts on bulk orders of this book.
For information, please contact:
Manager of Special Sales
Butterworth–Heinemann
225 Wildwood Avenue
Woburn, MA 01801-2041
Tel: 781-960-2500
Fax: 781-960-2620

For information on all Butterworth–Heinemann publications available, contact our World Wide Web home page at: http://www.bh.com

Printed and bound in the United Kingdom

Transferred to Digital Printing, 2011

Contents

Acknowledgments

Preface

Disclaimer

Although the author has attempted to provide an up-to-date and factually correct description of DCOM and its functionality in this book, features and functions may change over time, particularly as some of the functions described have only just been released and, as all developers are aware, the features of software products in particular can change very rapidly over time.

The author, therefore, cannot accept responsibility for any errors or inaccuracies in this book and cannot accept responsibility for any loss or damages occasioned as a result of decisions made on the basis of this book. Although this is not an "official Microsoft textbook," Microsoft staff have seen the basic notes for the book and agreed on its accuracy at the time of preparation.

This book covers the DCOM features provided as part of Windows NT 4. Although mention has been made of the Active Directory being provided in Windows NT 5, this book does not otherwise cover the features likely to be in Windows NT 5, such as distributed time, as at the time of writing it was unclear in many cases how they would be provided or whether in fact they would eventually be provided. If this book proves popular, an update will be considered once NT 5 has been released and is stable enough to discuss in detail.

Acknowledgments

The author would like to thank all the staff at Microsoft who provided information for this book, as well as the staff of Digital and Software AG who also provided useful information during the investigation.

Particular thanks are due to Mike Platt of Microsoft UK, who provided extensive help, support, and technical details.

Introduction to This Book

What Is This Book About?

This book describes the functions of DCOM—Microsoft's Distributed Component Object Model—and the services based on DCOM, which can be used to build distributed applications.

The aim of this book is not to teach you how to develop distributed applications using DCOM, but to explain what functions DCOM provides so that you are able to use DCOM more effectively, understand the options open to you when using DCOM, and understand something of the types of application that can be built using DCOM.

We have concentrated also on explaining on which platforms besides Windows NT the services are found so that you know more about the limitations and possibilities of developing with DCOM.

Who Is It For?

Technical designers will find this book useful, as will systems analysts, systems designers, programmers with an interest in design, technical architects, and possibly technical managers and project leaders. If you really have little idea what DCOM is or does and want a simple-to-read overview of what you can do with it—this book is for you!

Any Bias?

Many books on the market about COM, Microsoft technologies, CORBA (the OMG's Common Object Request Broker Architecture), objects, and so on are written by the vendors' employees. On the one hand, this has the advantage that the information in them is "from the horse's mouth." On the other hand, the information you get may be biased toward the products they are describing—perhaps a glowing picture is painted of the merits without much attention being paid to the problems. It has been particularly noticeable that books about CORBA have often included some quite savage criticisms of DCOM.

This book contains no such bias. First, I haven't worked for the vendors of either DCOM (that is, Microsoft!) or the vendors of CORBA products. Perhaps of more importance, however, is that my job involves intensive examination of these products for evaluation purposes. Thus, on the one hand, I have access to the technical details of the products, but on the other hand, I am in the happy position of being able to give you a balanced picture of the advantages and disadvantages of DCOM and how it compares with CORBA.

Not only will you be getting a description of DCOM from this book, but it will be a balanced, independent one.

2

What Is DCOM?

> ▶ **DCOM** is an **architecture** on which services to build distributed applications are based
>
> ▶ It provides a range of services to **support distributed processing at runtime** and to support the developer when building distributed applications
>
> ▶ The purpose of the DCOM runtime services is to provide an environment which is **secure, available, reliable,** and gives **good performance**
>
> ▶ The purpose of the DCOM development environment is to **save the programmer effort**

Microsoft's DCOM (Distributed Component Object Model) is based on Microsoft's own COM (Component Object Model). COM defines how components interact and is an architecture for simple interprocess communication. It defines a basic model of communication using Microsoft's equivalent of objects—components. DCOM supports the same model of component interaction, but supports *distributed* interprocess communication. Thus DCOM is an architecture that enables components (processes) to communicate across a network.

The architecture includes *two types of service*—services provided at runtime and services the developer can use to develop distributed applications.

Examples of the sorts of service provided at runtime include security services (authorization, authentication, and encryption), load balancing, guaranteed delivery, deferred delivery, triggering, automatic multithreading, shared memory management, distributed transaction support, message queuing support, broadcasting, multicasting, time services, synchronization (support for asynchronous and synchronous communication), context bridging, routing, plus many more.

Very few people realize just how extensive the service support in DCOM is until they "get under the covers." DCOM enables the developer to completely avoid having to write complicated communication code at the low level sockets or network software level. Thus DCOM takes care of all the communication between machines. DCOM is also supplied with a set of runtime libraries that handle all the functions of communication—session handling, synchronization, data format translation, buffering, and fault identification and handling.

We will be describing what each of the services means, what it aims to do, and how Microsoft has tackled the problem in this book. The main objectives in providing these services are first, to save the programmer the effort of having to write all these services; and second, to provide a secure, resilient, reliable, available, high-performance environment on which to build a distributed application.

Distributed processing is particularly prone to things going wrong. The network can go down, machines can fail, remote databases can fail, performance can be diabolically slow—hundreds of new possible problems can occur because the environment is a distributed one. The services in DCOM either ensure the errors or problems are handled automatically or, if they cannot be handled automatically, errors are trapped and the program is informed.

Anyone who has written a distributed application knows that without this sort of support software, hundreds and possibly thousands of lines of code (difficult, complex code) have to be written by the programmer to support the distribution. By using DCOM, all this effort is saved.

DCOM Is Middleware

DCOM is just one of a whole range of products which can be classified as *middleware*. Middleware is *"off the shelf connectivity software, which supports distributed processing"* at runtime and which is *"used by developers to build distributed software."* It is the software that binds the parts of a heterogeneous system together.

Whereas network software handles the communication between one machine and another, middleware provides the developer with services that support process-to-process communication across the network. Processes can be running on machines of different makes and, in most advanced middleware products, processes can be running on machines using different operating systems.

The effect of the middleware, then, is to make all the machines appear as though they were one "virtual machine." For example, a process on a Sun SPARC machine running Solaris can communicate, using middleware, with a process on, for example, the IBM MVS mainframe or, alternatively, a process on a Compaq machine running Windows NT. The processes can also usually be in different languages.

Figure 2.1
Middleware enables processes to communicate across a network

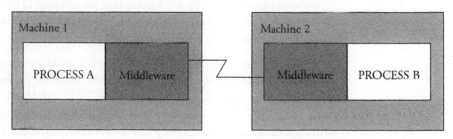

DCOM was not originally a cross-operating system architecture. When it was first released, it could only provide internetwork communication between Microsoft Windows NT- (and 95-) based machines.

Microsoft has, however, extended the support of DCOM to other operating systems by using partnerships with third party companies to either port DCOM services to Unix and the mainframe or provide access from these platforms to DCOM services. Four companies have so far become involved—Software AG, Digital, Hewlett Packard, and Level8. We will be seeing how these "versions" of DCOM inter-operate with DCOM on Windows NT in Chapter Eleven.

This said, however, most of DCOM's full functionality is to be found only on Windows NT, and DCOM services are tightly integrated with Windows NT. In fact, some of the services we have come to expect from middleware products are provided by Windows NT in the Microsoft environment. We will see in Chapter Ten how Microsoft is gradually including all the services we might call middleware services in the Windows NT operating system.

DCOM and Other Types of Middleware

There are hundreds of middleware products on the market. Perhaps the best known category of middleware products are the database connectivity products provided by companies such as Intersolv, Information Builders, Shadow, Oracle, and Sybase with their ODBC (Open Database Connectivity) drivers and gateways.

Other types of middleware include MOM (Message-Oriented Middleware), ORBs (Object Request Brokers), RPC (Remote Procedure Call), and DTPM (Distributed Transaction Processing Middleware). Other well-known middleware products include Tuxedo and TOP END (DTPMs); MQSeries, BEAmessageQ, VCOM, and PIPES (MOM); Orbix, DSOM, VisiBroker, and XShell (ORBs).

So how can one classify DCOM—is it an ORB, a DTPM, a MOM product, an RPC, or a database connectivity product? The answer is that DCOM is unique because it is a complete hybrid of all these types.

There are five main strands to Microsoft's middleware service offerings—its database connectivity services, its MOM services, its transaction processing services, its links to the mainframe (CICS and IMS), and its RPC services. The MS RPC provides the foundation for all the other services; although the developer sees only the component based interface, he or she has no need to program to the RPC mechanism.

Thus, DCOM provides distributed messaging services, object request broker services, distributed transaction services, and data connectivity services all layered over its own RPC mechanism. Microsoft, therefore, does not provide a set of completely disparate and unconnected set of products, but one integrated solution with multiple capability. The user does not have to choose a product or more than one product to support applications, nor does a user have to learn different product approaches or philosophies. He or she uses one set of services, which are already available if he or she is using Windows NT.

Messaging capability is provided by the Messaging services in DCOM, transaction services are provided by the Transaction Server in DCOM, database connectivity is provided by the database connectivity services, and so on. The developer could use several services together, accessing the queues in the Messaging server and data in various data sources and putting all of these under transaction control.

DCOM is thus a special product and unique on the market. Microsoft's aim is to provide the developer with all the services needed to develop a distributed application from one single source and using one common interface—that used in COM.

3

Main Concepts Used in DCOM

- ► Globally Unique Identifier
- ► Classes, Objects, and Components
- ► Class IDs
- ► Interfaces
- ► Polymorphism and Encapsulation

- ► Inheritance
- ► Interface Containment and Aggregation
- ► IUnknown
- ► Monikers

All Object Request Brokers (ORB) conforming to CORBA use the same conceptual model. Microsoft's model of object-based processing—COM—is, however, different, and it is worthwhile understanding the concepts Microsoft uses, as it affects the capabilities of DCOM and the sorts of application a developer can build.

Thus, although it is not, strictly speaking, essential that the developer has a detailed grasp of the concepts used in COM, a basic understanding helps in any discussion. This chapter thus provides a brief overview of the main concepts used.

We will be introducing other concepts such as Outgoing Interfaces, IDispatch, and all other terms in the context of the functions they provide. The terms you see here are the basic building blocks on which everything in COM is based.

GUID

GUIDs are Globally Unique Identifiers for things. The things in question can be anything—interfaces, classes/components, programs, and so on, but within

DCOM they are used specifically for classes and interfaces. The important point about a GUID is that it is unique, whereas a name (however long) may not be. The number used is a 128 bit/16 byte value which is created automatically by DCOM services. Microsoft's GUIDGEN.EXE and UUIDGEN.EXE both automatically generate GUIDs.

Different mechanisms can be used to create the identifier so that it is unique, but the one most commonly employed uses a combination of the IEEE machine identifier of the host used to create the thing, (this is obtained from the network card and subsequently has no meaning), the date/time of creation (to nanosecond level), plus, if need be, an incremental counter. The resulting GUID then has the sort of format shown below:

00000001-0000-0000-C000-000000000045

The resulting number has no meaning, but the use of the network card number ensures that the resulting number is unique. For systems without network cards, other algorithms are used to generate the value.

GUIDs are the same as the UUIDs (Universal Unique Identifiers) used by the OSF (Open Software Foundation—now the Open Group) when they developed DCE (Distributed Computing Environment). We will be learning more about DCE in a later chapter.

Programmers do have to know about GUIDs, but in their programs they do not have to use them directly—they can use the names of things, which are then cross-referenced within their programs to the GUIDs themselves. We will be seeing later how this works. But DCOM doesn't use names at all; it relies entirely on GUIDs because of the need for uniqueness (especially in a cross-company or even intercompany context).

Classes, Objects, and Components

Anyone used to object programming will know already that the basis of this paradigm of processing is some "thing" which is identified by the methods or functions it supports. So, we might have a customer "thing" with functions which "update the customer name," "query the address," "calculate the credit limit," and so on. Each method has parameters input and output to the method in much the same way we might make a subroutine call in a conventional program. So, one obvious example may be the method "update customer name" with an input parameter of the customer's new name.

A *component* is the generic name given by Microsoft to this type of thing and its methods. A *class* is a block of machine code based around some concept and which has methods which can be invoked.

Figure 3.1
The customer component with its methods and parameters

CUSTOMER
      Update Customer name
            IN: New-Customer-name
            IN: Customer-ID
            IN: Old-Customer-name
            OUT: Result
      Query Customer address
            IN: Customer-ID
            OUT: Customer-address

In practice, component and class tend to be used almost interchangeably by developers because for each component there is one class. The main difference is that the term component is used for the thing throughout its life—from design concept to source code to machine code. Class refers to the component at a certain point in this cycle—when it becomes machine code.

Microsoft also defines a class as "a particular implementation of certain interfaces," which means that theoretically you have to know what the interfaces are before you can define a class. Classes are *executable blocks* of machine code (or interpretable code), as opposed to source code—thus the use of the term "implementation" in its definition.

Machine resident blocks of code are called *objects*. An object is thus a single binary version of a component which has been compiled for that platform, which runs on that platform and that can be found in an actual DLL or EXE file. The word class is thus used as a generic term for an executable block of code implementing a set of defined interfaces. The occurrences of those blocks of code are termed objects. Objects are usually given the same class name and class identifier to show they are effectively the same "thing."

Thus in COM, the most important concept is actually the class rather than the object or, for that matter, the component. Developers know of the existence of classes, not their implementations in files or libraries.

CLSID

The *Class ID* (CLSID) is the identifier of the class. CLSIDs are in effect GUIDs—unique global identifiers used to identify the class—and are generated in exactly the same way as GUIDs. Not all classes need a CLSID. Only classes that need to be invoked from external processes need to be identified.

Interface

The interface defines the class, one or more methods that can be invoked on a class, as well as the parameters for the method. Client processes invoke classes via interfaces.

For example:

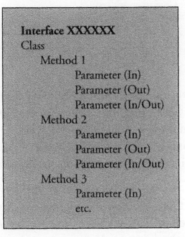

Figure 3.2
Example of an Interface

Interface XXXXXX
Class
 Method 1
  Parameter (In)
  Parameter (Out)
  Parameter (In/Out)
 Method 2
  Parameter (In)
  Parameter (Out)
  Parameter (In/Out)
 Method 3
  Parameter (In)
  etc.

Every interface has a name (which by convention usually begins with I). The name is used in the program source code, but internally, all interfaces have identifiers based on the GUID. Interfaces are described using Microsoft's *Interface Definition Language* (IDL). More details of this are provided in Chapter Five.

Unlike CORBA, a class can have more than one interface. Each of the interfaces describes only that class, but each interface can describe a sort of view of the class's methods and parameters.

All interfaces are "strongly typed" which means that once they have been implemented they cannot be changed. (Microsoft uses the term "immutable.") They obtain an identifier and a name, and once the GUID has been allocated the contents must remain fixed.

If used correctly, clients see only the methods they use in an interface. We can see that this approach is exactly the same principle as that used by DBMSs when they use "sub-schemas" and "views." So what happens if the class is enhanced to support more methods or the operation of an existing method is changed?

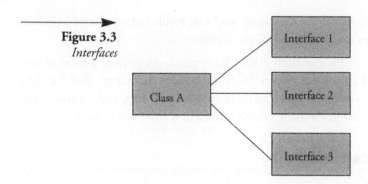

Figure 3.3
Interfaces

Where new methods are added, a new interface to the class is added. By doing this any existing client using the class can continue using the existing interface without needing any change to its code, but new clients that use the new methods can be added.

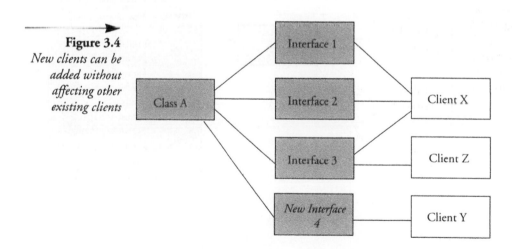

Figure 3.4
New clients can be added without affecting other existing clients

Where the existing method of the class is altered, the developer must see which interfaces are affected and then find all the clients that use these interfaces to see if they still operate correctly. These sorts of changes may result in recompilation of classes and clients with the new interface.

Thus, new methods may not affect a client, as it can be shielded from change by the creation of new interfaces. But changes to an existing method (new parameters, new error messages) may well result in both a new interface or even interfaces and change to all the clients.

The purpose of this approach is thus fairly clear—to provide a form of version control and to protect clients from some types of change. But the class developer has to ensure he keeps all these interfaces in step, and he also needs to know which clients are using which interfaces if there is a change.

Polymorphism and Encapsulation

Microsoft states that all interfaces are *polymorphic* in DCOM and also support *encapsulation*. Polymorphism describes the ability to have a single statement invoke different function implementations at different times. As such, COM interfaces are polymorphic because the developer can replace the methods/functions in the class over time but still keep the same interface.

Similarly, the interface encapsulates the behavior.

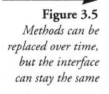

Figure 3.5
Methods can be replaced over time, but the interface can stay the same

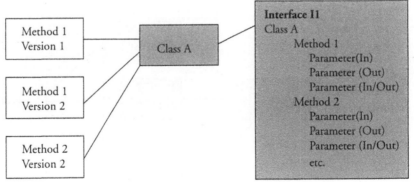

Inheritance

The word inheritance in object-oriented programming is usually used to mean that one "object" inherits from another object. Thus a little red widget, for example, may inherit its actual code (methods) from a perhaps more general object called the widget.

This is inheritance of the code itself and is designed to help save effort when programming. The programmer writes a general purpose object, then gradually specializes it with inherited objects each with their own special methods, until a hierarchy of objects results. The main widget, for example, may depress when clicked by the mouse (method "depress"), but the little red widget may turn red when clicked and also emit a sound such as a piercing shriek (methods, "turn red" and "emit piercing shriek").

This approach has obvious advantages, but it is a problem to control. If one programmer decides to change the base object, all the other objects will be changed automatically even if their programmers didn't want them to be. If the widget designer added a method to emit a beep when the widget was pressed, the little red widget would not only emit a piercing shriek but a beep as well!

If object inheritance is used you need a really good change and version control system to keep things under control. Microsoft believes that this approach to inheritance is perhaps too risky and thus decided that they would not support object (in their case class) inheritance.

Instead, they recommend that to achieve similar results without the possible side effects, the best approach may be to copy the class and rename it, adding to it or adapting it as necessary, or alternatively use the base class and simply invoke other extra classes if additional functionality is needed. This latter approach provides similar effects to inheritance, but uses the concepts of containment and aggregation (more in a few paragraphs).

Although class inheritance is not supported, Microsoft does support interface inheritance. Interface inheritance is only applied to reuse the definition of the base interface. The programmer may start from one base interface, then add a new one with new methods which is, in effect, inherited from the base one. If one interface inherits from another, it includes all the functions that the other interface defines.

All interfaces, however, inherit directly from IUnknown (of which more later).

Interface Containment and Aggregation

A class can delegate some of its functionality to other classes.

Where the interface to the calling class describes only its methods, not those of its called/delegated classes, the COM model refers to this as *containment*.

Where the class actually exposes some of the functionality of the called objects in its interface, COM refers to this as *aggregation*.

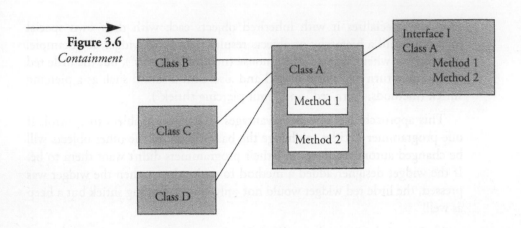

Figure 3.6
Containment

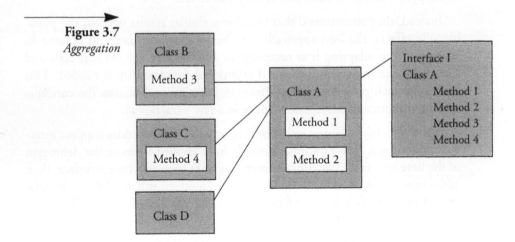

Figure 3.7
Aggregation

IUnknown Interface

The IUnknown Interface is a fundamental interface containing basic operations common to all classes and interfaces. IUnknown has three methods—QueryInterface, AddRef, and Release.

QueryInterface is used to find out what interfaces a class supports. The client first uses an Interface Name to start the process. Clients will have been given the name of the interface they should use, as the starting point of the invocation process. COM then returns the pointer to this interface.

The client can then use this pointer and the QueryInterface method to find out what other interfaces exist on the same class. As Microsoft puts it: "The GUID of the interface is input and what returns is an interface on itself through an accompanying output parameter typed as a generic void!" This facility can be used both to find out the other interfaces and also to see if an interface is still valid.

The **AddRef** and **Release** methods are used to keep track of how many occurrences/instances of an object there are on that host. We will look at the mechanics of how this works in the section on triggers, but it is important to understand that the count of occurrences is done by the classes themselves, not COM, using these method calls. In effect, the class has to be written so that it both keeps a count of how many instances there are and also makes sure the class is released once it is no longer used.

It is worth mentioning that if aggregation or containment is used, the developer needs to implement one set of IUnknown functions for all the interfaces, not just the main class's interface.

Monikers

Monikers are alias names that can be used to provide alternative names for files. In general, file names don't provide any information about what is in the file—it could be an executable, paragraph in a document, range of spreadsheet cells, range of data, or even a query on a database.

A Moniker is a class/component which encapsulates what the file is. In effect, the name itself becomes a component accessed via the IMoniker interface. Clients always work with names through this interface, not the names themselves, and the Moniker class defines operations which are used to locate components or perform some action on components of that type. Each Moniker class has a different CLSID and its own semantics as to what sort of class and operations it can refer to.

Microsoft has defined its own types of moniker—files, items, and so on, but clearly new ones can be added. Generic moniker operations include the ability to bind to an object to which it points, binding to the class's storage and *reduction*—rewriting itself into another equivalent moniker.

4

The Main Services of DCOM

DCOM is much easier to understand if you first see how all the different parts that make up the "middleware" services fit together and what they are. In this chapter I describe each service in brief, showing where it fits in relation to the others. In the following chapters each one of these services is described in detail.

I always believe a picture helps enormously in an explanation. Below you find a diagram I will be using throughout the rest of the book, which shows the parts of DCOM in overview.

DCOM is an architecture that groups a set of services used to build distributed systems. Unfortunately what constitutes a DCOM service and what doesn't isn't that precise within Microsoft's own literature, but we have defined it to mean *any service capable of being used to build distributed systems,* then we get round the problem of whether MSMQ is DCOM or not, whether MTS is DCOM and so on.

COM Interface

All the services of DCOM are accessible via the COM interface—a *component-* and *interface*-based interface to all the services of DCOM—not only application components. Put another way, DCOM services are invoked in exactly the same way as a developer may invoke the methods on an application component.

Thus, to access security services, for example, the programmer invokes security methods on security classes. Similarly, to use the Transaction services in MTS, the programmer uses classes and methods specifically designed to handle distributed transactions. In effect, the paradigm used by the developer for building applications is exactly the same as that he or she will use to invoke the services in DCOM.

Figure 4.1
*Overview of
DCOM services*

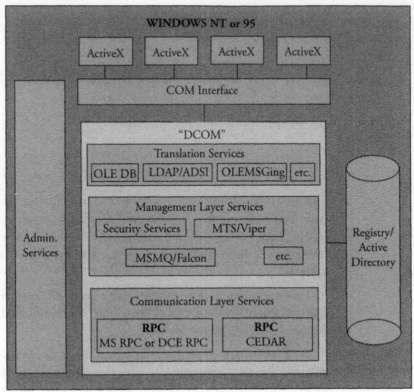

Windows NT

As we have shown it in the diagram, DCOM is a fundamental part of Windows NT and Windows 95. In fact, DCOM services are, in effect, embedded in Windows NT and are free with it, but this does not mean that DCOM services are not available on other platforms. In fact, there are limitations at the moment with the picture for other platforms looking more like that shown below, but this could change in the future.

One of the difficulties of the embedded approach to service provision, however, is that it makes it much more difficult for companies trying to port DCOM onto other platforms to both decide whether to provide a service and to provide the service itself. When a service is tightly integrated with an operating system, it can be difficult to unscramble the logic enough to provide the

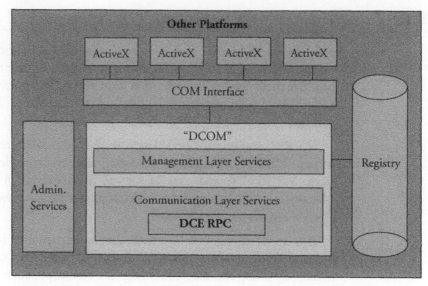

Figure 4.2
*DCOM on other
platforms*

equivalent on other platforms. We will see that this is particularly the case with features such as threading support.

There are services in Windows NT, such as its time clock, which are very useful when building distributed systems (and thus ought to be considered a part of DCOM), but which are not provided in the same way on other platforms and which are not part of the plans of other vendors in their ports of DCOM. We will be looking at both the services provided by Windows NT and the services on other platforms in separate later chapters.

ActiveX

Clients invoke the methods on DCOM services or invoke application components. These application components can be *ActiveX* components or *OLE Automation* components. ActiveX components are perhaps the more interesting because they are intended to be portable—capable of being developed for more than one platform. So expect to see ActiveX components on Solaris, HP-UX, even the MVS mainframe in the future! A separate chapter explains the difference between ActiveX and OLE Automation components and describes the tools which can be used to develop components. Note that Microsoft is now downplaying the term ActiveX in favor of "just class," but I believe it is useful to discuss the tools and concepts by using the ActiveX term.

MS RPC

MS RPC is Microsoft's core Remote Procedure Call technology. It is based on the OSF's DCE RPC standard. Microsoft did not use the OSF's code to produce their implementation, but used the API and developed their own code. The implementation is thus DCE compliant, but is not OSF sourced.

MS RPC can be used by a developer, but Microsoft prefers the developer to treat MS RPC as enabling technology hidden from view by other interfaces. MS RPC should thus be viewed as a foundation product used by Microsoft and their partners to build other enabling software or middleware. It is the foundation for DCOM.

It is worth noting that Microsoft developed their own implementation in order to avoid having to pay OSF license fees (and keep core technology in house). By doing this they could keep the cost of products such as Windows NT and DCOM services down. On other platforms communication with MS RPC is achieved by other implementations of DCE RPC. We discuss DCE and RPCs in the chapter on MS RPC.

OLE DB and Active Data Objects

OLE DB and Active Data Objects provide class, interface, and method-based access to data—data in tables, data in databases, data in files, and so on. The aim of OLE DB is to provide a common API with which to access data of various sorts—thus it could be relational data or data in flat files or even data in spreadsheets or hierarchical file systems.

OLE DB is not a replacement for ODBC, but supplementary to it. The ODBC (Open Database Connectivity) standard was developed by Microsoft but was intended to be used for access to relational DBMSs. Microsoft supplies a number of ODBC drivers (translation products that convert the ODBC dialect to the dialect of SQL used by each vendor) and its own driver manager (which routes requests to the correct driver).

OLE DB extends this basic relational database connectivity solution to incorporate access to data sources of other kinds—not just relational databases. OLE DB is thus a more powerful product. The reason this category of service is described with the overall box called "translation services" is because there has to be translation of the method invocations from an "object invocation"–based approach to an "API" approach—whether this is translation to SQL or translation to some other data manipulation language.

MTS (Microsoft Transaction Server)

Microsoft's distributed transaction processing service was code-named VIPER and is now called Microsoft Transaction Server. MTS enables a developer to write applications that access multiple distributed and different DBMSs (MS SQL Server, Informix, DB2/6000) or "Resource Managers" (like file systems or queue managers) under transaction control. MTS coordinates the update of data on these different DBMSs and ensures that either all the data is updated successfully on all the DBMSs or none of the updates are made. To do this it uses the well known approach of two-phase commit.

MTS uses a standard called the **XA** standard from the X/Open Group and Microsoft's own object-based approach called **OLETX.** Unlike the CORBA-based products, Transaction Server does not support OTS (Object Transaction Services).

Transaction Server is based on DCOM, providing a value-added service based on the DCOM model and using all the other DCOM services. Thus, for example, the developer could use the services of OLE DB to access different databases and files in a "transparent" way, but also put the updates of the data in all these different files under transaction control.

MTS was originally priced separately, but is part of Windows NT 4 at no additional cost. It uses the same COM object-based interface to build transaction-based applications out of prebuilt components written in different languages.

Cedar

Cedar is the internal code name for the Microsoft technology, technology which works in conjunction with Microsoft's Transaction Server (MTS). It has just been renamed COM TI (Transaction Integrator) but as most Microsoft literature still refers to it as Cedar, I have used this name in the book. Cedar makes CICS and IMS programs appear as though they were MTS components. Thus IBM CICS and IMS programs running on MVS mainframes can be placed under the control of transactions running under Windows NT. MTS and Cedar communicate with one another to translate CICS and IMS calls to the equivalent MTS calls. Microsoft has a "zero mainframe footprint" strategy, which means that all mainframe interaction is achieved from a Windows NT platform base using gateways and proxy components—no modules are needed on the mainframe.

Cedar is based on technology from TransAccess. TransAccess technology (it supplied an RPC product) was acquired from Netwise in November 1995, and the original TransAccess product is still being supported by third-party companies. But TransAccess technology was used to develop Cedar and now underpins its operation.

MSMQ (Microsoft Message Queue Server)

MSMQ, originally code-named Falcon, is a message queuing service. MSMQ is short for the full name now given to the service of Microsoft Message Queue Server.

Message queuing is not the same as mail messaging. Certainly the approach taken is similar, because there is store and forward capability built into MSMQ, but the difference is that whereas mail messaging handles mail between people, MSMQ handles messages between computer processes—messages that the receiving process uses in its processing. Thus, MSMQ enables one *process* to communicate with another *process* using messages that are stored along the route they have taken on queues.

If we think for a moment about the possible ways one process could communicate with another, we can see that one process could call another by name—in effect invoking functions (this is the default approach used within DCOM), or we could have a form of processing whereby one process does not directly invoke the other process, but sends it a message (the approach used in MSMQ). The approaches are complementary—both are useful means of communication.

Message queuing services don't request processes to be activated with input and output parameters. Instead, message queuing products provide a much looser form of communication whereby the data needed by the receiving process is stored in the message and the message is then sent; there is no direct invocation of the process.

Whereas the invocation of a process often has to be quite tightly coupled with the sending of data and receipt of the reply synchronized, processes which send messages can be very loosely coupled. The process sending the message can continue with its processing after the message has been sent— acting asynchronously.

Microsoft released the beta test version of FALCON, as it was then known, in the third quarter of 1996. It was released in December 1997. MSMQ is part of Windows NT 4 at no additional cost and is due to be fully integrated into DCOM as part of Windows NT 5.

LDAP/ADSI and the Active Directory

The Active Directory is the store or database holding information about the location of components, the users and groups in the system, the passwords of those users, the components that those users can access, plus other data needed to drive the system at runtime. In the same way that practically all commercial applications need data in databases in order to operate, DCOM uses the Active Directory to drive its operation. The Active Directory is due to be a replacement for the Registry files used at the moment.

LDAP (Lightweight Directory Access Protocol) and ADSI (Active Directory Service Interface) are simply APIs and the means by which developers can access the Directory services. More than one option is provided, and we will be seeing in the chapter on Directory services that Microsoft is providing access to other Directory systems as well as their own via these interfaces. This is the reason we have placed the service box under the heading of "translation" since although access via ADSI to the Active Directory requires no translation of the API, access to other Directory services will.

Security Services

Security services—the ability to control who has access to the system and which components they can access—is a key requirement of software to support distributed computing. It is of little use if the platform on which the user signs on has checks, but the moment the user is transferred to another computer via the underlying middleware, none of the security checks are transferred along the way. Security services need themselves to be distributed so that there is "end to end" security checking.

DCOM's security services are currently provided primarily by Windows NT, but plans for security mean that in the future DCOM's security services could indeed be end-to-end and cover other platforms besides Windows NT. We will look at both the current checks and the future in the chapter on security services.

OLEMSGing

We have not included a lot of detail about this service in this book, as it is probably of lesser interest than the other more powerful services. OLEMSGing, however, provides component-based access—access using the DCOM style of invocation of methods on an interface—to the services of Microsoft's mail products. It means that a developer can access data, for example, and then compose an e-mail message using the data, from the same program, and all using the same interface and programming paradigm.

In Summary

Perhaps key to the understanding of DCOM is that Microsoft does not provide a set of completely disparate and unconnected set of products, but one integrated solution with multiple capability. Thus, for example, Transaction Server and MSMQ are in fact just services that are part of one integrated architecture—DCOM.

This is an enormously powerful concept. It is worth pointing out that no other middleware products on the market are integrated in this way with all the services a developer may need to build a distributed system integrated within one product and with one interface.

In general, if the developer is using other products and wants to build applications that need distributed transaction processing capability, for example, he or she uses a *Distributed Transaction Processing Middleware* (DTPM) product like Tuxedo or TOP END. If he then needs to send messages using store and forward capability, he uses a message queuing product such as MQSeries, BEAmessageQ, or VCOM.

If our developer uses DCOM, however, he or she does not have to choose a product or more than one product to support applications, nor does he or she have to learn different product approaches or philosophies—our programmer uses one set of services (which are already available if he or she is using Windows NT), one common interface, and uses the needed services. If messaging capability is needed, our programmer uses the Messaging services in DCOM; if transaction services are needed, our programmer uses Transaction Server in DCOM; if database connectivity is needed, he or she uses OLE DB; if security services services are needed, he or she uses the security API, and so on.

One might assume that such a powerful and all-inclusive "product" was developed using some grand strategy—where Microsoft devised the complete architecture of the product with all its services before they started to build the parts. In fact, the architecture has evolved and grown as much out of pragmatism and customer demand than as a result of some grand preconceived strategy.

Certainly a strategy does underpin all development that is the use of components, the use of a common interface to access services, and the use of a common model—COM. But DCOM was built on Windows NT because it made more sense for Microsoft engineers to reuse what they already had. Similarly, Transaction Server and MSMQ were built using COM and Windows NT because it was the most pragmatic and cost-effective route.

Perhaps equally surprising, given the integrated nature of DCOM, is the fact that development of the various products described in this report is not the responsibility of one particular group within Microsoft. In practice, the development has been distributed over the whole organization, with COM and DCOM being the responsibility of the OLE group based in Redmond; the networking components of DCOM being the responsibility of the networking group; the Directory being the responsibility of the Windows NT group; and Falcon being the brainchild of Jim Allchin. The DCOM architecture was designed by Bob Atkinson and Kraig Brockschmidt—both long-serving Microsoft employees.

So what you are seeing described in this book is something of a phenomenon. An integrated middleware product based on Windows NT, which was developed by a number of separate teams within Microsoft but which remains an integrated product, and a product which is unique on the market in covering the services it does—messaging, database and data connectivity, distributed transaction processing support, object/component-based access (ORB-like services), RPC services, plus other middleware services.

5

COM

> ▶ Same object/component-based interface used to access all services
>
> ▶ All services built using COM
>
> ▶ Components invoke methods on other components—these components can be user or services
>
> ▶ Interface based on MIDL (based on DCE IDL)
>
> ▶ Approach can be "static"(using stubs and proxies) or "dynamic" (using Type Libraries)

We saw in the last chapter that all applications access the services of DCOM as well as the components themselves using the same class and interface-based approach. In other words, all the services are accessed via a common object-based interface or "API." The API is implemented in the COM Library.

In this chapter we explore this concept further by looking at the concept of the client at the two ways in which interfaces can be used, via the use of stubs and VTables or using Type Libraries. We will also be briefly covering the IDispatch interface.

Application

Microsoft uses the term application in a generic way to mean either a client or a server or a collection of clients and servers. All applications (clients or servers) have some set responsibilities whether they are clients or servers. On application startup they must:

▶ verify the COM library version

▶ and initialize the COM library

Figure 5.1
*The COM
interface*

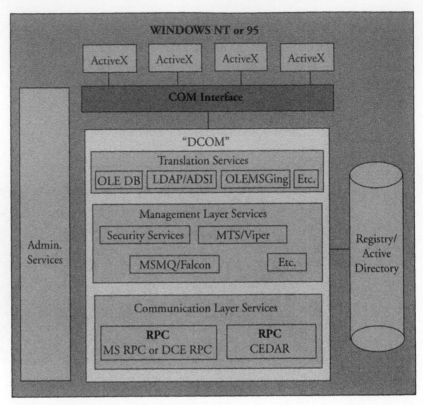

On application shutdown they must "uninitialize" the COM library.

All applications must also perform their own memory management during processing, and we will see how DCOM provides commands to help in this in a later chapter.

Client

A client is any application requesting for an object to be instantiated via DCOM/COM; as such the term "client" really describes a role. Clients are responsible for:

▶ creating instances of objects

▶ initializing the object via its Initialization interface

▶ and calling the object's release function when the client has finished with it

Server

A server is a collection of one or more classes that can be invoked by clients.

A server enables components/classes to be grouped together into packages that execute in the same address space. Servers can be deployed as a single unit and where services such as Microsoft Transaction Server are used also share security. (Within MTS servers are component packages.) Servers exist partly to help improve performance but also to aid fault isolation and ease administration.

There are two main types of server—a Dynamic Link Library, which can be loaded into and will execute within the client's address space—and EXEs—standalone executables.

DLLs are often referred to as "in-process" servers because they execute in the address space of the client. EXEs are often referred to as "out-of-process" because they execute out of the address space of the client—either on the same machine or remotely on another machine. Where the EXE is on a different machine than the client it may be referred to as a remote server to differentiate it from an EXE on the same machine as the client where it may be called a local server.

IDL–Interface Definition Language

We saw in the second chapter that an interface is the contract between the client and the server. The client invokes methods on a class in the server using the interface. The interface defines the class, one or more methods which can be invoked on a class, as well as the parameters for the method.

All interfaces are defined using a purpose built language called *MIDL* or Microsoft's IDL (Interface Definition Language). Microsoft's IDL (MIDL) was based on the DCE RPC IDL from the OSF (Open Group). It is a C++-like language but is actually language independent and built to be language independent. Its specific role is to define the interface. Microsoft added extensions to the basic IDL provided with DCE first, to make it more "object oriented" and second, to ensure it supported COM. At one time, Microsoft also supported another language called MODL (Microsoft Object Definition Language) to define interfaces aimed at type libraries but this has been discontinued.

The format of the header to an interface in IDL defines:

▶ the Interface name—the programmer uses the interface name

▶ the key word "object" to show it is a COM interface

Figure 5.2
The Interface

Interface XXXXXX
Class
    Method 1
        Parameter (In)
        Parameter (Out)
        Parameter (In/Out)
    Method 2
        Parameter (In)
        Parameter (Out)
        Parameter (In/Out)
    Method
        Parameter In)
        etc.

▶ the GUID of the interface—this is generated when the developer requests that a GUID be allocated to the Interface. Because the GUID is specified within the Interface definition, when the developer uses the interface name in his program, the GUID can be used internally by DCOM.

▶ an optional help string which can be used to find out more about the class when it is stored in a Type Library or in the program source code

The methods and parameters—input only, output only, or input and output, are then listed.

It may seem blindingly obvious to the programmer used to distributed processing, but it is not always so obvious to the complete novice, that the interface has to define all the data needed by the class, as, of course, no memory can be shared. The data defined in the interface thus cannot be pointers to memory; it has to be a data type with a defined structure that the programmer sets up as part of the invocation. If the developer wants to reuse definitions he or she uses the keyword "import." This acts like the C++ preprocessor command #include.

MIDL Compiler

After the interface has been defined using the MIDL, it is run through the MIDL compiler. The purpose of the compiler is to produce language-dependent files which can be incorporated or read by the client and server programs. There are two ways in which a client can access classes in a server—

"statically" from stubs in the client or "dynamically" at runtime using Type Libraries.

In the former "static" case the IDL is used to generate blocks of code called stubs and proxies, which are actually compiled with the client and server programs.

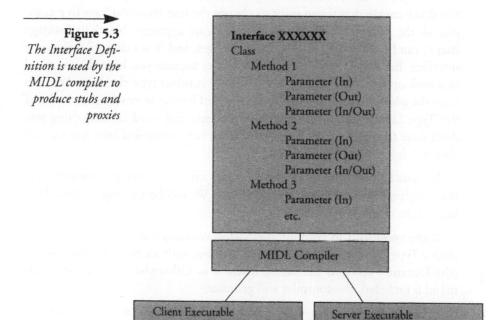

Figure 5.3
The Interface Definition is used by the MIDL compiler to produce stubs and proxies

The details of the interface in this case have been "embedded" in these blocks of code, and the interface has thus been used to generate code that will specifically handle that interface and its contents, for example, the data being passed and the GUID. This code performs operations such as data format conversion and packing of the data into buffers automatically (we will see this in more detail later in the MS RPC chapter).

In the latter case, the IDL is used to generate entries that go into a Type Library, which is accessed at runtime dynamically whenever a client requests an interface by name. In this case, the details of the interface have effectively been stored in a sort of "database" containing the details of the interface rather than being embedded in the client and server code.

The code in the client and server is thus not interface specific but instead does runtime handling of the information it obtains when it looks at the Type Library, such as the extract of the GUID and packing of the data and data format conversion. As its name suggests, the Type Library contains type information about the interface as a whole in compiled (binary) form.

Clearly, the "static" way of using interfaces is potentially faster, but it has the disadvantage that if you want to change the interface, you have to recompile all the programs that use it. The dynamic approach has the advantage that it can be used with interpreted languages, and it is easier to change the interface. But the dynamic interface is slower because you have the overhead of a look-up to a Type Library and you have runtime type checking. You also have the additional administrative overhead of having to ensure that copies of the Type Library get distributed to the clients that need it, something you don't have to worry about if everything has been compiled into one executable as it is in the static case.

In some cases the use of the Type Library isn't an option; it is the only way the programmer can achieve certain things. We will be looking at this a little later in the chapter on Cedar.

If the command to compile the MIDL contains the "library" statement, then a Type Library will be generated together with an entry in the Registry (the Directory services) indicating where it is. Otherwise, if no library command is included, the compiler will generate:

▶ A header file in C, C++, Java, and Visual Basic that contains declarations of the interface defined

▶ A file in C that defines the GUIDs used

▶ A file in C that implements the proxy and stub

Proxies and Stubs

A *Proxy Object* is an in-process object which acts on behalf of the object being called. In effect, the proxy object acts as a "front-end" to the remote server's interface. Proxy objects are generated when the interface (IDL) is processed.

The proxy object resides in the client address space and packages (marshals) the parameters in the call ready for transmitting. One proxy object exists for each object called, and the proxies are invisible to the client. The proxy object makes an RPC to the remote (or local) object. The RPC library (of which more later) then handles the transmission of the data across the network.

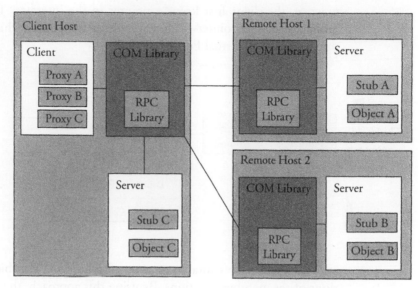

Figure 5.4
Communication
across the network
is handled by the
RPC libraries

The same interface/IDL is also used to generate the *stub*—a small object residing in the same process address space as the server. The stub picks up the RPC calls from the proxies, unmarshals the parameters, and turns them into function calls to the real objects. After the object has completed processing, the stub passes the return values back to the proxy via an RPC call and the proxy then returns them to the client.

The main difference between the proxies and stubs used in DCOM and the stubs used in RPC calls is that proxies and stubs need to be able to handle multiple function calls on an object—RPCs only handle one function call. It is also worth noting that the approach is somewhat similar to the approach used in CORBA, but the terminology is different—CORBA uses the terms Stub and skeleton.

Vtables

Microsoft often uses the term "binary call standard." This term refers to the standard that defines the layout of the call stack for all method invocations—a call stack called a Vtable. Vtables hold the pointers to where methods can be found.

Vtables are used for the compiled "static" approach to interface generation.

As we saw, each class can have more than one interface. Every client wanting to use an interface keeps a Vtable in memory for every interface it uses. In practice, the client first keeps a pointer to the interface. This pointer then points to another pointer—known as the pVtbl pointer, which itself points to the Vtable—the Virtual Function Table.

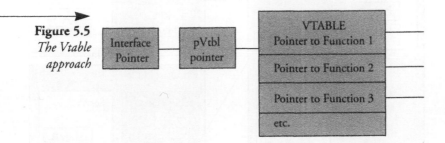

Figure 5.5
*The Vtable
approach*

The Vtable then contains an array of pointers to the object's implementations of the member functions. By using this approach, the client can use the name of the interface (the first pointer) and does not have to use any other pointers.

Clearly, if an object has more than one interface, other Vtables are created for each of the interfaces. If the client invokes methods on many objects, it will have sets of Vtables in memory for every one of the objects and methods it invokes.

So, where do the final pointers to the function implementations point to?

Clearly, the functions could be part of "in-process" objects. Where the object is an in-process object, the Vtable function pointers in the table are actual pointers to the implementation—so a function call from the client to an interface function directly transfers execution control to the member function.

But, if the process is out of process whether local or remote, the pointers in the table cannot be in memory because they cannot be shared between processes. In this case, the pointer points to the Proxy Object.

Who creates these tables? Perhaps of most importance is that the C form of the interface generates the same binary structure as the C++ interface does. But C++ is more convenient for an object implementation because the compiler automatically generates the Vtable and the object structure pointing to it in the course of instantiating the object.

A C object implementor must define an object structure with the pVtbl first; explicitly allocate both object structure and interface Vtbl structure; fill in the fields of the Vtbl structures, and point the Vtbl field in the object structure to the Vtbl structure. There is thus much more explicit coding needed if C is used on the client. In C++, the compiler handles pointers to the Vtbl pointer and also sets up pointers on the stack. If C is used, extra code has to be added to do this.

Type Library

We saw that the Type Library is a language-independent replacement for the C++ header files with a content the same as the C++ header file. The Type Library contains type information about interfaces (methods classes and so on) and is stored in compiled binary form so that details of the interface can be accessed by program at runtime.

By using the Type Library, interfaces can be accessed dynamically and type checking done at runtime. This feature is particularly useful if you are using an interpreted language such as Visual Basic, Java, or similar language where the VTable cannot be accessed in an interpreted manner so cannot be used as the means of finding the functions.

In fact, the general approach recommended by Microsoft is to use VTables if you are using any form of compiled language and the Type Library for interpreted code. Visual Basic hides much of the underlying code of this invocation anyway if you use the normal commands—in fact, you never really see what is happening underneath.

The Type Library first has to be specifically loaded by the client. Once loaded, the developer gets the information he or she needs about the interface from the Type Library and then uses the IDispatch interface to get information about the location of the functions in it. A Visual Basic programmer doesn't have to worry about IDispatch; this is hidden from him or her and happens under the covers.

IDispatch

When a client uses IDispatch in order to execute a function, it first gets the ID of the function using a method on the IDispatch interface called GetIDsofNames. This ID isn't a GUID; it is a convenient string with which to identify the function.

After the ID has been obtained, the "Invoke" method on the IDispatch interface is then invoked! The arguments (parameters) used in the invocation include the function ID just obtained, the actual parameters of the function being invoked, the type of function being called (normal, function of put

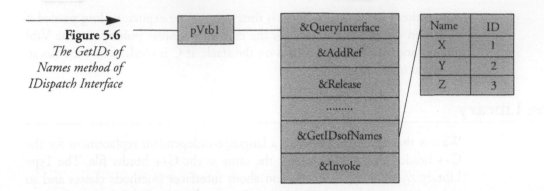

Figure 5.6
The GetIDs of Names method of IDispatch Interface

property, function of put property by reference, etc.), a pointer to the field that should hold the results of the function, and a pointer to the structure that should hold exception information. The function arguments/parameters can be obtained from the Type Library information.

The effect of the "Invoke" method is to cause DCOM to use the IDs to either find pointers to the functions themselves (Disp interface) or find a separate Vtable that points to the functions.

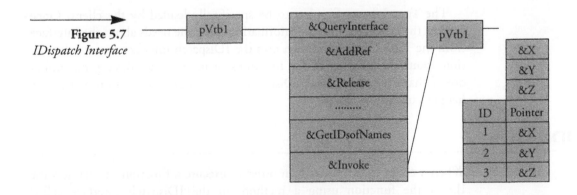

Figure 5.7
IDispatch Interface

Where a component can offer two ways of getting to its functions—directly and indirectly via the Invoke function—the interface is known as a Dual Interface.

Components that implement the IDispatch interface are known as *Automation Servers.* COM clients that communicate with Automation Servers via

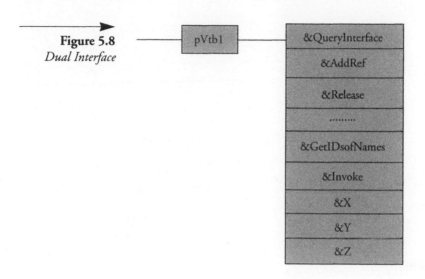

Figure 5.8
Dual Interface

the IDispatch interface are known as *Automation Controllers*. In effect, Automation Controllers use IDispatch to indirectly call functions in an Automation Server.

In Summary

COM enables a developer to define interfaces to components using a language called the Microsoft Interface Definition Language. The MIDL description is used by the MIDL compiler to generate C, C++, Visual Basic, and Java files, which can be used to create entries in a Type Library and used to form the stubs and proxies in clients and servers.

Where the stubs and proxies are compiled statically with client and server programs, the functions (whether these are the functions themselves or their proxies) are found using VTables. Where information about interfaces is found dynamically at runtime, the programmer uses the Type Libraries and the IDispatch interface to find the functions or proxies.

Dynamic invocation is useful for interpreted languages, and Visual Basic has been specifically set up to hide many of the complexities of dynamic invocation. Static invocation is useful with languages such as C or C++ that you want to compile into an executable for use at runtime.

6

ActiveX

- Written in Java, C++, C, Visual Basic, OOCOBOL
- Can be developed using...
- Visual Studio 97
  - Delphi – Borland
  - Micro Focus – Object COBOL
  - Obsydian – Synon
  - Fujitsu COBOL
- All Windows tools (NT, 95)
- Work underway to get Win32 APIs to work on other platforms
- Active Group work relevant here

The generic term for any piece of code that can be invoked via methods and interfaces is termed a component, and we have seen that automation servers are one form of component capable of being run on many platforms. Clearly, they might need to be recompiled to get them to work on other platforms using native compilers (we will see why I have said "might" later on in this chapter), but in essence the same component *source* code should be capable of being compiled to run on any platform supporting DCOM without needing to be changed (ActiveX components, however, are of special importance to DCOM because they work over the Internet and are intended to be portable).

Figure 6.1
ActiveX

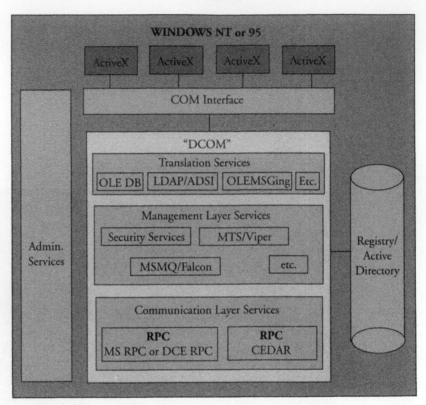

About ActiveX

ActiveX components are a key part of Microsoft's strategy. ActiveX components are like normal components in all respects, but as we have seen, they can be distinguished from normal components because they are intended to be portable.

In the future it should be possible to run ActiveX components on any platform supporting DCOM, as long as they use the COM model, communicate using DCOM services, and use the Microsoft Interface Definition Language to describe the interfaces.

A developer should be able to describe the interfaces and generate the source code for the stubs and proxies, write the component in his language of choice, then deploy it on the platform of choice by using the native compiler to convert the source code to executable code.

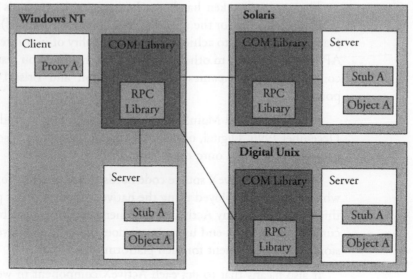

Figure 6.2
*ActiveX compo-
nents can be
deployed on many
platforms*

Thus a client on a Windows platforms should be able to invoke ActiveX components on a Solaris platform, for example, or a Digital Unix platform. Similarly, a client using a web browser should be able to download ActiveX components for use on a Windows machine.

The ideal, of course, would be a "Java" type model whereby the developer wrote the code once and then could deploy it on any platform with no changes, but there are four main blocks to the complete portability of ActiveX components at the moment:

▶ Win32 APIs

▶ Compilers and language differences

▶ Underlying thread support

▶ Memory management

Win32 APIs – Where an ActiveX component uses the Windows GUI, clearly other platforms such as the OpenVMS or Digital Unix platform do not—they use the Motif GUI. Where an ActiveX component needs to be run on Unix platforms there thus needs to be some form of translation software which takes the Windows calls and either turns them into native Motif calls or alternatively emulation of the Windows GUI on other platforms.

The approach taken has been the latter with emphasis placed upon the same look and feel for the user (the Windows look and feel) on all supported platforms. In order to achieve this commonality of user interface, the Win32 API is being ported to other platforms. By the time you read this it could be complete with companies such as MainSoft and Bristol working on the ports.

Software AG and MainSoft formed a partnership to trade technologies in December 1996. Digital, on the other hand, is working closely with Bristol to port the Win32 API onto their platforms.

Compilers–ActiveX source code needs to be compiled for the platform on which it is to be deployed using the native compiler of that platform. Clearly, this does not stop any ActiveX component developer distributing binary executables to potential end users, but it does mean he will have to send out versions of the component for each platform.

It also means that to get each ActiveX component to work on each platform, some changes may have to be made to the source code before it is compiled. As we all know, compilers are different and versions of the languages—even so-called standard languages are also different—so a developer needs to ensure that that version of the ActiveX source code—destined for a particular platform—will actually work on that platform.

Even this hurdle may start to become less of a sticking point as companies start to provide direct support for Microsoft's languages of development. Digital, for example, is currently working on providing native Digital Unix compiler support for both Microsoft C and Microsoft C++.

In the future, ActiveX components written in Visual Basic may be totally portable, as Microsoft is toying with the idea of developing a Visual Basic Virtual machine.

Thread support–This is undoubtedly the biggest hurdle to overcome.

Let us see why.

DCOM supports multithreading rather than multitasking. In fact, as an architecture it is based on the premise that developers will balance the load on server components using threads. DCOM on the Windows NT platform uses the Windows NT threading service—a service we will be examining in our discussion of Windows NT itself. A vendor porting DCOM to other platforms has three main options open to him in order to provide a threads service. It can:

▶ Port the Windows NT thread service to the other platforms it is aiming to support

▶ Use the underlying thread service of the operating system and provide a "veneer" to hide this service—translating the Windows API to the operating system API

▶ Use a portable threads service—one that has been used in other middleware, for example, and again use a veneer to hide the difference in APIs

All three approaches may be used in the long term. Software AG is actually porting the Windows NT thread service for use in their Unix implementations. Digital is considering the use of the DCE threads service—a service based on POSIX threads and one which gives portability across Unix and other platforms supporting DCE—for their OpenVMS platform.

Clearly, if the Windows NT threads service is ported, the ActiveX component will be portable. But, if the underlying operating system thread service or the DCE thread service is used, we do not believe the threading service can be made completely "transparent" to the developer.

In basic DCOM the programmer has to directly use the thread service, understanding how the threads are created, the different models of thread support given, and the differences in the locking strategies used. Other threads services behave differently, so even though the same API is used, the developer may still have to understand the implications of that API on that thread service—the effects of the locking, the effects of the threads.

So, if the programmer creates ActiveX components for Windows NT which use threads, he or she *may* have to rewrite this bit of code if he or she wants to use this component on other platforms besides Windows NT. Massive rewrites are not required and rewriting code for every change of platform is not required, but he or she may still have to do some adjustment to get it to perform well on that platform. It would have been so much easier if Microsoft had used the DCE threads service as well as the RPC because they would then have had a portable cross operating system threads service and none of these problems would have occurred.

Memory management – Memory management is also a service of the operating system in Windows NT, and as memory management is a fundamental function of most programs, the lack of a portable service does pose problems. Again, memory management in DCOM is exposed to the developer, it is not automatic, nor are the commands the programmer must use hidden from him. The rules used are also quite complex, which means the programmer must understand the implications of what he is doing.

The same three options which could be used for threads are not open to vendors who port DCOM, and the vendors are having to port the memory management services within Windows NT (Win32 APIs) in order to provide equivalent services. This is clearly a problem for the vendors but should solve the portability problems for the developer.

Languages of Development

ActiveX components can theoretically be written in a number of programming languages—C++, Java, Visual Basic, OOCOBOL, or C (though as we saw more work is needed with C because it is not object oriented). ActiveX components written in one language can communicate with Active X components written in other languages, as long as MIDL and DCOM are used.

I say theoretically for two reasons. First, components have to be written in a language supporting the notion of function pointers. The language used must also support "structures" containing "double indirected access to a table of function pointers" (because of the Vtable). Since the binary Vtable can be generated easily by most C++ compilers, Microsoft states that the most convenient language to use for components is C++ and is better than, for example, C. Remember, however, that interpreted languages can be supported using the Type Library concept.

Second, we need to remember that when components communicate with one another, they will be passing data from one component in one language to another. The data structures and data types used by one component have to be recognizable by the program language of the other component, so you may have to do some juggling around in your program to enable the data structure sent by a C++ program, for example, to be recognizable by a Java program. Alternatively, the easier approach is simply to only send data of a type recognizable in both languages.

Microsoft's attitude to Java deserves a special mention. Microsoft sees Java as a potential language of development for all sorts of applications—client, server, and so on, but not the only language. In fact, Java to them is simply another OOPL. Their third-party component builders have used C++, Java, and Visual Basic to build components, and these will coexist with new components built in other languages.

ActiveX and Standardization

The ActiveX interface is clearly key to the successful widespread use of DCOM, and as such, Microsoft has placed control of ActiveX technology in the hands of the Open Group. The decision to place ActiveX with the Open Group was taken at a meeting of 84 companies in late 1996. The decision was overwhelmingly in favor of the Open Group (63 voted for, 19 preferred a new group, and 2 abstained, of which Netscape was one).

The new group set up within the Open Group to control ActiveX and license ActiveX technologies is called the "Active Group." This group is controlled by a Steering Committee appointed by and including Microsoft itself. The list of technologies which the Active Group has within their control actually covers more than ActiveX—COM, DCOM, MS-RPC, the Security Provider Interface, OLE Structured Storage Format, the Registry, and Monikers.

Microsoft is equally interested in the Open Group's Pre-Structured Technology Process, which is a framework for collaboration rather than standardization. One of the first PST initiatives, which was approved by the Open Group members, was geared to integrating ActiveX with DCE services—in reality ensuring DCE services could be invoked from the ActiveX interface, as well as or instead of the DCOM services. This may be especially important in the areas of security. Five or six companies are due to fund this first initiative.

The Component Market

One area in which everyone is hoping a market will develop is in the provision of third-party horizontal and vertical components—components which can be reused in applications. A number of groups within Microsoft have already started development of ActiveX components for both horizontal and vertical applications. The Office Components Group (OCG), for example, is developing ActiveX components for use with Office.

The object/component market is an intensely confusing one at the moment, however, because there are so many different types of objects. If a company is to use objects in an application, it needs to be able to use objects from third parties, its own developers, other companies, and so on. Most developers make the assumption that an object is an object and that the development of an application is simply a matter of "plugging in" the objects from all these sources. But it is not as simple as this.

As we have seen, to "plug in" an object you need middleware (or its tool equivalent) to support the interobject communication, and the key to intercommunication is the interface the object presents to the middleware. *Middleware products are geared towards the acceptance of only one type of interface.*

The way the interface is defined is thus key to interoperability between objects. If the interface and IDL are the same, then all objects, whether they come from Microsoft, CORBA vendors, Netscape, Lotus, JavaSoft, IBM, or any other company, will be able to communicate with other objects using any middleware. If the interfaces differ, the customer will only be able to use the middleware which supports that interface and will only be able to use objects with that type of interface.

Unfortunately, what we have seen over the years is a proliferation of the ways in which objects can be defined until we now have numerous incompatible means by which object interfaces can be expressed. The ones I have identified are:

▶ CORBA IDL–and CORBA objects

▶ DCE–XIDL objects

▶ Microsoft IDL–with OLE, ActiveX, VBX, OCX, OLE Automation objects

▶ OpenDoc–from IBM/Apple

▶ JavaSoft's Java Beans components

▶ Netscape's LiveConnect objects

▶ IBM's PARTS (for use with Visual Age)

▶ SOM Objects–which are different from CORBA objects

▶ Tool vendor's objects—every tool has its own definition of an object

▶ Proprietary ORB objects—each of which are defined using different interface definition languages—OIL, CDL, and so on

▶ IBM's PartPaks objects—which are also based on Visual Age

With this number of object types around (and the list is growing), third-party object market may never get off the ground because third-party companies will be totally confused as to which standard to go for, and people like yourselves—the buyers—won't know what they are buying.

I suspect that Microsoft themselves may end up being the best source of reusable components in the future with a few smaller vendors adding niche horizontal market widgets rather than vertical market widgets. This suspicion is supported by the companies which currently provide ActiveX components. Practically all of them are providing widgets for use in the GUI interface rather than vertical market application components. The companies providing widgets include:

▶ ABACO (CAD functions)

▶ ADDSoft (scheduling)

- ► Apex Software (grid)
- ► Blue Marble (mapping)
- ► Bits per Second (graphics engine)
- ► Classic Software (Btrieve access)
- ► Contemporary Software (Calendar, Date, etc.)
- ► Crescent Software (numerous from statistics to curve fitting to grids and queries)
- ► Crystal (reports)
- ► Distinct
- ► dLSoft (barcode)
- ► FarPoint (buttons, spreadsheet, tabbed card)
- ► KL Group (charts)
- ► LEAD Technologies (image handling)
- ► MediaArchitects (image handling)
- ► MicroQuill (database access)
- ► ProtoView (charts, date, time, gauge, button controls, Explorer add-ons)
- ► Sandstone (lexical analysis and parsing)
- ► Sax Software (Exchange add-ons)
- ► Software Fx (charting)
- ► Sheridan (calendar, indexes, notebook)
- ► Smithware
- ► VideoSoft
- ► Visual Components

Tools

Keys to the success of ActiveX and the use of components in general is how many tools help the developer to build ActiveX components. Although I recognize that this sort of information quickly gets out-of-date, I decided it would be helpful to show you which tools can be used at the time of writing to develop ActiveX components.

ActiveX components can currently be developed using:

▶ Microsoft Visual Studio 97–which includes Microsoft Visual Basic 5.0, Microsoft Visual C++ version 5.0, Microsoft Visual J++, Microsoft Visual FoxPro 5, and Visual Interdev

▶ Delphi–Borland

▶ Micro Focus Visual Object COBOL

▶ Synon Obsydian

▶ Fujitsu COBOL

(Note that PowerObjects from Oracle and Power++ from PowerSoft/Sybase can *host* ActiveX controls which are installed as custom controls but cannot be used to build them.)

Microsoft states that as long as their Visual Studio 97 set of tools is used, Win32-based applications can be developed that will run on all Windows 32 platforms (95, NT workstation, and server) as well as over the Internet. Notice, however, that all these tools essentially run on the Windows platform currently, so the developer is likely to have to do his or her development on the Windows NT platform, then port and adapt the components when he or she deploys them on other platforms. Although languages such as Visual Basic 5 provide considerable automated support for the development of the DCOM commands, on the whole, the programmer does need to know how DCOM works in order to get it to operate effectively—for example, the use of threads.

In non-Windows environments, there are no short-cut GUI-based widgets, wizards, or tools to hide the IDL, the API, or any of the other interfaces to DCOM itself—transaction server, MSMQ, security, and so on. You do have to know what you are doing to use DCOM, and to get the best from it you need to understand every command and interface and how it is used.

Microsoft recognizes that the DCOM interfaces used by developers are currently quite difficult to use and may not be capable of being mastered by programmers used to procedural (and simpler) languages or 4GLs. As such they are concentrating effort on hiding the object-based interface with tools—their own and third-party tools. It is still early days here—more improvements in Visual Studio as well as third-party tool improvement should be expected.

Visual Studio 97

Visual Studio is Microsoft's tool suite for building DCOM and Internet applications. It was code-named Boston before its launch.

Most of the tools within the suite had been released before the final launch of the tool suite—Visual J++, for example, code-named Jakarta, had been released in August 1996. Visual C++ had of course been available for some time. But Microsoft enhanced the existing tools for the launch of Visual Studio—the main enhancements were geared towards support for ActiveX creation, integration of the development environments, and improved performance. Visual Studio was launched early 1997.

The following paragraphs describe the tools within Visual Studio in more detail.

Visual Basic 5.0–Visual Basic version 5 is an improved 32 bit version of the VB 4 development environment. Improvements made include better performance, more ease-of-use features, compilation to native code (again which improves performance), and support for the creation of ActiveX controls. After ActiveX controls have been built they can be installed in the Visual basic toolbar for reuse or placed in the Visual Component Library. Forms can be exposed as "active documents" and used with Internet Explorer.

VB's Books Online is included together with an improved code editor (popup syntax, and help, auto complete of property and method names); new wizards; docked windows; a toolbox for customization; and tabs to organize components.

In addition to Visual Basic itself, Office 97 has standardized *Visual Basic for Applications* (VBA), which is like Visual Basic but cannot be used to build stand-alone applications. What the developer can do, however, is to program Word, Excel, etc. 97 objects (paragraphs, bookmarks, drawing shapes, cells, etc.) using ActiveX. These objects can raise events, and the developer can write code to respond to them. Office documents can contain ActiveX documents, and ActiveX components can be used in forms. VBA can also communicate with databases using the data access objects.

Visual C++ version 5–Version 5 of Visual C++ went into beta in January 1997 code-named Orion, with a planned release to coincide with the launch of Visual Studio. Visual C++ is Microsoft's own primary development tool and geared towards programmers needing high performance, debugging, and access to the latest Windows APIs. Visual C++ uses Developer Studio, the same Integrated Development Environment used in Visual J++, and Visual Interdev. The environment is now "scriptable" using VB Script and exposed for automation.

The new features of Visual C++ are a better heap manager contributing to faster executables, compiler extensions to support COM, and a new version of the Microsoft Foundation Classes reflecting the inclusion of the Active

Template Library. (MFC is the C++ class library that encapsulates the Windows API.)

Perhaps of greatest importance to an ActiveX developer is the inclusion of the Active Template Library. The ATL is a way of creating ActiveX controls. New wizards in Visual C++ create skeleton ATL projects making it easier to get started. By adding this enhancement, Visual C++ can now support "thin" applications (over the Internet), and support ActiveX (where before it had been limited to MS Foundation classes).

Visual J++–Visual J++ comes with Microsoft's Java Virtual Machine and Internet Explorer 3. The Web Browser is used to debug applets. The main aim of the tool is to provide a coding and debugging tool, and as such it acts like a normal integrated programming environment. The developer can view projects as classes or files and can move through these to the source code, which can then be edited using the built-in editor. The debugger can be used to watch variables with data tips, modify variables on the fly, and view and suspend threads. The developer can also "compile" the code and see the virtual machine byte code.

Visual J++ Books Online provides Sun's Java reference documentation, a user guide, and a tutorial. The tools come with a Java wizard to start off the Java applet or stand-alone applications and create an HTML text page. The developer can also use a visual editor to define resources, and these are converted into Java code (the tools have the same look and feel as those in Visual C++).

Visual Interdev–Visual Interdev is used to create Web applications. It needs an Internet connection to a server on the network, or the developer can use the Personal Web Server, in which case development can be done on the PC. The developer works with:

▶ HTML files/documents

▶ ActiveX layouts (forms containing ActiveX controls), together with Visual Basic Script or Java Script to drive the interface. These layouts are themselves ActiveX controls

▶ Active Server pages–the special HTML pages that contain scripts that execute on a server

▶ Global file–which contains event handlers so you can write code that executes at the beginning or end of user sessions with your Web project

▶ Media files–images, sound, video in standard format

▶ Active Data Objects

ActiveX controls could be Java applets created using Visual J++ and inserted into the pages using FrontPage (see below). To run your application you navigate to the page on your site using Internet Explorer.

Visual Interdev has a color-coded HTML editor, an enhanced layout designer, and tools to help edit and add files. It does not yet have a debugger. Visual SourceSafe is used for team working, and it includes ActiveX controls that generate data access scripts for Active Data Objects. Where the developer wants to edit HTML pages, he or she can also use Frontpage, which is integrated with Visual Interdev.

Visual Interdev was released with Visual Studio. Microsoft had worked for some time on its own homegrown Internet Authoring tool code-named Blackbird. The initial release of this tool destined for MSN was cancelled. Microsoft then announced it would be converted to work with HTML pages under the name of Internet Studio, and an early version was previewed at the March Internet conference. The final version renamed Visual Interdev was included in the launch of Visual Studio.

FrontPage–FrontPage is a tool acquired from Vermeer Technologies and is an HTML authoring tool which enables a whole Web site to be visualized, navigated, and created. FrontPage also comes with a personal Web Server so that sites can be tested on a local PC. The tool comes with two main components— an Explorer and an Editor.

The Explorer is used to create the Web site. It uses a graphical layout to enable the developer to see the overall structure of the site. The tool can spot broken links and will automatically update links if pages are moved around. The Explorer can also deal with page updates from different people so it can be used by a team of "webmasters." A Web Import Wizard can be used to import an existing site into Explorer.

The Editor enables the developer to edit Web pages without needing to use HTML, although HTML code can be edited directly if the programmer wants to. The Editor can be used with Explorer to create pages for the site, or on its own to create single pages. Double clicking the Web Page in Explorer opens up the FrontPage editor, which enables the content to be edited without resorting to HTML code. Many different sorts of HTML tag are supported—marquee text, sound, table, cell, background color, and images.

Convertors included in the tool enable documents from Microsoft Office and other file formats to be converted to Web page format. The tool employs a drag and drop approach to page creation and includes a spell checker and thesaurus. Perhaps of greatest importance, in the context we are looking at the tool here, is that FrontPage 97 supports ActiveX components.

Visual FoxPro–ActiveX components cannot be created using Visual Fox-Pro so we have only provided brief information here. Instead, Visual FoxPro applications can be clients for ActiveX controls and OLE Automation. (Although ActiveX support has been improved in version 5, compatibility problems are not unknown.)

Other Tools

Tools are also available from third parties that could be used to build ActiveX components.

Borland's Delphi 3 uses a Visual Component Library (VCL), which is a Pascal Class Library that encapsulates the Windows API. A new ActiveX control expert enables the developer to convert a VCL component and turn it into an ActiveX control to use in Visual Basic, etc.

Select Software's **Select Component Manager** can be used to store components—both the source code and the binary code, locally, or remotely. This tool comes with its own object browser.

7

MS RPC

> ▶ Microsoft's DCE RPC implementation
>
> ▶ DCE compliant but not OSF sourced
>
> ▶ Can work with DCE RPC
>
> ▶ Invisible to developer
>
> ▶ Provides "distributed" capability in DCOM

DCOM is entirely reliant on MS RPC to provide its distributed capability. In fact, it is MS RPC which turns COM into DCOM. Understanding what this key service does is thus essential even if much of what is achieved is done "under the covers."

What Is an RPC?

A *Remote Procedure Call* (RPC) is a procedure that, when called, executes a function on a remote machine and returns with results from that function when completed. Remote Procedure Calls mimic the structure of a simple C function call, with the function's name, its arguments when called, and its returned value or structure, giving the programmer the impression that he or she is making calls to routines on the same processor.

From the programmer's perspective, calls to routines on other systems seem no different to calls to, for example, local C functions. If processes communicate using RPCs, one process calls another process as though it were a part of the original process's code.

MS RPC, like its sister in import Remote Procedure Call (RPC), MS RPC is a set of routines and development tools which enable the developer to build distributed applications using RPCs.

Figure 7.1
MS RPC

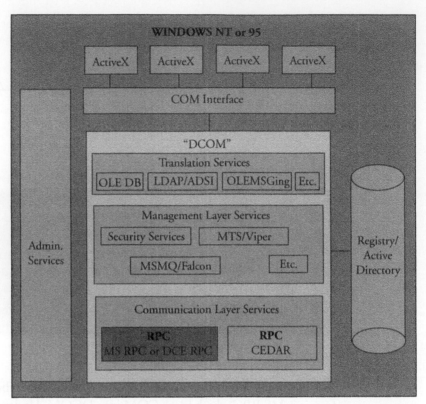

Distributed processes pass control and data between application processes just as they do for local procedure calls. But there is an obvious difference between the way distributed applications pass data when compared to single processor systems.

Single processor systems can pass data between procedures by passing only the address or the name of the data item. Because they run in the same execution environment, the data is effectively shared because storage format and data structures are usually the same. The data in this case may be in shared memory. If an application is distributed, data must actually be packaged and moved across the network with the call, in order for it to be usable by the called process.

And MS RPC?

MS RPC is Microsoft's software to support Remote Procedure Calls. Thus, MS RPC is a set of runtime libraries and development tools which enable the developer to build distributed applications using RPCs.

MS RPC can thus be regarded as middleware in its own right. It can be used without any of the rest of DCOM to support distributed processing. In other words, the developer could use MS RPC right now to build distributed applications. But in the DCOM context, Microsoft uses it to support their own remote function calls across the network, and MS RPC becomes invisible to the application developer. Thus, in the context of DCOM, MS RPC is enabling middleware used by Microsoft.

What Does MS RPC Do?

MS RPC's prime function is to ensure that the request for a function with its parameters and the resulting reply are transmitted across the network. The MS RPC runtime environment reduces the data structures to be passed into a buffer for transmission, converts the individual data elements to a format used during transmission, and then makes calls to the network interface using the appropriate network protocol, to coordinate the sending of the packaged data to the called process.

The middleware software at the called end receives the inbound request containing the packaged data and then unpacks the received buffer, recreating the data structures. It then converts the individual data from the format used for transmission into the local format and starts the processing. Once processing is complete, the middleware then reverses the process to return control and results back to the calling process.

The network software acts as the transport agent between machines, but it is the MS RPC which handles transport between the processes. MS RPC also provides a number of functions which save the developer effort—in this case the Microsoft developer. The RPC software, for example, hides the network commands that remain as an invisible layer, saving the programmer from having to write tedious low-level network code.

Without the MS RPC service, the work associated with packing and unpacking the data structures, data format conversion, error handling, network software communication, session handling, and so on has to be coded by the programmer. Once MS RPC middleware is used, all this is handled by the middleware on behalf of the programmer. We will be looking at the specific services provided by the middleware later in this chapter.

MS RPCs and Interfaces

When a developer wants to build an application based on remote procedure calls, he or she first defines the *interface* to the function. The interface has an almost identical meaning to that used in COM—it is a contract between any client and the function which defines the function itself together with the parameters to that function. The interface to MS RPC might describe:

▶ the parameters to the remote call and how they are used—input, output, input/output

▶ error message and return codes

▶ the name of the process

This interface is described in an *IDL—Interface Definition Language*. Now where have we seen this before? It should be obvious that many of the concepts used in COM and DCOM were borrowed from RPC technology (a technology, incidentally, that actually goes back to the 1970s).

An IDL generator or "compiler" then reads the IDL and generates code. The MS RPC IDL compiler generates a standard language such as C. When the C source code is generated, it is effectively machine independent and can then be compiled for the target environments. The compiler may also generate header files and make files.

In addition to the header files and make files the other main code generated by the IDL compiler are *client and server stubs*. Again, where have we seen this before? Of course DCOM supports the notion of client and server stubs and proxies, although the proxy has an extended role in DCOM to the stub we see in the MS RPC stub. On the whole, however, DCOM produces client and server stubs because MS RPC does.

The generated stubs are usually compiled and linked with both the client and server programs. It may be possible to use DLLs (Dynamic Link Libraries) to store the code, or the code may be directly compiled and linked to provide a single executable client or server program.

The client and server then communicate at runtime with an RPC library, which is provided as part of the MS RPC middleware.

The generated *stub code* performs functions associated with the manipulation of the data structures. The reasons why should be obvious. The stub code is generated from information you give it about the interface—in effect the structure of the data going across the network. It is obvious that the code is thus going to deal primarily with data structures. Hence, for example, it does things like:

▶ Pack and unpack the data structures

▶ Convert individual data items into a format which can be both passed across the network and converted from one machine format to another

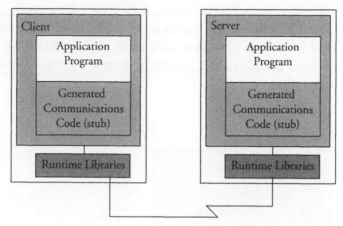

Figure 7.2
IDL compiler used to generate stubs

(if an intermediate common protocol such as the *ASN* (Abstract Syntax Notation) Basic Encoding Rules has been used, both conversion to the common format and conversion from the common format may be performed)

The runtime library functions, in contrast, are responsible for functions such as:

▶ Handling network communication errors—and recovering from the errors

▶ Coordinating the request/reply messages between client and server managing all network synchronization of clients and servers, establishing connections, and coordinating transmission

▶ Managing sessions between multiple clients and server processes

In essence, the stubs perform data-related processing and the runtime library performs communication-related services.

MS RPC and DCOM

So how does all of this relate to DCOM? What happens to turn a method call into an RPC? When a programmer uses DCOM, he or she invokes a method on an interface using certain arguments. The method call is *translated* within DCOM into a call to a remote procedure call. The procedure in this case is equivalent to a method found within a component.

Similarly, when a DCOM service is invoked using a method call on a DCOM interface, this, too, is translated internally into a remote procedure call—a call on a method within a DCOM service component. This translation is easy because the paradigms used for component invocation and that used for remote procedure calls are so similar. When the programmer uses components he or she is actually looking at a group of methods described by an interface.

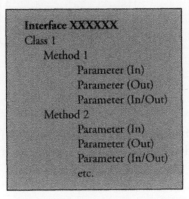

Figure 7.3
Interface on a class or component

When the programmer uses a remote procedure call he or she is looking at only one of those methods. As Procedures are also defined by Interfaces, the similarities between RPCs and Component invocations are obvious.

Figure 7.4
Interface for an RPC

In fact, the only difference is that the interfaces used for component invocation group methods together around the concept of the class. Whereas, with RPC Interfaces, no grouping takes place, each method has one interface.

MS RPC and DCE RPC

MS RPC is based on the OSF/Open Group's DCE RPC. Why is this important? It is of exceptional importance because it is via the DCE RPC mechanism that communication with non-Windows platforms is being achieved.

In effect, on Windows platforms, Microsoft uses their own MS RPC mechanism to support distributed processing across machines and across the network, but where communication is between a Windows machine and a non-Windows platform such as Solaris or Digital Unix, the DCE RPC mechanism is used.

DCE RPC and MS RPC can communicate with one another because Microsoft based MS RPC on DCE RPC. Microsoft did not use the OSF's code to produce their implementation but used the API and developed their own code. The implementation is thus DCE compliant but is not OSF sourced. Some differences in approach between MS RPC and DCE RPC did creep in during the development of MS RPC, but these are being sorted out by the DCOM vendors themselves, so the developer does not need to worry too much about this.

So What Is DCE?

DCE stands for Distributed Computing Environment. It is a standard developed by the OSF (Open Software Foundation), now the Open Group. DCE is not a specification, however. It is provided to potential vendors as source code, which they then adapt to ensure the code works successfully on their platforms.

Altogether DCE is now ported successfully to about 30 hardware environments including not only numerous flavors of Unix, but many "proprietary" operating systems such as GCOS and VMS. DCE is middleware in its own right, and many people are using it to develop distributed applications. It was designed for use in an enterprise-wide capacity—a middleware product that could support many types of application across the enterprise, and many of its features are geared towards enterprise level use—its Directory services, its thread support, its security support, and so on.

The architecture of DCE is shown below, together with its relationship to other software such as the application. Software outside the scope of DCE is shown using dark shading; software within the scope of DCE, but which is still being developed, is shown using light shading.

Figure 7.5
*Architecture
of DCE*

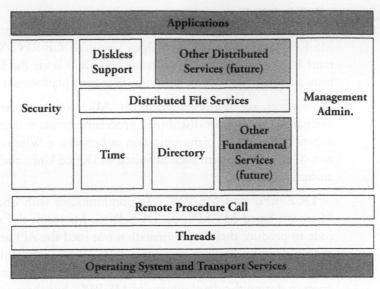

As can be seen from the picture, DCE is far from just the RPC mechanism which Microsoft uses DCE actually includes a Threads service, security service, Directory service, time services, as well as Distributed File support. Microsoft has, in effect, used only a small part of DCE—its RPC mechanism—to develop their own MS RPC.

Although this book is not about DCE, I will, in the next few paragraphs, provide you with a brief description of DCE so that you can see what it does and how it works. This may seem irrelevant to you if you want to use DCOM, but you need to bear in mind:

▶ First, that your company may be using DCE anyway and you may have to interface to it when you are developing your DCOM applications.

▶ Second, that companies providing DCOM implementations on other platforms are going to be using some of the DCE services in their ports to provide equivalent services for security or thread support, for example.

▶ And, third, that Microsoft is actively thinking of using some of these DCE services themselves anyway—particularly the security services—so in the future you will need to know how they work.

DCE Services

DCE is a set of specific management services with a communication layer based on Remote Procedure Calls. In effect, the Remote Procedure Call technology provides the foundation of DCE, and the rest of the services implement various management-related tasks such as security, threads, time synchronization, directory services, and distributed file services.

The architecture is layered bottom up from the most basic supplier services such as the operating system to the highest level of consumer services—the application. DCE is a layer of software that sits on top of the host operating system and network services and offers its services to the applications above.

The RPC and Threads services are base DCE services that are available on every system on which DCE is installed. All the other services use these services. So, for example, when a call is made to the Directory service, it is transported using the RPC mechanism. Furthermore, increases on the load to the Directory service are handled internally by DCE using its own thread service—the Directory service simply multithreads itself using the Threads service—complicated but efficient.

DCE's services are layered so that the user can use one or more services separately or in combination. The application uses only the APIs it requires and does not have to use all DCE's APIs. It is possible, for example, that a user could use the threads, RPCs, or security service and not use the time or Threads services. It is this ability to use only one or a selection of services that made it possible for Microsoft to simply extract the RPC mechanism and use it on its own for use in DCOM.

DCE services are divided into Fundamental services and Data Sharing services. Fundamental services are aimed at the developer of systems and help him to develop distributed applications. These services include the RPC, directory service, time service, security service, and Threads service.

The Data Sharing services build upon the Fundamental Distributed Services and require no programming by the developer. They include a distributed file system and support for diskless workstations. The services provided and their function are described below:

Time service–The DCE Distributed Time Service (DTS) synchronizes host clocks in LANs and WANs. By having clock synchronization, distributed applications are able to determine the sequencing, duration, and scheduling of events, independently of where they occur. DTS is transparent to the end users of a system and users cannot access DTS directly, but applications which use DTS can schedule events for the user; for example, a conference call scheduling application can use time zone information to determine the best time to schedule conference calls that span multiple time zones. The time service could also usefully be used in transaction processing applications.

Microsoft could have used this time service with advantage when developing DCOM but instead use their own time service in Windows NT. No equivalent service for DCOM on other platforms exists, so if the developer needs a time service he or she may find it useful (if his company uses DCE) to use this service directly.

Directory service–The Directory service is a key component of DCE and acts much like a telephone directory assistance service that gives a person's telephone number when given a person's name. By using the Directory service, any resource—person, disks, print queues, servers, and so on—can be contacted anywhere on the network by using their unique name. When the Directory service is given the name, it returns the network address of that resource along with other information associated with the name.

Microsoft, as we will see, does not use the DCE Directory service and uses their own Registry and in future Active Directory service. We will be seeing what happens with DCOM on other platforms in the chapter on other platforms.

DCE RPC–The client RPC runtime routines provided with DCE:

▶ Gets the call arguments from the program and prepares then for transmission. This is called "marshaling" in DCE speak.

▶ Determine which network transport to use for communication. In reality, DCE only supports TCP/IP at the moment, but DCE was designed to support more than one network transport.

▶ Search the directory service for the server's host address. When an application server initializes, it places its host address in the directory—so the Directory always knows where a running server is. When Microsoft used the DCE RPC code, this code had to be adapted to use their own Registry service.

▶ Connect to and transmit the RPC to the server.

The server RPC runtime routines provided with DCE run continuously in wait for an incoming call. When the call arrives, the runtime library dispatches the call to the proper procedure in the server stub. The stub "unmarshals" the data by converting it to the form needed by the server machine, changing byte orders, converting 16 to 32 bit data, and so on, turning it back into a normal argument list. Once the procedure has executed, the program passes the argument back to the calling code in the stub, which calls the RPC runtime routines that marshall the data and transmit it back to the client. As we can see, therefore, Microsoft has used the DCE RPC mechanism almost in exactly the same way with only very minor changes.

Threads service–DCE Threads is an implementation based on the POSIX 1003.4a standard, which includes realtime priority scheduling. Threads and the use of multithreading is well known in the world of high transaction systems. Multithreading saves memory space, as well as improves performance where a very large number of users or "clients" may be wanting to use the same process simultaneously.

Multiple threads of a process use the same address space, so they share all static and external data, as well as open files and any other services available to the whole process. They execute concurrently and in parallel, which improves performance, whereas single thread processes execute serially. They do not require the process to be duplicated, however, and this is how memory is saved.

DCE Threads enables the programmer to write client and server processes that incorporate support for multithreading, with protection of shared resources, synchronization of the threads, scheduling of activities, and resolution of Unix signals and errors. Perhaps of most importance, however, is that this service is the same on all platforms on which DCE runs. So, if a client or server wants to multithread, they can, knowing the resulting application will be portable. As we saw earlier, Microsoft did not use the DCE Threads service in DCOM, but it is more than likely that some of the other suppliers of DCOM on other non-Windows platforms will, particularly for non-Unix platforms.

Security services–DCE provides authentication and authorization services and can support encryption. *Authentication* services enable the client to prove its identity to the server. *Authorization* services are used by the server to regulate access to resources. Once the client has proved it is authentic, a check is then made to determine whether the client is authorized to use the services/ resources requested. DCE Security service uses the Data Encryption Standard (DES) to support encryption.

The system works on the basis that every client must prove it is authorized to use a server to the server itself. Because access to every DCE resource— directories, files, printers, and so on—is controlled by the server, the server's demands for authentication and authorization provide the network security required.

Security checks are applied not only to application servers, but also to DCE servers such as the Cell Directory Service. In effect, every time any client—be it a DCE client or an application client—requests a service, its authenticity and authentication are checked and optionally the requests and replies are encrypted. Encryption is a developer-controlled service and is only provided if requested.

Microsoft did not use the DCE security services in DCOM, but used the Windows NT services. There are plans, however, to support DCE's security services as one option—we will be looking at this in the chapter on security.

The Distributed File Service (DFS)– actually works much like an application because it uses the underlying DCE services for distribution. It provides a single integrated file system that can be used by all DCE users to share files and the information in those files across a network of machines running different operating systems. When you install and configure a DFS server on a host, the DCE Local File System exists alongside the native file system.

Everyone using DFS has their own directory in the file system and uses the same interface to move around it. End users use native operating system commands to control directory and file operations. So, for example, a Unix user would use *cd* to change directories, *ls* to list directory contents, and *mkdir* to create new directories. DFS also has some extra commands to show things like the location of files.

To speed operation and provide some resilience to network failure, DFS has a cache manager which stores versions of the retrieved data in a portion of the local disk and then writes it back to the file server after the application has finished. Microsoft did not implement DFS and has no apparent plans to do so.

The Functions of the RPC Service

We have looked at what an RPC is, what MS RPC is, and how it relates to DCE RPC and the DCE standard. Now we will take a specific look at what the MS RPC actually does in more detail—the functionality it provides. The main functions provided by MS RPC are, as we saw, to:

▶ Pack and unpack the data in the message

▶ Perform data format conversion

▶ Pack and unpack the data into buffers ready for transmission

▶ Establish sessions

> ▶ Handle the network calls
> ▶ Coordinate transmission
> ▶ Handle faults

Packing/Unpacking the data in the message

The code generated by DCOM in the proxy objects and stub objects handles the packing and unpacking of the data for the developer. Developers define the object, the functions to be called, and the data to be input and output using the Interface Definition Language. The data structures supported thus depend on the structures supported by that language; there are no specific restrictions on the types themselves.

But, since MIDL is C++ like, its support of data types is also going to be C++ like. This means that data types used in other languages such as Java hash tables, primitive data types, vectors, bit numbers, and high precision numbers that have no equivalent in C++ could not be exchanged. There are normally no limits to the length of the call data.

Translation of data formats (from sending to receiving machine format)

Procedures in distributed applications often run on machines which use different data storage formats, which again requires application code to translate the formats. The conversion performed by a product such as an RPC system sorts out the differences between data formats. Thus, for instance, Tandem and DEC define byte positions within a 16 bit word differently. The middleware contains library routines called by the stub code that convert data formats between the systems from ASCII to EBCDIC and from big endian to little endian.

You may think that this is trivial code, but those who are using middleware that does not support data format conversion, or building distributed systems without using middleware, can tell you that data format conversion is anything but trivial. In practice, two formats are used by DCOM as the "on the wire" formats for transporting the data—NDR and UDR.

> ▶ *NDR*–NDR—Network Data Representation—is used for communication between MS RPC and DCE RPC and, as such, between DCOM on Windows NT and DCOM on other platforms. DCOM uses the DCE standard to handle data format translation. NDR is a neutral in-between format in which the reader "makes right." Conversion using NDR is achieved at both the client and server ends into this neutral format.

▶ *UDF*–UDF—Uniform Data Transfer is the format used to exchange data between objects on the same machine or between machines of the same type.

Data format conversion is made easier because the stub has the format of the data being passed—it knows what data is being sent and returned and its format. In messaging systems, where a message is sent across rather than a call to a function, the middleware has no idea what data is being sent across and data format conversion has to be tackled in other ways. We will be looking at this problem in the chapter on MSMQ, as it provides a message queuing service.

Packing into and unpacking from the buffers used for transmission

The packing and unpacking of data into buffers is performed by MS RPC and is transparent to the programmer. One of the options open to a middleware developer is to add features which handle very long messages more efficiently (by splitting them automatically and reconstituting them automatically) or grouping very short messages into buffers. Another feature often provided, where the network software may not offer the feature, is to offer optional automatic compression and decompression of the buffer to speed transmission.

DCOM does not support compression or decompression of messages, nor does it split or group messages. It relies on the underlying network software to do this.

But DCOM does use a novel method of minimizing network traffic called *box-carring*. It is the nature of object-oriented and component-based communication that a large number of method calls are needed to set up the final request/reply between client and component. In comparison with an RPC call where the request/reply is one action, in object-oriented processing the actual sequence of calls may be—connect to object; query its functionality; create the object; and send it the method call. Each individual method call involves a round trip and as a consequence affects performance. Box-carring groups these multiple-method calls into a single invocation. The proxy object on the client side intercepts the multiple-method calls from the client and bundles them into a single RPC.

Transmitting the message—establishing sessions

Although network software may handle sessions between machines, sessions between processes have to be handled by the middleware. A number of options exist as to how those sessions are handled, each having their own advantages and disadvantages, and each having specific purposes.

A connection can be created by the middleware between two communicating processes, for example, where name-to-address resolution occurs only once at session inception. Sessions are then typically multiplexed over the underlying network transport mechanism to avoid exhausting network resources.

Alternatively, a connection may be created by the middleware in which name-to-address resolution occurs with every message sent. These sorts of sessions might be used when only a few messages are being sent during a short time period to the same process.

Within DCOM, a session is established between *DCOM nodes*, not between applications. The session and connection is then used for multiple request/reply communications between clients and servers on the two machines. DCOM is able to pair up request and reply, and is also able to pair up requests from threads with replies from threads.

Handling the network calls

Where middleware is not used, the developer has to create code to communicate with the network software; in other words, he or she has to code to the network transport protocols. This means he or she has to add numerous low level calls using the network-specific API into his client and server code. If the application is moved to a new network, then this aspect of the application has to be recoded. DCOM MS RPC runtime libraries include this code for the developer; no coding is needed.

Coordinating the transmission

DCOM MS RPC establishes the connection, coordinates the transmission, and synchronizes with the network. The programmer does not have to do anything.

Handling faults

One of the most tedious and time-consuming aspects for a programmer developing distributed applications is handling errors. Without middleware, the developer has to write all the code to trap the errors, interpret what went wrong, and then try to build in the code to correct or act on the fault. In some cases, the application may be in no position to actually find out what went wrong as it may be the one isolated by the fault. All these problems conspire to make error and fault handling in distributed applications a very tricky job.

Middleware handles this, and various levels of fault handling can be provided, from useful error trapping mechanisms to fully automated recovery mechanisms with automatic restart for the servers and clients, automated transfer from failed servers on failed machines, retries, plus many more automated mechanisms. DCOM offers a set of services halfway between the very basic error trapping to some support for automated procedures.

Client request failure–In DCOM, when a client makes a request and the network has failed, the server's host has failed, or the server itself has failed, MS RPC will try to deliver the request a set number of times and then return an error message. The number of times MS RPC retries is configurable for the entire network as is the retry delay per server and queue length. But where the server has failed, DCOM will not search for alternative servers.

Server reply failure–Where the server fails before sending the reply, or the network goes down before the reply has been sent, the client will time out. The time out period is configurable.

Where the server tries to send a reply, but failure of the network (or client) causes the send to fail, MS RPC will also try to deliver the reply a set number of times and then return an error message to the server (which has to then recover itself, if need be). The number of times MS RPC retries is also configurable.

Client alive–DCOM uses a pinging protocol to detect if clients are still "alive" in a connection. Client machines send ping messages at two-minute intervals. Only if the entire client machine is idle with respect to a given server does it send ping messages. DCOM uses a per-machine keep-alive message. Thus, if the client uses many components on the server machine, a single ping message keeps all the client connections to components alive. DCOM considers a connection broken if more than three ping periods pass without the server's receiving a ping message.

DCOM also uses an approach called delta pinging to minimize the size of the ping messages. It creates "meta-identifiers" that represent groups of clients—if the clients in the group change, the delta is changed. DCOM piggybacks ping messages onto regular messages.

Error codes–Most failure conditions within DCOM are signaled by error codes. DCOM has no automatic error correction features—servers are not restarted, nor are connections transferred, but the error code is used to indicate what error has occurred so that the programmer can take appropriate action.

The COM interface functions and COM Library API use specific conventions for error conditions that the client must pass back with the reply. Where the reply is used, the return value, status and error information (for example, a Boolean result of true or false), and a failure/success field must be specified. It is illegal to throw an exception across an interface invocation because errors need to be platform independent.

The key field used in DCOM error reporting is the **HRESULT field**—a simple 32 bit field that is used by DCOM to report communication errors, RPC errors, and so on. It is used rather than the parameter return values in the interfaces and is structured as follows:

► Severity code–0 = success, 1 = error

► Reserved (for later DCOM use)

► Facility–a code classifying the error—some facility codes are MS defined but they can be user defined as well. Examples include—RPC (error resulted from underlying RPC); Dispatch (error from Dispatch interface); Storage (persistent storage error); Win32; Windows; Control (OLE control error)

► Code–the actual error code

Failover–Is not supported in DCOM. That is, DCOM does not have the ability to actually transfer calls from clients to the same application on another machine if the application on a machine fails, even if the call is mid-process, or to also transfer any connections the application had with other software along with the call. In other words, in true failover, the middleware can transfer the call and the links to the databases the application is using too.

In Summary

MS RPC, based on the OSF's DCE RPC, is a key and vital piece of technology. It is what puts the D in DCOM; without it there would be no support for distribution.

You rarely see the effects of what MS RPC is doing for you. The handling of sessions, network synchronization, network calls, and data format translation are all handled automatically for you by this piece of clever technology, but you do get the results of one of its services—the error handling services. Only here are you actually communicating with MS RPC and using its services directly, and only here is the service not automatic. Rather than thank Microsoft, we should perhaps be thanking the OSF for putting together such a useful piece of code.

8

Cedar

> ▸ Based on technology acquired from TransAccess/Netwise
>
> ▸ Provides nonintrusive access to IMS and CICS programs on MVS
>
> ▸ Works with MTS (Microsoft Transaction Server)
>
> ▸ Transactional control of CICS only at moment
>
> ▸ Alternative to Software AG's DCOM on MVS

MS RPC provides access to other platforms via its links with the DCE RPC. But what if a company has an IBM mainframe with CICS or IMS and does not want to use DCOM on the mainframe? The answer is to use Cedar—a product integrated within the DCOM architecture providing nonintrusive links to programs in CICS or IMS on the mainframe. Remember that Cedar is now called COM TI (Transaction Integrator), but as it is still widely referred to by its code name, I have used Cedar instead of COM TI.

What Is Cedar?

Cedar (Cedar is the internal code name for the technology) provides clients component-based application access to programs written using IBM's CICS and IMS.

Developers using MTS can include CICS programs within an MTS transaction; however, Cedar does not currently support transactional involvement of IMS programs. Where developers need to access IMS/DB databases under

Figure 8.1
Ceder or
COM TI

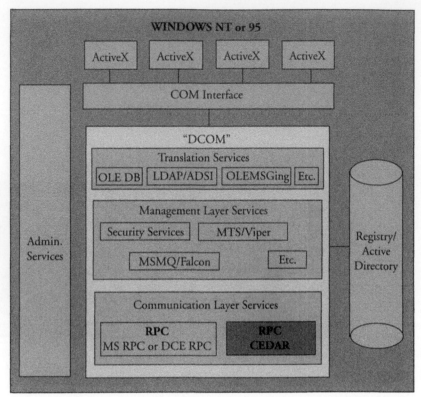

transaction control, Microsoft advises that the developer use CICS to access the DBMS.

What does it consist of?

Cedar consists of three main components:

▶ **runtime**–which intercepts the method calls to the mainframe and uses the Cedar-type library to perform the actual conversion and formatting of the method parameters

▶ **Interface Builder**–provides application developers with a GUI tool for creating Windows-based-type libraries. The IB also enables the developers to start from or create the COBOL data declarations used in the mainframe CICS and IMS programs. The developer can install the Interface Builder as an add-in to the Microsoft Visual Basic version 5 tool, or can use it as a stand-alone tool.

▶ **administration**—used to install program files, collect information about the user environment, and configure Cedar for the particular Windows NT server and MVS mainframe.

How is it configured?

The client application can be running on a computer running Windows NT Server, Windows NT Workstation, Windows 95 (or other platforms supporting DCOM and Automation). Cedar can also be used with Web-based clients connected to the Microsoft Information Server (IIS).

Cedar supports clients that use the Automation interface only.

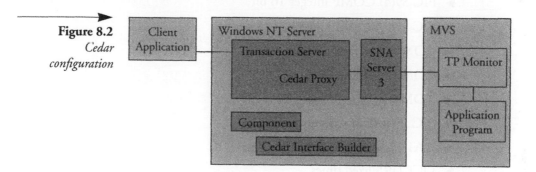

Figure 8.2
Cedar
configuration

Cedar does all of its processing on the Windows NT Server. As such, there is no executable code required to run on the mainframe. Cedar then acts as a generic proxy for the mainframe. It intercepts object method calls from the application and redirects those calls to the TP Monitor running on the MVS mainframe. Cedar also handles the return of all output parameters and return values from the mainframe. In all cases, developers can send and receive optional meta data and rowsets.

It uses standard communication protocols (LU 6.2) for communicating between the computer running Windows NT Server and the mainframe TP Monitor. Microsoft SNA server 3 is used as the bridging software to handle the protocol exchange. Cedar supports MVS version 4.3 and later.

What About Data Conversion?

When Cedar intercepts the method call, it converts and formats the method's parameters from the representation understandable by Windows NT server into the representation understandable by the mainframe. Cedar uses the technology acquired from TransAccess. It has the job of changing the format of data structures from both sending to receiving language format, but also has the job of transforming the machine formats from ASCII to EBCDIC.

The developer uses the Interface Builder tool to define the mappings which must take place between data types, and Cedar then uses this information at runtime to do the conversion. The developer pastes the COBOL copybook acquired from the mainframe into the Interface Builder. The IB then analyzes the copybook and asks the developer a series of questions to define the methods and parameters and the corresponding data type mappings. Cedar can support the conversion of the following data types:

▶ PIC S9(4) COMP integer 16 bit

▶ PIC S9(9) COMP integer 32 bit

▶ COMP-3 packed decimal

▶ COMP-2 float 8 byte

▶ COMP-1 float 4 byte

▶ PIC X with or without translation

▶ DATE and TIME packed decimal

▶ OCCURS fixed times

▶ OCCURS depending

The developer can change the default mappings between COBOL data types and automation data types, and Cedar supports the following automation data types:

▶ 2 and 4 byte signed integer

▶ 4 and 8 byte real

▶ Currency (8 byte fixed point)

▶ Decimal

▶ Date 8 byte real

▶ Variable length string

▶ Boolean

▶ 1 byte unsigned integer

▶ Arrays of any of the previous types

When the developer has finished doing the mapping, he clicks "make typelib," and this then creates the Cedar-type library. Machine format and language format translations are completed simultaneously using these libraries at runtime. Cedar will handle all the complexities that the remapping from one language to another results in—blank padding where needed and packing decimal data.

And What About CICS Calls?

We will see in the chapter on MTS that MTS uses two-phase commit to control the execution of distributed transactions. By using Cedar, CICS programs can be included within the transaction. Thus, for example, a programmer could define a transaction to be the execution of updates on two DBMSs (say) and the successful execution of a CICS program. If the DBMS updates failed, or the CICS program did not complete successfully, the transaction and its updates would be abandoned. If, on the other hand, the updates could complete successfully and the CICS program completed successfully, the updates would be committed under two-phase commit control.

To include CICS (and in the future IMS) programs within a transaction, Cedar converts between Windows two-phase commit and the mainframe-based Sync Level 2 transactions. Cedar uses CICS Distributed Program Linking (DPL) or Advanced Program to Program Communication verbs (APPC), and IMS applications use the IMS Message Queue.

In the CICS environment, programs can communicate with each other using an EXEC CICS Link or straight LU6.2 (non-linked model). When a link is used, IBM's Mirror Transaction handles the protocol and creates a communication area (COMMAREA), which it passes to the program being linked to. At runtime, Cedar sends the appropriate LU6.2 data stream to the CICS Mirror Transaction. The requested CICS program is then executed and receives its input parameters in the COMMAREA. The mainframe TP Monitor processes the input parameters, places any output into the COMMAREA, and issues an EXEC CICS RETURN.

In a non-linked connection, the modules use only the LU6.2 protocol to communicate directly with each other. At runtime, Cedar sends the appropriate LU6.2 data stream to send inputs to the mainframe TP Monitor. The TP Monitor receives the inputs, processes them, and uses the APPC verb set to send the outputs.

The IMS environment provides two ways to pass parameters between programs—implicitly or explicitly. Cedar currently supports only implicit passing. When passing parameters implicitly, a program uses the IMS message queue to access parameters, and IMS handles the LU6.2 protocol behind the scenes. The IMS TP monitor does GETs for the input parameters, processes them, and does INSERTs for the output parameters. (When passing parameters explicitly, a program uses the APPC/MVS API verbs to access the parameters and interact directly with LU6.2.)

Any Other Functions?

We saw in the last chapter on MS RPC that the software handled sessions, synchronization, network calls, "marshalling," transmission, and the buffers. Cedar's role is to act as a "broker" between DCOM and CICS so that all these aspects are "converted." Thus, for example, Cedar provides conversion software so that arguments are marshalled in the form expected by CICS. Similarly, where CICS handles sessions in one way, Cedar acts as the broker to coordinate the sessions between CICS and DCOM. Thus, effectively, Cedar also provides equivalent functionality to MS RPC through its links with CICS and IMS.

Why Not Use DCOM on MVS?

I have already mentioned a number of times that DCOM will be provided on other platforms by companies such as Software AG, Digital, and HP. The MVS version of DCOM is provided by Software AG, and the developer is right to ask the question—why not use Software AG's DCOM to communicate with the mainframe?

The answer is that Cedar and Software AG's DCOM are alternative approaches to connectivity, providing different solutions, depending on the requirements of the purchaser. Software AG's DCOM implementation on the MVS mainframe uses DCE RPC code to communicate with Microsoft's MS RPC on Windows NT.

"Programs" on the mainframe must be COM components, and if existing programs are to be used, they will need to be "wrapped." Furthermore, on MVS, the developer must have the POSIX compliant version of MVS and be using TCP/IP. Thus, if you are happy to "wrap" your existing programs and use the POSIX compliant version of MVS, then you should use DCOM. By using DCOM you will get all the benefits of the DCOM approach as the programs on the mainframe will look exactly like components and behave like components.

But, if you do not want to go to the trouble of wrapping your existing programs, prefer a nonintrusive solution with no DCOM on the mainframe, and want to continue to use LU6.2 and CICS, then Cedar is the obvious choice. We will be saying more about wrapping in the chapter on other platforms.

In Summary

This is a short chapter, but an exceptionally important one for mainframe users. Microsoft's entire development of Cedar was driven by customers' demand for connectivity to the mainframe. Very few companies can afford to redevelop the systems they have on their mainframe and so called legacy hardware.

There is still a vast number of machines out there with operating systems such as MVS, VME, and VMS all running key core applications, all supporting vast databases of crucial data. These applications also work. To call them legacy applications is an insult—as one of my colleagues once said, they should be called "heritage," not "legacy."

Although vendors of software may not have caught on to this, few if any customers want to remove these systems, few if any have any real need to remove them. But they do want to reuse the data stored and updated by those systems and they do want to add new functionality which may cross system and hardware boundaries. Middleware is there to help the developer do this. By using middleware, applications and hardware platforms can be linked together to add new functionality to existing working systems. The fact that Microsoft has added Cedar to make this easier for the customer is a step in the right direction. I will have more to say about this when we look at support for other platforms.

9

Other Communication Functions

> ► Triggering
> ► Context Bridging
> ► Broadcast and Multicast

MS RPC and Cedar provide specialized services related specifically to the transport of invocations across the network. There are other services, however, that we might loosely think of as services that help in communication, but that are not part of either MS RPC or Cedar.

In this chapter we will look at these functions, what they do, and how they work.

Some are automatically provided for the developer by DCOM—such as context bridging. Some are provided automatically but require developer involvement—such as triggering, and some are services the developer can use to help him or her write component-based applications such as multicasting Where the developer is involved, however, all these services are accessed via the same COM interface.

Triggering

Components in DCOM can be running permanently in memory—loaded and waiting to be used—or they can be stored somewhere in a library. Where they are stored in a library, when a request is made for them, they need to be loaded into memory and started. This latter process is termed "triggering," and DCOM is able to trigger components.

The advantages of triggering are that if the developer has literally thousands of components to use on a machine, he or she can save memory by storing

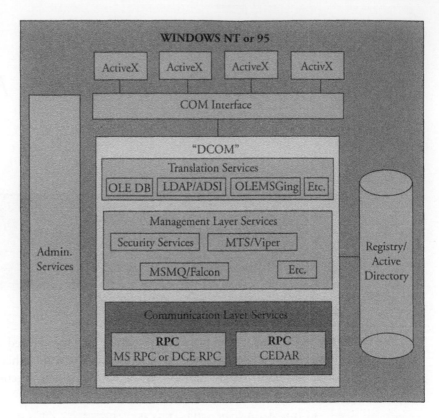

Figure 9.1
*Other
communication
services*

them on disk and only triggering them when needed. This aspect is especially useful if you only have a small machine—it makes better use of the small amount of memory you may have available, while at the same time still providing a client process with a rich array of functionality.

The disadvantage with triggering is that it is slow. To load a component from a library takes time, so if you need a fast response, triggering may not be such a good idea. This is the reason many Distributed Transaction Processing Monitors such as TOP END and Tuxedo do not support triggering—a slow transaction processing application just wouldn't "cut the mustard" as we techies say! In fact, transaction processing and triggering are incompatible.

Microsoft, however, does provide you with the choice. You can decide to have servers permanently running in memory or, if the server is not running (that is, it exists in the library but not as a running task), DCOM will trigger the server by automatically creating an instance of the server. Thus servers/ objects are triggered automatically by DCOM.

But the programmer does have some work to do. DCOM must be directed to create an instance using the Class Factory (we will be learning more about this in the chapter on the Directory), and the programmer has to keep **a count of the instances**. So how does he or she do this?

As part of the process of creating the instance, the client is passed back a pointer to the IUnknown interface. All objects "inherit" (in reality share methods with) the IUnknown interface. This interface uses two methods which must be called by every client as they use the **object** instantiated by DCOM. In other words, a count is kept for each object in a server, not of the server. The **client must call the methods each time it uses a new interface pointer on the object.**

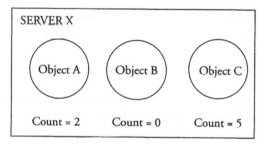

Figure 9.2
DCOM keeps a count of the numbered instances of objects

When the client calls the object it calls the **AddRef** method. This method increments a reference counter maintained by DCOM, which keeps a count of how many clients are using the object. When the client stops using the object, it must call the **Release** method. The Release method decrements the same counter.

For example, when a client first creates an object, it receives back an interface pointer to an object that, from the client's point of view, has a reference count of one. If the client then obtains *another interface* pointer to the same object, the reference count is two. The client must release through *both pointers* to decrement the reference count to zero before the object as a whole can release itself. In effect, every copy of any pointer to an interface requires a reference count on it.

In the simplified case, AddRef must be called for every new copy of an interface pointer and Release called every time an interface pointer is destroyed, but more complex rules can apply so that addref and release actions are properly paired and the object is not released before all the methods called have been actioned. (Clearly a wrong action could cause a code

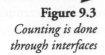

Figure 9.3
*Counting is done
through interfaces*

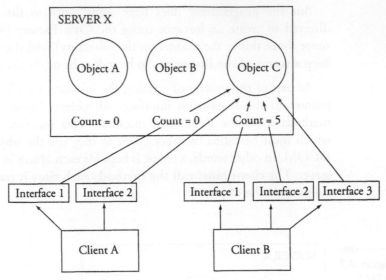

crash.) For example, when a global variable is used, it must be independently counted, as calling functions might destroy the copy in global memory while the local copy was still alive. Nested and staggered/overlapping pointer lifetimes or backpointers also have to be carefully managed.

Clearly, there is the potential here for the counter to get out of step with reality if the client fails, the line goes down between client and server, or the client simply does not respond. We saw that DCOM uses a pinging protocol to detect if clients are still "alive" in a connection. DCOM considers a connection broken if more than three ping periods pass without the components's receiving a ping message.

If the connection is broken between a client and a server, DCOM automatically decrements the reference count, which keeps track of how many clients are connected.

The treatment of the server, as opposed to the objects "encapsulated" by the server, is different. When a server has no objects to serve, no locks, and is not being controlled by an end user, then the server unloads itself.

The way this is done differs depending on whether the server is an EXE or a DLL.

DLLs wait for "someone else" to explicitly unload them, and the server tells this someone else it can be unloaded via a function that must be coded by the developer—DIICanUnloadNow. EXEs unload themselves by terminating.

Context Bridging

Context bridging is the ability to transfer messages between network protocols transparently. The important point about context bridging is the complete transparency of the service—the service not only passes the message on between software products but also handles the transfer between network stacks.

DCOM supports TCP/IP, UDP (which is used internally between Windows NT machines), IPX/SPX, and NetBIOS network protocols. Appletalk support is planned—may even be available by the time you read this book (with the release of DCOM on the Macintosh). Microsoft uses the connectionless UDP subset of TCP/IP to improve performance—by using UDP low-level acknowledgement, packages can be merged with actual data and pinging messages.

DCOM supports context bridging between all the protocols it supports. Three-way bridging is also possible, in addition to the normal two-way bridging. In addition to the normal support provided by DCOM, the use of Cedar adds additional support for the IBM LU6.2 protocol. Cedar uses standard communication protocols (LU 6.2) for communicating between the computer running Windows NT Server and the mainframe TP Monitor. This time, however, as we saw in the last chapter, Microsoft SNA server 3 is used as the bridging software to handle the protocol exchange.

Broadcasting and Multicasting

The default communication approach supported by DCOM is what is termed *one-to-one* or *point-to-point* communication. In DCOM's one-to-one communication approach the developer uses an invocation of a method. This form of conversation is termed *request/reply*—a client requests that a method is invoked and a reply is expected.

So called *one-way* communication where the client sends a request but no reply is expected is not supported by DCOM. This contrasts with CORBA, for example, which does support one-way communication. Even though this style of communication is called one-to-one, a client can communicate with one or more components. Similarly, a component can receive requests from more than one client.

But the request/reply, one-to-one form of addressing is not the only approach that DCOM supports.

What if the client, for example, wanted to send details of an event, but wanted the servers to register their interest in the event? In this case, the client should not need to know all the addresses of the servers that had registered an interest; all it should need to know is that it was supplying an event as opposed to a request.

This type of communication is called *broadcasting* (all servers on the network receive the event) or *multicasting* (only those servers registering an interest get to know of the event). DCOM supports broadcasting and multicasting using a special form of interface called the *Outgoing or Event Interface*.

Where a normal interface is used, the interface is used for incoming calls to methods in a class—the client calls methods via the interface using a request for the method invocation. If the Outgoing or Event Interface is used, the server/class can inform clients of an event via this outgoing interface. If a server has this interface, it is called a *connectable object*.

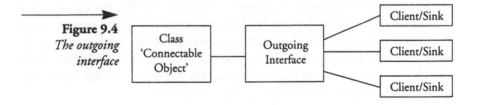

Figure 9.4
The outgoing interface

A client that uses the outgoing interface on an object is called a *sink,* and a special process is implemented within the client to handle incoming calls. From the sink's perspective, the interfaces appear to be incoming and the sink listens through them.

Interfaces in this case are composed of a series of "functions," which are actually events, notifications, or requests.

Events and **notifications** are used to tell the client that something has happened and no reply is expected (one way). A **request** is used to tell the client something, but a response is expected (two way). A class (connectable object) can distribute event details to multiple client sinks, and those client sinks can be connected to any number of outgoing interfaces—in other words, listen for multiple events.

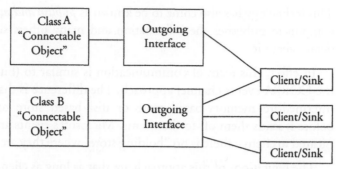

Figure 9.5
A client can be connected to multiple outgoing interfaces

The mechanism used to handle registration within the component is called a "connection point." The connection point allows callers to connect a sink to the connectable object, to disconnect the sink, or to enumerate existing connections.

Connection points are subobjects of the connectable object that are owned by it but that are separate. The reason Microsoft has used this approach is to avoid "reference counting" problems (see Triggers). The sinks connect and disconnect themselves from the outgoing Interfaces, so the component itself does not need to know which clients have registered an interest in knowing about an event.

By connecting themselves to the Interface, the client is effectively registering an interest in all events in the interface. But since a component can have multiple interfaces, it is possible (where a component can generate multiple events) to split up the events into groups and allocate each group to a different interface. In this way the clients need only be informed of the events in which they are interested.

What does all this mean in practice? It means that a component can either "broadcast" or "multicast" details of an event to all the clients interested in the event without needing to know the name or address of those clients. This is a useful feature because it means new clients can be added or old clients removed without needing to alter the component generating the event.

So, a component could be written that monitored the stock value of a share, for example, and once it had reached a certain value any client interested in this event could be informed. Perhaps one type of client was connected to customers owning the share, another type was connected to stockbrokers, another to the actual owners of the company with the share, and so on. All these could register an interest and then write their own processes to act on the information.

This technology has also come to be known as *publish and subscribe* because one component publishes the information and many others subscribe to receive details about it.

In effect, this form of communication is similar to (but not the same as) the CORBA events channel approach. The difference is that CORBA uses an intermediate memory-based store or disk-based store to hold the events before it sends them off to the clients. Microsoft's events are directly communicated to clients; there is no "holding store" where they are temporarily held.

The limitations of this approach are that as long as clients are **up and running** and registered with the connection point they will be informed of the event via their sink. If they have been shut down or have temporarily failed, they will never know. The event isn't stored for them. This means that if our customer, for example, was unfortunate enough to have gone for lunch when the share price rose to an all-time high and the process written to handle the share price event wasn't running, he or she would never know about the event.

We will be seeing in a later chapter that Microsoft's message queuing technology gets around some of these problems and provides an alternative way of broadcasting events that need to be safely delivered to all interested clients.

In Summary

The additional communication services provided within DCOM in addition to the ones provided by the MS RPC and Cedar mechanisms are triggering, context bridging, and broadcast/multicast delivery. Context bridging requires no programmer involvement—it is automatic and is used to bridge network protocols.

Triggering requires programmer involvement, although the actual triggering—loading—of the server is done by DCOM. I rather wish it needed no programmer involvement as this counting stuff could surely be done by DCOM. Perhaps in the future we will see more automation in this area.

The broadcast/multicast communication service clearly needs programmer involvement because it provides an alternative form of communication to the normal one-to-one communication, which is provided as a default with DCOM. This is a useful service and one which can be used to good effect in certain special cases by the programmer. You may want to look, however, to see how the messaging service works before deciding to use the outgoing interface because MSMQ may provide a more robust means of achieving the same thing.

10

DCOM and Windows NT

- ▶ DCOM is embedded in Windows NT
- ▶ But some other services needed to build distributed systems are embedded in Windows 95 and Windows NT 4—not part of DCOM
- ▶ Knowing about these services is important—to help in building distributed systems and to understand the implications on portability

DCOM is embedded within Windows NT and 95, and, at the moment, it is possible to classify what constitute DCOM services and which services are not DCOM, but provided by the operating system. But some services we need to build distributed applications are classified by Microsoft itself as services of Windows NT and not DCOM. This confuses the issue.

We use DCOM to build distributed applications. But, in reality, what we see is that occasionally we are going to have to go outside DCOM and use Windows NT to get the services we need. Knowing about these services is important because if we start to build applications for other platforms, DCOM ports may not provide these services for us.

Even if equivalent services are provided, the suppliers of these ports may be using a different mechanism, which may in turn require changes to our code and limit portability.

About Windows NT

Windows NT was first launched in July 1993; since then Microsoft has sold well over 15 million copies. It was designed by Dave Cutler, creator of Digital's

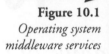

Figure 10.1
Operating system middleware services

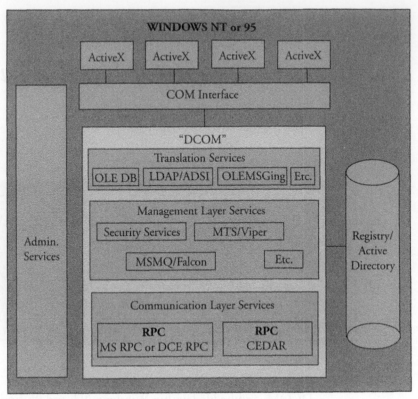

highly successful VMS operating system for the VAX, and it provided, on its launch, full 32 bit operation, preemptive multitasking, virtual memory, C2 level security, and built-in networking.

At the time I wrote this, Windows NT was on version 4, but the key and most important version of Windows NT to affect DCOM will be Windows NT version 5.0. Windows NT 5.0 is due to enter beta testing late 1997, with a launch in 1998.

DCOM is embedded within Windows 95 and both Windows NT 4.0 Workstation and Windows NT Server. DCOM will play an even greater role in Windows NT 5.0.

Windows NT and DCOM

Windows NT is important to any developer needing to build distributed applications because some of the services needed to build a distributed application are found not within DCOM but within the operating system. What are these services? The main services provided within the operating system rather than defined as DCOM services are:

▶ Threading service

▶ Security service

▶ Distributed File service

▶ Memory management

▶ Shared memory service

▶ Time service

▶ Directory service

The Directory service and Security services are of such importance that we have allocated them chapters in their own right, but the other services—threading, shared memory, memory management, distributed file, and time—will be described in this chapter.

To complicate matters further, many of the obviously DCOM services such as MSMQ and MTS use the Windows NT services we have described above. MSMQ, for example, uses the Registry/Directory to store its queues, as does MTS (the buffer pool). All the services use the threads service; some of them use the Directory service. DCOM is thus far more integrated into the operating system than other middleware products might be.

This is going to make it far more difficult for the vendors providing ports to other platforms. Perhaps of most importance is that Microsoft themselves places absolutely no importance upon whether a service is classified as DCOM or not.

As far as it is concerned, all the functions are really functions of the operating system—it just so happens some of them support distribution over a network. Unfortunately, this argument leaves the vendors of DCOM ports with an even more difficult task because they have their job cut out to untangle what in effect is a highly integrated set of operating system services, to produce a set of coherent equivalent middleware services on other operating systems.

Multithreading

DCOM and the threads service

One of the complexities of describing the threading service is that it is Windows NT that provides the threading service but DCOM services use it. First, they use it themselves to improve their own performance, increasing the throughput of their own services. Second, however, a DCOM programmer uses the interfaces defined in DCOM to invoke the services of the thread service.

Surely, you might ask, if it is accessed by a DCOM interface this isn't it a DCOM service? The problem with this argument is that the threads service exists and can be accessed outside of the DCOM approach. DCOM has just added to the existing service, creating a COM-based approach to access the service, a new terminology for the functions provided, and added-value functions built on top of the service.

In the following paragraphs we look at what is meant by multithreading, why threads are useful in general, and then go on to look at how they work in the DCOM context.

What are threads?

A process instance (a running process) can support multiple threads. We could think of a thread as a piece of figurative string through the process, not needing duplicate code (copies of the code) to exist in memory. Thus one copy of the process exists in memory, but multiple executions of that code may be proceeding in parallel.

Threads support simultaneous access to shared resources. Multiple threads of the same process use the same address space and share all static and external data as well as open files and any other services available to the whole process. If multithreading is used, locks have to be placed on shared data, and resources and locking is the responsibility of the programmer.

The use of threads

Threads serve two quite distinct purposes within a distributed application:

▶ They can be used to provide support for asynchronous processing

▶ They can be used to improve performance

Asynchronous processing support–Normal communication between clients and servers using DCOM is synchronous with the client sending a request and then waiting with its thread blocked until the reply is received. By using the threads service, however, asynchronous communication can be supported—the client spawns a new thread to handle any additional processing while the existing thread waits for the reply.

There are alternative means by which asynchronous processing can be supported. One of these ways has already been described—the Outgoing interface.

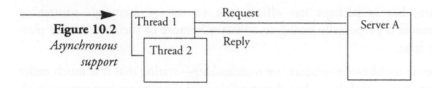

Figure 10.2
Asynchronous support

All events sent to outgoing interfaces are by their nature asynchronous because the event is sent to DCOM and server processing can then proceed.

Another way is to use a **call back object**. In this case, a special call back object is created to handle any replies. Note, however, that the initial reply from the called object still has to be waited for even if it is only an acknowledgment.

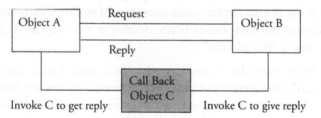

Figure 10.3
Using the call back object to support asynchronous processing

We will also see in the chapters on MSMQ and MTS that they offer their own specialized form of support for asynchronous processing. So, there are ways the programmer can use to avoid having to use threads to achieve asynchronous processing. To improve performance, however, the thread service must be used.

Performance improvement–When applications are distributed, many clients may be requesting the same component. If some means of increasing the number of server copies available is not available, the client either has to wait in a queue to be processed (if one exists) or in the worst case, it could be simply turned away. To achieve the highest throughput on a single machine, developers must be provided with a means of duplicating servers on the machine.

Microsoft employs a multithreading rather than a multitasking model to increase the number of available servers. Multitasking would have been an option, but is perhaps less efficient in its use of memory—something Microsoft is perpetually trying to conserve because of their traditional platform base.

Some middleware vendors use multitasking—stating that it is much easier to program (which it is), but they traditionally support environments which use larger machines (not PCs) where memory is not a particular problem.

In DCOM, as the number of clients needing to access a server increases; the server is multithreaded to handle each client in parallel.

Thread creation in basic DCOM is *not automatic*. Without MTS (which we will be looking at in a later chapter and which does support automatic thread creation) the programmer is responsible for creating his or her own threads. Thus, the programmer will use a special set of interfaces provided within DCOM itself to create new server threads. The programmer also has to control locking. Functions such as CreateThread, ResumeThread, WaitForMultipleObjects, WaitForSingleObject, CreateMutex, and CreateEvent are used to handle threads. The programmer then uses the features supplied with the thread service—mutexes, critical sections, and semaphores to protect access to the data. Basically the developer generally needs to ensure the component is "thread safe."

With any object-based model, Microsoft had a choice as to what to thread—the server, the object/component, or the method. In DCOM, the developer can "free thread" a component if desired. In free threading, each object invocation may be handled by a separate thread.

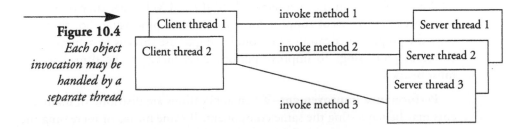

Figure 10.4
Each object invocation may be handled by a separate thread

What this means is that one client thread can be communicating with multiple server threads, each one handling a different invocation from that client. At one time, Microsoft restricted a client thread to one server thread; DCOM removed this restriction. Dispatching is handled by the COM library in conjunction with the MS RPC runtime library.

How does Microsoft's thread service work?

DCOM uses an unusual approach to thread provision. A thread pool, managed by DCOM, is set up for incoming requests. On multiprocessor machines, the thread pool is optimized to the number of available processors. The number of threads in the pool is preallocated by the administrator, but in principle the number of threads in the pool can be as large as the administrator wants—there is no DCOM imposed limit.

In response to a request for a component, DCOM allocates a thread from the pool, calls the component on that thread, and, after the call completes execution, returns the thread to the pool. As requests arrive, the number of actual threads in the pool is increased up to the preallocated maximum number.

In summary

Microsoft bases all their DCOM services upon a multithreading model of processing rather than a multitasking one in order to improve memory usage. Servers and client can be multithreaded, but the programmer must control threads, creating them, removing them, and handling the locking.

It is worth noting that we have avoided going into the types of thread model— apartment and free threads—because we feel this is too low a level for this book, but the type of threads does affect the approach taken by the programmer and to what extent he is supported. The apartment model of threading used for user interfaces provides slightly more support than the free threading model used for all other types of processing.

Distributed File Services

The aim of a distributed file service is to provide one unified integrated file system that can be used by all users to share files and the information in those files across a network of machines running different operating systems. A DFS enables a collection of heterogeneous computers to share files as though all the computers were homogeneous. It is thus a global file system with a single shared file space. The files can contain anything the user wants—text, audio, video, data, etc., but it will obviously need to be interpreted/accessed by whatever package/software created it, where the data format is software defined.

Users should be able to share files, copy files, maintain, update, and remove files, as though they were all local to their machine. Users (end users or developers) should have no need to know that the files are distributed.

Windows NT 4 has a distributed file system, where files in the network are presented as a single hierarchical view, accessible across the network. An even fuller version of the file system with more features is expected in Windows NT version 5.

But the Windows NT DFS is not a cross-operating system. Microsoft did not implement the DCE DFS and has no apparent plans to do so. Furthermore, the vendors porting DCOM to other platforms also have not stated any plans to provide such a service. As such, although Windows NT has a distributed file service, we can say that DCOM does not and is unlikely to get one. Does this matter?

DFS is not a service used by developers to build applications and is thus a sort of periphery service to many people. Many developers consider that middleware should just provide services to build distributed applications and support them at runtime afterwards.

But DFSs are useful. The DCE DFS, for example, has been used to support some of the most demanding file access applications yet developed. IBM's 1996 Atlanta Olympic information service was underpinned by DFS, and although IBM had problems with the quality of information being entered on the system, it had no problems with providing the information to journalists and reporters across the world, with very acceptable response times.

It is something of a pity, therefore, that Microsoft doesn't use DCE's DFS or provide more support for distribution of their own on other operating systems. But we must be careful here about the limitations of Microsoft's approach. What cannot be achieved via DCOM may be achieved in a different sort of way via the Internet.

Microsoft's vision is to have a single user interface for all access to server data. Effectively, they want to unify the world of the Internet, intranet, and enterprise so that the same interface is used whatever method of communication is used. That interface will be the Windows interface combined with Microsoft's Web Browser. Web Browser and Windows will eventually be indistinguishable. The Web Browser will be used to browse the World Wide Web and to browse your PC's files or the files in PCs of others on the network.

A user, for example, will be able to open files and folders on his or her own machine using the same approach as that used in Web Browsers—so local or remote internal files will look like Internet Web pages. Just like pages in an Internet file, the developer will be able to create internal bookmarks that will enable the end user to jump about the files as they can with Web pages. Users will be able to navigate though the files as though they were Web pages and open them with the same paradigm—a single click as though they were a "hot spot." A developer, for example, will also be able to create Web pages in

HTML (more about this in a later chapter) and include them in the Directory as though they were normal files.

Conversely, Internet pages will look like local files, arranged in a hierarchical way to look like your directory. All Internet files will simply be filed under the Directory heading of "Internet." In effect, there will be the equivalence of external and internal storage space.

The Internet will appear to be just an extension of your hard disk, with frequently used pages cached or simply accessed invisibly via the Internet through the browser capability. The same task bars will be used to navigate files and the Internet. The Find option on the task bar Start button will enable you to search for information on your hard disk and search for information on the Internet. (For more details see http://www.microsoft.com/ie/ie40/integrat/).

Thus, although Microsoft does not have a Distributed File System which covers several operating systems, they do have a distributed file system—an integrated distributed file system—that covers their operating system and any files on the Internet. Thus, a user could create files on both the internal network and external networks in "Internet format" using HTML pages on operating systems other than Windows NT and access them using the new Windows interface.

By using Microsoft's approach to distributed files, users should be able to share and look at files but they won't be able to copy files, maintain, update, and remove files, in the same way that you can with a full distributed file system. Nevertheless, the use of the Internet format as a means of supporting distribution is quite inspired, as the end user is assured of having a common readable format for information.

Memory Management

Generally speaking, programmers building distributed applications without using middleware have to handle the memory allocation and deallocation themselves.

For novice or inexperienced programmers, this can often cause problems as they are often not sure when to deallocate the temporary memory needed to handle a call, when the call has finished, and whether it is their responsibility to free memory or not.

The result is what is called "memory leak" where memory is continually allocated by the program, but not deallocated. In other words, programs allocate more memory than they subsequently free. Distributed applications are particularly prone to memory leakage on both the client and server side.

Some middleware products provide functions which handle memory allocation and deallocation automatically for the programmer and thus avoid memory leak. One particular product's memory management functions are controlled by knowing the state of the RPC call. The memory management functions are thus triggered by the state of the RPC.

Where Microsoft's tools are used, memory management can in some cases be handled by them. Where tools are not used, although the management of the Vtables is handled by DCOM, all other memory management has to be handled by the programmer using commands provided with DCOM.

The DCOM library provides a number of APIs which are used to get and free memory, as well as an interface through which methods can be called. The **IMAlloc** Interface has methods to allocate, reallocate, free, get the size of, and minimize the heap. The shortcut API commands also provided are **CoTaskMemAlloc** and **CoTaskMemFree**.

The way parameters are handled is dependent on whether they are in parameters, out parameters, or in/out parameters (used for both input and output). The rules are shown below:

▶ In parameters are allocated and freed by the caller.

▶ Out parameters are allocated by the called object and freed by the caller.

▶ In/out parameters are initially allocated by the caller, then freed and reallocated by the called object. The caller is responsible for freeing the final returned value.

In error returns, out parameters have to be set to a value which can be cleaned up without any action on the caller's part, and all in/out parameters must either be left by the caller or be explicitly set as in the out parameter error return case. Thus, although memory management is supported by Windows NT with commands (interfaces really) to help the programmer manage his own memory, no automated services are provided. (It would be nice to see more help here. Memory management is such a pain in the neck it could use more support.)

Shared Memory

One of the useful services which a middleware product can support is distributed shared memory. Distributed shared memory is the ability to access an area of shared memory on one machine from processes on other machines where these other machines may be running the same or different operating systems.

Distributed shared memory acts like a bulletin board with processes able to share memory across the network, posting data into memory, and accessing or retrieving data from it. Read and write operations should be serialized automatically and should be guaranteed to act atomically.

Generally speaking, the shared memory services provided by middleware products are better than those provided by operating systems. Where Unix is used, for example, the programmer has to program his application to serialize data access when using native operating system shared memory services.

By using the distributed shared memory services in middleware products, programmers should also be able to apply access controls to the data and lock the data. Byte level read or write access limits should be able to be imposed on all or parts of memory segments. Particular areas of segments should be able to be made read only or inaccessible for given time periods.

All or parts of memory segments may also be locked at byte level so that updates can be performed on the area. Read or write operations attempted against a locked area of memory are then prevented until the memory is subsequently unlocked. This feature has particular use on high performance applications to replace a DBMS.

Distributed shared memory services are not provided with DCOM, nor are they provided with Windows NT, and as such they are not likely to be provided with DCOM on other platforms. Windows NT does have support for shared memory on a single host. This provides a virtual memory system which enables up to 32 processes to read shared memory on the host (as long as the manufacturer's HAL drives are installed).

The memory looks as though it is a file and supports paging, caching, buffering, and locking. Where SMP is supported, applications can share between processors. But this is not the same as distributed shared memory.

Timing Services

There is only one middleware product (as far as I'm aware) that supports distributed time services and that is DCE. Windows NT has a clock, but it doesn't provide distributed time services.

To be a truly distributed time service, the times on each computer must be synchronized in the network to a recognized time standard. This could be an internal and largely arbitrary time, or it could be an external source such as that obtained through a hardware device that receives time from a radio signal or other public source of time. Furthermore, there needs to be constant resynchronization of the clocks to ensure they stay in step.

In Summary

As we have seen, Windows NT is important to any developer needing to build distributed applications because some of the services needed to build a distributed application are found not within DCOM but within the operating system. The main services we believe *should* be provided to build distributed systems which are currently provided within Windows NT rather than defined as DCOM services are:

▶ Threading service

▶ Security service

▶ Distributed File service

▶ Memory management

▶ Shared memory service

▶ Time service

▶ Directory service

The security service and Registry/Directory service are described separately in later chapters. We will be seeing that the Registry service is being ported to other platforms by other vendors of DCOM, but the security services may not be "end-to-end."

The Registry is so fundamental to the operation of DCOM that it has to be ported, and as such it makes the development of distributed applications possible. The absence of a full "end-to-end" security service may cause problems as the applications will not necessarily be totally secure as a result. The success of the security services may well depend on how the developer uses third-party products.

The memory management service is being ported to other platforms by vendors of DCOM, so this service will end up being a distributed one and will support the development of distributed applications on platforms besides Windows NT. The threading service, as we have seen, may be ported, or an alternative service may be used. Either way a service of one sort of another will be available to build distributed applications.

The Distributed File service is a fully distributed service on Windows NT but is not being ported and, as such, will not be available with DCOM on other platforms. As DFS is not a service normally used to develop applications or support them at runtime, this may not be a problem for many developers, but as we have seen, it does deny developers a useful service if it is not available.

The new Windows interface will provide a unified distributed file service for ready access to information in files and pages on the Internet and across local and remote Windows servers giving a good compromise solution, though not fully distributed file service functionality. But, there are two services on Windows NT that are not only not going to be ported, but even on Windows NT are not fully distributed—the time service and shared memory service.

This means that DCOM is missing some useful services—services which could be used to build distributed applications. Where developers need a time service, they could use DCE's Time service instead, using the fact that both DCOM on Windows NT and DCOM on other platforms are supported by the DCE RPC, and as such, as long as the service is available on some of the platforms, it can be accessed—albeit with an RPC call rather than a method invocation. All of which brings us on to our next chapter—DCOM on other platforms.

11

DCOM and Other Platform Support

- ▶ DCOM is being ported to other platforms
- ▶ Services will be a subset of the full set
- ▶ Software AG, Digital, and Hewlett Packard are main players
- ▶ Timescales 1997/8
- ▶ AIX, HP-UX, Solaris, Linux, Digital Unix, Sinix, SCO UnixWare, OpenVMS, OpenMVS, OS/400

If you want to build a distributed application, the last thing you need is to be told is that the middleware you have available, to act as the infrastructure, only runs on Windows with links to the IBM mainframe. Given the number of other perfectly good (even excellent) middleware products there are around, no one would blame you for deciding to use TOP END, Tuxedo, or DCE instead, for example, which run on numerous platforms, so would provide no limit on your design or how you connected up your existing systems and databases. DCOM may be free with Windows, but if it doesn't work with the other platforms you need to incorporate in your design, it isn't a lot of use.

You shouldn't have to migrate your systems—your heritage systems, your working systems, your working databases—to new platforms. Really good middleware enables you to link them all up. Your company's investment in those systems can be preserved, and you can be saved the tedium of pointless migration (a thankless task at the best of times as most end users consider it a waste of money and time).

So this chapter is particularly important for those of us that believe the D in DCOM should stand for more than distributed over a Windows network.

We will be seeing that DCOM is being ported to other platforms, but the number of platforms is still limited and the functionality is not as rich as on the Windows platform itself.

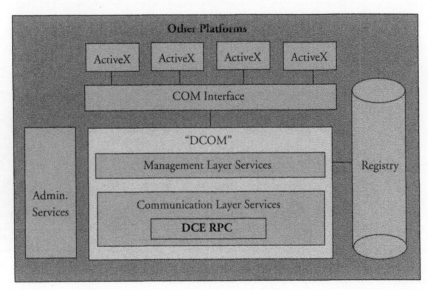

Figure 11.1
DCOM on other platforms

What Platforms?

Let us start this chapter by first looking at what platforms DCOM already exists on or is being ported to. DCOM was released with **Windows NT version 4** (Workstation and Server) in 1996. DCOM for **Windows 95** was put into beta in mid-1996 and released towards the end of 1996. A beta version of DCOM for the **Apple Macintosh** was made available in 1997 (running under Windows).

The draft version of the COM specification was released for third parties in October 1995. DCOM was by this time already in development, but the specification was for use by external third parties. The specification was a joint development by Digital and Microsoft.

There are four companies involved in the porting at the moment—Digital, Hewlett Packard, Software AG, and Silicon Graphics.

Digital–is porting DCOM to **Digital Unix** and **OpenVMS**. Note that it will only be OpenVMS on the Alpha, not VAX/VMS, and there are no plans to support the VAX. The ports are actually being based on Software AG's port. Source code is also being supplied by Microsoft. Work started on the port in August 1996, and when I wrote this the ports were due mid-1998.

As part of the port, Digital plans to also provide compiler support for Microsoft's C and C++ as well as providing a Java Virtual Machine on Open-VMS. They intend to support the Win32 API using (probably) Bristol technology's software.

The ports will be limited to the TCP/IP network protocol because DCE is being used as the underlying infrastructural software to support the ports. Digital is having to do some work to get Microsoft's MS RPC to talk to the DCE RPC, particularly adding NTLM authorization to OpenVMS to provide the equivalent authenticated RPC mechanism which Microsoft uses. But you don't need to worry about this too much.

You also won't need to worry about installing DCE when you use DCOM on the other platforms; it will come as part of the port. If you want to find out more about Digital's ports, they have a Web site—**http://www.openvms.digital.com/openvms.**

Software AG–was the first company to get involved with ports of DCOM and it terms these additional ports DCOM FTE (For the Enterprise).

It is concentrating on developing ports of DCOM for midrange Unix and mainframe systems. The ports it is planning to release or has already released are for **Solaris, Digital Unix, OpenMVS, Linux, AIX, Sinix, OS/400**, and **SCO UnixWare.** Further ports to **HP-UX** and **OpenVMS** are also planned though this may change with Digital and HP's involvement. On MVS, the developer must have the POSIX-compliant version of MVS.

Microsoft entered into the partnership agreement with Software AG at the time Windows NT version 4 was being developed. The partnership wasn't announced until October/November of 1996, by which time Software AG was well underway developing the ports of DCOM to other platforms.

Software AG in the United States worked with Microsoft's Windows NT team to develop the ports, and a test version for Sun Solaris 2.5 was made available in October 1996, where it could be freely downloaded. At the time, the versions for Digital Unix and OpenMVS were under development.

IBM OpenMVS, Linux (on Intel), and Digital Unix beta kits were released in the first half of 1997. Platforms scheduled to begin beta testing in 1998 were the OS/400, OpenVMS, and SINIX.

Software AG and MainSoft have formed a partnership to trade technologies based on DCOM. Under the agreement, announced in December 1996, Mainsoft was responsible for putting the Win32 APIs onto Unix. Software AG also used MainSoft's DCOM automation technology and structured storage system. Both companies are Microsoft source code licensees.

As we saw earlier, DCOM on the Windows NT platform is highly integrated with basic operating system services such as thread management, memory management, and I/O functionality. On Windows NT these services are provided by the kernel system and typically present a callable interface in the Win32 set of functions.

DCOM FTE contains an implementation of a subset of the Microsoft Windows NT Kernel services (Win32 service routines). This implementation provides the basic services required for the DCOM FTE runtime environment on Unix. Rather amusingly it has been dubbed the "Mutant," so if you hear anyone asking if you have a mutant on your Unix machine, they're not talking about Turtle games, they're talking about DCOM!

The Mutant provides the system services required by DCOM FTE plus additional APIs, which Software AG feels are needed for DCOM applications. When I write this, support for Win32 GUI–related APIs (Windows, Windows Messages, Drawing, primitives, and so on) weren't supported, but no doubt they will be in the course of time.

Their Web site for more details about the Software AG ports, particularly the timescales for the ports, can be found on **http://www.sagus.com**. This Web site also contains downloadable versions of DCOM for the ports available in beta.

Hewlett Packard–is intending to port DCOM to HP-UX. The announcement was made in May 1997, when Hewlett Packard announced their intent to provide COM technology, including DCOM features, on HP-UX "within the year." A summary of the planned platform support is shown below in the table.

One important aspect worthy of special mention is that the other ports of DCOM on the platforms shown generally work only with Windows NT, not Windows95. This means that the developer needs a three-tier architecture to use DCOM, with Windows NT or 95 clients accessing a Windows NT server which can then, in turn, communicate with other platforms. In fact, this is the sort of architecture Microsoft is encouraging, with other platforms acting more as servers and the Windows NT platform acting as a sort of hub.

Table 11.1 *Platform support*

	Operating system	DCOM	Who
UNIX	AIX	Planned	Software AG
	HP-UX	Planned	HP, Software AG
	Solaris	YES	Software AG
	SINIX	Planned	Software AG
	Linux	YES	Software AG
	SCO UnixWare	Planned	Software AG
	Digital Unix	Planned	Digital, Software AG
	IRIX	YES	Silicon Graphics
PC	Windows95	YES	Microsoft
	Windows NT WS	YES	Microsoft
	Windows NT Svr	YES	Microsoft
	Macintosh	YES	Microsoft
Propty	Open MVS	YES	Software AG
	OS/400	Planned	Software AG
	OpenVMS	Planned	Digital, Software AG

Figure 11.2
Windows NT acts as a hub in three-tier architecture

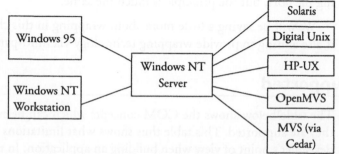

Furthermore, the network protocol supported is TCP/IP to all platforms except MVS when Cedar is being used.

What Is Provided?

DCOM on other platforms is provided as a runtime environment and a Software Development Kit (SDK).

The runtime environment comes as a set of shared runtime libraries (DLLs or equivalent) used for supporting the applications at runtime together with a set of administration tools, such as a utility to enable servers (proxy and stub libraries) to be registered, and installation utilities. Be aware that the runtime takes up over 20MB of disk space.

The SDK consists of a set of tools, libraries, and examples which typically include:

▶ An MIDL compiler—which can be used to generate stubs and proxies. Sample files are often provided with the ports

▶ An ActiveX Template Library—a Unix implementation of the Microsoft ATL

▶ GUIDgen (the tool to generate GUIDs)

▶ UUIDgen—this looks up the registry to get the address of the network interface card in the way we described in the chapter on GUIDs

▶ header files—a set of header files for inclusion in source files for compilation

▶ make files—the makefile utility is provided as a Bourne shell script in Software AG's Unix port, for example. The utility generates a C++ module that has to be compiled and linked with the shared libraries.

▶ mktyplib—the make type library utility

These are generally command line driven at the moment rather than being GUI-based tools. Clearly the actual tools provided depend on who is providing the port, but the principle is much the same.

We will be saying a little more about wrapping in this chapter, but Digital is also aiming to provide wrapping technology via third-party companies.

Concepts Supported

The table below shows the COM concepts which can be supported and how they are supported. This table thus shows what limitations there are from the developer's point of view when building an application. In the next section we will show the functions available.

Table 11.2 *Concept support*

Concept	Supported?
Component	YES
Interface	YES
Moniker	YES (registering, stringification, binding file, and composite, etc.)
Automation	YES (IDispatch and the type library)
Aggregation	YES
MIDL	YES

Services Supported

In this section we will look at the services supported. The tables in the following pages have been organized first around the general headings I have used for the types of service and second around the service names I have used in this book so far to show the functionality of DCOM. In the following lists, I have described Software AG's and Digital's approaches separately.

Communication-level services

Table 11.3 *Communication-level services*

Service	Supported?
Pack/Unpack	YES (including "custom marshaling," though a developer is recommended not to use it)
Translate Data formats	Generally yes, although these early releases are having difficulty with Microsoft's Unicode. Use standard marshaling (not custom marshaling)
Buffer packing	YES
Session management	YES
Network calling	YES
Transmission coordination	YES
Fault handling	YES
Triggering	YES

Table 11.3 *Communication--level services (Continued)*

Service	Supported?
Context bridging	NO
Broadcast/Multicast (Outgoing Interface)	Not clear at the time of writing
Memory Management	DCOM FTE contains an implementation of a subset of the Microsoft Windows NT Kernel services (Win32 service routines). This implementation provides the basic memory management services required for the DCOM FTE runtime environment on Unix.

Management layer services

Table 11.4 *Management layer services*

Service	Supported?
Threading	**Digital**–Is using the underlying DCE thread service to support multi-threading on the OpenVMS platform. Their Unix port is based on the Software AG version for Unix and as such will mirror the approach used by them.
	Software AG–DCOM FTE contains an implementation of a subset of the Microsoft Windows NT Kernel services (Win32 service routines). This implementation provides the basic threading services required for the DCOM FTE runtime environment on Unix.
Security	**Digital** is using the GSSAPI interface to DCE security to provide security services on OpenVMS. But, they also aim to enable a developer to use NT security.
	The user will be able to log on using NT users and passwords and authentication will be achieved via the NT host. Access control is likely to prove more difficult and Digital envisages that two sets of identifiers may be needed for the Windows NT and the OpenVMS platform because it is difficult to combine Access Control Lists.
	Software AG is also using a third-party Security Service Provider.
MTS	Not supported by Digital or Software AG
MSMQ	Not supported by Digital or Software AG

Translation services

In the following table we have not included an entry for ADSI and LDAP as this is covered by the next table under the heading of Directory services support.

Table 11.5 *Translation services*

Service	Supported?
OLEDB	Not supported by Digital or Software AG. Both Digital and Software AG will be able to provide support, however, for structured storage (see chapter on OLEDB).
OLEMSGing	Not supported by Digital or Software AG.

Other services

Software AG is providing a Registry which can be edited using a "regedit" tool or a tool called the "sermon" tool. Both tools are provided with the Mutant.

The Registry edit tool is a Motif application with a similar look and feel to the Microsoft Registry editor and is GUI based. The sermon tool is a command line application which can be used to operate and monitor the registry service itself at runtime.

Table 11.6 *Other services*

Service	Supported?
Administration	**Digital** is porting the Windows event logger and providing tools to help with administration. But administration will not be of the entire configuration of Windows NT and other platforms. Thus no unified centralized administration tools will be available.
	Software AG's tools are also not capable of supporting the entire configuration; they are platform specific.
Directory	**Digital** will be supporting the Registry. A Digital group is looking at the developments in the Active Directory.
	Software AG is supporting the Registry. More details are provided below.

Software AG supports both a disk-based and memory resident registry. When the configuration is started, a utility loads the registry from disk or creates it automatically using default settings. It then checks on a regular basis to see if the memory resident registry has changed, and if it has, the disk-based registry is updated. The utility also creates a backup of the disk file. The Registry provided on the Solaris platform is a multiuser registry.

We will be seeing in the chapter on Directory services that DCOM uses a component called the SCM—Service Control Manager—to handle requests for components on other platforms. This SCM keeps a list of the servers actually running in a table—called the Running Object Table. Software AG has implemented both the SCM and the ROT. Any machine wanting to run a server application must have these services on it. The SCM on the Unix machines can offer its services to both applications on Unix and applications on Windows NT—so the two types of SCM do talk to each other to find a component.

Wrapping

One of the main themes of Microsoft's approach to other platforms is that the connectivity being provided by the ports of DCOM is there primarily to enable the developer to link to existing applications. Microsoft is not keen on developers writing lots of new components on machines running Unix or MVS, for example, for the simple and very obvious reason that it prolongs the life of these operating systems, when Microsoft wants the world to use Windows.

Digital and HP, of course, do want you to write lots of new applications on their Digital Unix, HP-UX, and OpenVMS machines for the equally obvious reason that they want to prolong the life of these systems this is one area where Microsoft and its partners don't agree. Anyway, talk to Microsoft and they will actively discourage you from putting new components on these other boxes and operating systems, while encouraging you to access your legacy/heritage systems on these boxes.

If you want to invoke or use legacy code from an object-oriented application, however, you have to give it an object-oriented interface—make it look like a component and adapt the logic to respond to object-based calls. Generally speaking the legacy code acts as a server for client requests, so the wrapper code turns the legacy code into a "pseudo-object" (or objects) that can be invoked using object-oriented techniques. This process is termed "wrapping." A *wrapper* is a "software envelope for existing business functions that hides the implementation details of the function."

The functions of a piece of software can be accessed via screens or terminals, a callable API, a command line interface, or via other sorts of input such as transaction files. Wrapping technology works best when applied to software accessed via APIs or command lines and in practice, is better applied to application functions like an application package, software package, or in-house application. Both the API and Command line then represent the functionality of the internal code and the 'calls' are then translated into object-oriented invocations.

Many ORB vendors talk about wrapping as though it was a simple case of adding a few lines of code. The very word "wrapping" conjures up images of presents being wrapped in paper rather than the sort of complex problem-ridden task it actually is. The sorts of problems the developer has to overcome in practice are:

▶ the application state may need to be preserved between wrapper invocations

▶ object and method calls may not map one for one with function calls

▶ application error conditions must be mapped to wrapper code exceptions

▶ application and wrapper code threads have to be matched (they can become mismatched if not properly managed)

▶ input/output and the matching of data structures from OO to other structures can be complex

▶ there are implicit problems with performance as translation is involved

The developer must first decide which of the functions in the legacy code are "invokable" from the client. He then builds an interface which represents these as objects and methods. The interface can be generated in the normal way to provide stub code in C or C++, for example, but the developer must then map the C and C++ data structures to the internal data structures (in COBOL, say) and map object calls to function calls. It is the wrapper code which does this mapping and translating. Where the application is accessed via a command line interface, the wrapper code can invoke the application and execute application commands in an operating system specific script.

The wrapper code developed by the programmer may consist of a portion which takes the input from the server stub (unmarshalled data but in object-based form), a mapping portion to do all the translation needed, and a third portion which interacts directly with the legacy application. In practice the mapping section can become extremely complex—one to many, many to many, and many to one mappings between object invocations and function calls can occur. In some cases a separate "Interface Engine" is needed rather than a simple wrapper, which can handle multiple clients and servers.

Thus, Digital's search for third-party wrapping software to be provided with their ports is particularly welcome. I recommend that if you do want to access existing systems from a component that you do look for third-party products to help you. It is worth mentioning that Software AG has added some extremely useful automatic technology to their "EntireX" range of products, which enable Natural programs to be wrapped as ActiveX components.

In Summary

I think we can see from this chapter that Microsoft's partners are beginning to put the **D** in DCOM in a fairly major way. It is still early days, but in the course of time you will see DCOM appearing on the AIX, HP-UX, Solaris, SINIX, Linux, SCO UnixWare, Digital Unix, Macintosh, Open MVS, OS/400, and OpenVMS platforms in addition to the Windows 95, Windows NT WS, and Windows NT Svr platforms on which it runs now.

Support for services is also going to be fairly good, though not all the services will be supported. All the communication type services are likely to be supported with the exception of context bridging, which has no meaning in this context as all the ports use TCP/IP.

The threads and security services will be supported, but some doubts hang over the security services and whether they will be end to end. As we also pointed out, threads support may also not be completely uniform even though it is provided with a common API. Where threads are supported by ports of the kernel as they are in the DCOM FTE ports, threads services should be common.

Perhaps the biggest disappointment is the lack of support for MSMQ and MTS, both of which are fairly key services, but we may see changes here in the fullness of time.

No translation services are supported, but support is provided for structured storage.

The Registry—an essential part of DCOM even though it is a part of Windows NT—is being ported, but at the moment little is known of what will happen when Microsoft starts to introduce the Active Directory. Administration services are a real weak spot, with some services being provided by the port suppliers, but with nowhere near the functionality of the Microsoft administration tools, which are GUI-based and provide a large number of

GUI based functions. Worse, the administrator has no way of monitoring the entire configuration of Windows and non-Windows machines, so if the administrator has a problem, it is going to be incredibly difficult sorting out where it is. I have visions of a poor developer running between machines, accessing each administration utility trying to figure out why performance has dropped to a 50-second response time! I guess you'll have to build links to your system management software. You are using systems management software, aren't you? Of course you are!

12

DCOM and the Internet

- ▶ DCOM and ActiveX are intended to work with the Internet
- ▶ But Microsoft's approach to the Internet is different from other vendors
- ▶ The main products used are Internet Explorer and Information Internet Server
- ▶ Script languages used are VBScript and JScript
- ▶ The approach is unique to Microsoft

We have looked at the platform support for DCOM; the next big question most people are likely to ask is does it work over the Internet? This chapter thus looks at Microsoft's approach for supporting the Internet, the products it has, the strategy it recommends its users take, and the links with DCOM.

We will be starting this chapter with a description of the approach taken by some of the other middleware vendors so that you can contrast the approach Microsoft has taken with that used by them. Microsoft's approach is quite different, and we will be looking at the reasons why and the implications of this in this chapter.

How Do Other Middleware Vendors Provide Internet Support?

Several middleware vendors currently support the Internet—NCR with TOP END using a module called *Java Remote Client* services, Transarc with Encina using *DE-Light Web Client*, and BEA with Tuxedo using a module called *Jolt*. All of them use an identical approach—an approach which uses Java, Web browsers, and Web servers—and all of the above products are aimed at

Figure 12.1
DCOM and the
Internet

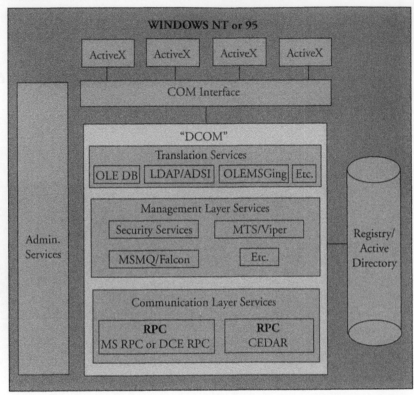

organizations wanting to support commercial transactions on the Internet using the Web.

The Internet and its protocols are normally unable to recognize the state of a transaction, which makes the multistep, often complex interactions which take place within a transaction largely impossible to support. DE-Light Web Client, JRC, and Jolt solve this problem by combining distributed transaction processing with software that can sustain transaction interactions over the Web.

Let me start by explaining the way the Web normally works. If you are a Web expert you can ignore the next few subsections, otherwise read on for an explanation of Web and Internet technology.

Internet Technology Explained

The Internet and the World Wide Web normally work using TCP/IP as the network protocol, Web browsers communicating with Web servers, URLs as the addressing mechanism, CGI to invoke programs, HTML to describe documents, and HTTP as the communication protocol. The Web is accessed using a Web browser on a client, which connects with a Web server. The Web browser (for example, Netscape's Navigator or Microsoft's Internet Explorer) running on a PC or similar machine is used as the user's point of access to the Internet. The Web server is located elsewhere on the network and handles the storage of information and retrieval on behalf of the client.

URLs

When a user wants to connect to a Web server, he uses a "logical" address name called the *URL–Uniform Resource Locator*. The URL is used for all Internet communication and has a format like that shown below:

aa://aa.aa.aa.aa/aa/aa/aa/aa.aa#aa

The first set of aas describe the data source/protocol. The Internet actually supports a number of protocols:

▶ a file accessible through the File Transfer protocol (ftp)

▶ a file accessible through the Gopher protocol (gopher)

▶ a hypertext document—typically an HTML file accessible through the HyperText Transfer Protocol HTTP (of which more later)

▶ mail

▶ a news group accessible through the News Transfer Protocol (NNTP)

▶ telnet

The Internet can thus act as an e-mail application, file transfer application, and data access application, among other things. The particular protocol used for Web access is the HTTP protocol.

The rest of the URL is then the address—in the case of Web access, the Web server name, the directory in which to find the Web page you're looking for, and even down to a particular spot in the particular page. The address, in other words, is not just the address of the Web server, it is the address of the particular bit of information you're wanting to look at on the Web server. This means that a company can set up a number of "Web sites" telling you about different things—support and help, general information, and so on.

HTTP

Communication from the PC to other nodes is via the protocol *HTTP–HyperText Transfer Protocol*. HTTP is just the particular protocol used for communication in the World Wide Web. It is not a network protocol, but an application protocol—it defines how Web browsers and Web servers talk to one another. The Internet is, of course, based on the network protocol TCP/IP.

Information exchanges on the Web happen in four parts all classed as message types for HTTP—connection, request, response, and close. These message types bear a strong similarity to the RPC mechanisms we have discussed in this book.

▶ Connection–When connecting, the browser will display status messages on the connection—connecting, for example, or timed out if it can't make the connection. The Web browser finds the server's IP address from what is called a local domain name server. The Internet is based on the TCP/IP standard and the IP address is a unique number for each machine on the Internet. IP addresses are physical addresses, for example, 193.1.1.19.56. The Domain Name Server converts the logical name the user has used to the physical IP address for the machine. In effect, the DNS is a Directory Service.

▶ Request–The client asks for the Web resource that it is looking for with the name of the protocol to use, the name of the object to find, and information about how the server should respond.

▶ Response–After the Web browser has made a connection to the Web server, it downloads a Web page (or pages). If the server cannot deliver the information as requested by the client, it sends back an error message explaining why it couldn't deliver.

▶ Close–After the information requested has been delivered, the connection between client and server is closed.

Once HTTP has completely transferred the information requested, it has done its part. The browser then takes over to interpret and display the information.

HTML

Web pages are created using **HyperText Mark Up Language (HTML)**. HTML isn't a programming language; it is a text formatting or "markup" language. The developer creates the text he wants to put in the page and then marks it up using HTML, either using his normal word processor, an HTML editor, or an HTML generator tool.

HTML does not behave like Postscript (which is a page description language). An HTML document consists of the text with **tags** that tell a browser how the text should appear on the screen, or how to do specific things like draw a horizontal line.

To make a Web page, the developer writes the words and then adds tags to say how they should appear. HTML uses various categories of markers to mark up the text, for example:

▶ Comment

▶ Document structure–for example, head, body, link

▶ Document headings–title, headings

▶ Links–anchors and hypertext links

▶ Layout elements–line breaks, preformatted text, horizontal rules

▶ Graphics

▶ Forms–blocks, widgets, text area, pick lists, selectable items

▶ Paragraphs

▶ Lists–directory, ordered lists, glossary lists, menu lists, etc.

▶ Text controls–bold, citation, font, italic, emphasis

By using HTML, the developer can also add pointers in the Web page to graphics files that get loaded as the page is read by the Web browser. These graphics files, sound files, or other "blobs" can be stored in local directories which can be accessed by the Web server. If the developer wants to add a new picture or a new piece of text, he or she loads or scans it into the local directory and modifies the Web page pointer to point to it.

Developers can add pointers in their documents that enable the user to jump about within a Web page or across pages. These points are called **anchors** in Netspeak and tell the Web browser where to go to get information when you click on it. Simple anchors can be used to jump to other points in the same document—in other words, to get the browser to jump about in the one Web page.

Another type of anchor is a **hypertext reference**. In this case, the user is taken to a different address on the Internet. The addresses of these files are invisible to the user but must be written into the HTML document. These addresses are described using URLs—Uniform Resource Locators—as normal. The main difference between these URLs and the URL the user uses to get access to a site is only that the user never sees these addresses; they are embedded in the marked up text.

CGI

Web browsers and Web servers were designed to be geared more towards dissemination of "multimedia" objects rather than tools that could access

DBMSs or perform application-type processing such as giving the time or date. Although the normal architecture is very effective for dissemination of infrequently changing information, it is less effective (in its basic form) for dissemination of database information, application information, or information derived from databases, which may be refreshed every minute (or second even).

The solution devised to solve this problem was the creation of the **CGI standard** (**Common Gateway Interface**). CGI is one means by which a Web browser (via its Server) can communicate with a separate program or application that can be used to provide customized information, up-to-date information from databases, or any application function.

Web servers normally access static files in directories. If CGI is used, the Web server can be made to access the CGI programs, which can then provide less static information. Similarly, the CGI can also be used to build interactive exchanges between clients and servers.

The importance of this concept cannot be overstated. The Web in its basic form provides none of the capabilities of a normal application—there are no accesses to databases, no calculations, no dialogues, or conversations between users and computer. By using CGI, the developer can go partway to providing this capability—albeit with some limitations.

Developers must write their own CGI applications that perform the processing they want to achieve. There is no difference between writing a CGI program and writing a normal server-based program except that developers seem to favor the use of C and Perl (an interpreted scripting language) above other languages for developing these programs. Apple users tend to use Applescript.

If the developer wants to access one or more databases, he or she must code the database logic to access the data, but **must also code the logic to format the resulting output so that it is in HTML format**. Some of the tools which can handle CGI programs work with ODBC drivers, for example, Allaire's Cold Fusion and Nomad's WebDBC.

CGI programs are also found using their URL. This means that a user could (without necessarily knowing it) directly ask for a CGI program using the URL of that program, or a Web page may contain the URL embedded in a page—in which case the user will not know the address of the program and will be unaware of the action behind the scenes. At runtime, it is the Web server which invokes the CGI program, based on the URL that points to the CGI program.

The CGI program performs whatever actions it has been built to perform using input from the browser request. The CGI program then returns the data back to the server in the form expected (e.g., an HTML page), and the server then passes the results back to the browser. If the exchange is part of an ongoing interactive Web session, these results could include additional form tags to accept further user input, along with a URL for this or another CGI program, and the cycle begins again. In this way, it is possible to have a sort of disjointed conversation over the Web, but without the session and context-based approach familiar in most applications.

Web pages and Java

Java is a combination of a programming language and an environment for executing that language, called the **Java Virtual Machine**. Because no operating system is assumed, each Java Virtual Machine has to use Sun's *Abstract Windowing Toolkit (AWT)*. The Abstract Windowing toolkit is a windowing system and defines the way the user interface looks on the Internet. It includes a set of desktop widgets that it believes to be common to all platforms—Sun, Macintosh, Windows, and so on. The Java interface will thus not be the same as the one the user uses when the Internet is not used.

The developer "compiles" the Java language, and the virtual machine then interprets these instructions at runtime. The aim of this approach is to ensure that Java programs can run on any operating system or hardware. Compiled Java programs can be run wherever a Java virtual machine runs, providing "instant portability" for any compiled Java program.

You may have frequently heard the expression "write once, run anywhere" used with respect to Java. Of course, the run anywhere capability depends on the existence of the Java Virtual Machine on that platform, and versions have not been developed for every platform. But they do exist for Windows and various flavors of Unix (Solaris is an obvious one).

Java programs which run in a browser are called **applets**. As we have seen, Web pages normally contain HTML and pointers (URLs). In order to accommodate Java, HTML has been modified to include tags that identify the Java code to be run and any arguments passed to it. What makes Java so special, however, is that when a page that points to a Java applet is downloaded, not only is the page downloaded to the client machine, but the Java applet is downloaded along with it.

This has obvious benefits. Using this approach, the IT department can always be sure that the user has the most up-to-date software on the client and has no need to continually distribute and update client software. It also means that a casual user can access and use your applications.

Applets are intended to be small, easily downloaded parts of an overall application.

When we say small, we mean small. If the user is accessing your applications across an external line as opposed to an internal network, even a medium-sized applet could take forever to download. The bulk of Internet connections to end users are still either 14.4 Kb or 28.8Kb serial lines. Assuming a generous actual average bandwidth of 2K bytes/second, even a 100K applet will take 50 seconds to download!

If you have an internal network, of course the problems may not be the same, but you probably don't want to have to write two versions of an Internet-based application—one for internal Internet use and one for external use. So on the whole, the rule is keep them really small.

Once the page is downloaded, the Web browser activates the Java classes, which then become an autonomous program running from within the confines of the Web browser. This concept of confinement is important to the whole way Java works and is worth a mention.

Once the Java applet starts working, it is allowed to work only within what is called its *sandbox*. A sandbox (where it can play!) is limited to the environment of the Web browser. The applet can't access the client files or external memory or muck about with code on the client machine interacting with existing applications or even applets on the client machine.

The Browser software and JVM prevent (or should prevent) access by applets to any resources on the client upon which it is running, and the applet is usually destroyed when the page is flushed from cache. Furthermore, Java applets cannot listen on a network for requests or open a network connection to any IP address other than the one from which the applet was downloaded.

The reasons should be obvious. If it is this easy to download software without the user's being aware software has been downloaded, the user is very vulnerable. A less scrupulous Web page designer may (if no restrictions are in place) send the poor hapless individual viruses, applets which read files and report on them, applets which steal data from files—anything really. The poor end user could be totally unaware that a rogue applet was wandering his or her hard disk. By having a restricted model of access, the user has some level of protection from the unscrupulous designer.

Other Middleware Vendors' Support for the Internet

All the middleware products described earlier—NCRs, BEAs, and Transarcs—replace the need for HTTP and CGI programs and use Java applets. By doing this, middleware runtime client libraries do not have to be preloaded on the client platform. All the potential user has to have is a Web browser and a Java Virtual Machine (normally embedded in the Web browser) to run an application as though he was connected in the normal way to the application.

The Web browser and JVM can be running on any platform—a PC, workstation, big box, little box, Unix, Windows, or whatever, as long as the Web browser and the JVM will run on that machine. So how does it all work?

The middleware in practice

Users wanting to complete a transaction from the Web first access the Web in the normal way using the Web browser. They find the appropriate page using the address of the page or by browsing until they get to the page they want. The page is then downloaded from the Web server in the normal way.

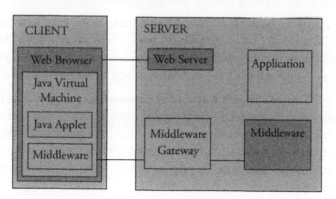

Figure 12.2
Other middleware support for the Internet

Within this page, however, (unknown to them) is a tag pointing to a Java applet, and when the user asks for the page, the Java applet gets downloaded onto their machine.

This Java applet is rather special. It consists of two parts—a part written by you, contains the application code you want executed, and a part supplied by your middleware supplier, which is a lightweight implementation of the normal middleware they supply—something that will supply basic connectivity for the end user but won't take an age to download.

The application part of the total client package contains the presentation logic, a link to the middleware Java class, and a small amount of application logic—possibly validation. Once downloaded, the lightweight middleware on the client bypasses the Web server and opens a direct connection to a middleware gateway, which runs on the company's Web server machine. This is an important point to remember—you have to have the middleware gateway running on your Web server machine for this to work.

Communication between the lightweight Client and the middleware Gateway server is then via TCP/IP, but the protocol used is not HTTP. Instead, a special protocol is used—the middleware vendor's own internal protocol, adapted for use over the Internet.

The gateway provides access to the fully functioned middleware running on the machine. The middleware client builds a string describing the RPC or other type of call it wants the gateway to execute on its behalf. The gateway then builds a true RPC or other type of call and passes it on to the fully functioned middleware to action. The fully functioned version will then do things like security checking, lookup of the Directory to see where the application requested actually resides, and transaction control.

Any application written on any machine on your network can be accessed. The user may be using a Web browser type interface, but he or she will actually be interacting with a real application accessing its functions in the normal way—no need for CGI or scripts or any other forms of complex access.

All communication is via the Gateway, so the Java class has no need to listen on the network for requests or open a network connection. Furthermore, an individual Java class can be identified uniquely over many different service requests, regardless of whether the network connection is maintained or re-established each time, so application state can be maintained, even when the network connection is released.

Java and three-tier architectures

Generally speaking, the vendors of these products recommend a three-tier architecture for use with this sort of application. The client invokes the transaction, a business logic server executes the transaction, and accesses data or other processes on behalf of the client.

The Java class's only function is to invoke a transaction and allow entry of data to support the transaction. As such it has no need to access files on the client or communicate with other applets. The architecture is vastly superior to a two-tier approach (which may actually be infeasible), as the transaction

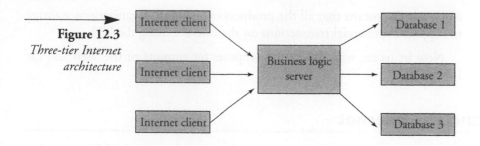

Figure 12.3
Three-tier Internet architecture

can be executed on a powerful machine with failover capabilities, ensuring that the transaction always completes as intended.

If the transaction is controlled directly from the client machine, with two-phase commit, for example, being controlled from the client, any failure of the client could cause problems. As users can be haphazard about the way they handle their machines, they could even turn the machine off before the transaction had completed—a disastrous situation—so three-tier is always to be recommended with Internet use. It also makes the control of security easier, as checks can be delegated to the gateway.

In summary

The modules that other middleware vendors have built to be used over the Internet provide a useful extension to their normal product range, enabling the same applications and services to be used either from a normal client under Windows, for example, or via Web browsers and the Internet. The important point to emphasize is that the developer has no need to adapt an application for use over the Web as long as he or she can adequately express the functionality of the client in a Java applet. The "business logic server" part of the application and data access portions can remain the same.

The reason vendors such as Transarc, BEA, and NCR chose Java for the client was to obtain portability—their Internet front ends should be able to run on any machine—a network computer, a windows-based computer, a NetPC, and so on. A casual user with any sort of machine (as long as it has the Java Virtual machine running on it) should be able to access the applications the company has on site.

The interface will also be the same for all users—irrespective of the machine they are using (a major advantage with a casual user), and the user interface—the browser interface—is easy to understand and use. The approach also means that all the products can support organizations wanting to support commercial transactions on the Internet using the Web.

Now let us see what Microsoft proposes for support of the Web and the Internet.

Microsoft and the Internet

Microsoft's interest in the Internet can be traced back to the Microsoft Network MSN, which supported the Internet and was launched in May 1995. The key event which marked Microsoft's full entry into the world of the Internet, however, was the Professional Developer's Conference in San Francisco in March 1996, subtitled "Building Internet Applications."

At this conference Bill Gates explained Microsoft's strategy for the Internet. The main thrust of this strategy was that there would be:

▶ **one interface** everywhere for file access, messages, pages, documents, and so on

▶ **the same metaphor** for browsing the Web as that used for browsing other devices such as the hard drive of the user's computer

▶ **a single standard** for graphics and multimedia

▶ **complete integration** of data and services across PCs and the Internet

What does all this mean?

In effect, Microsoft wants to treat the Internet like any other network. The developer will continue to use Windows as the client interface in the Microsoft world, but the interface within Windows will be adapted so that Web access, remote access from Windows to other machines, and local access will appear to be the same.

This is a fundamentally different philosophy to what we saw with our other middleware vendors. Java has no real place in the scheme of things here other than as an alternative language in which to develop components. There will be no Java middleware downloaded to a browser to perform connectivity and no Java interface.

The main concrete changes which were to take place as a result of the Internet strategy we saw earlier were that:

▶ Explorer would be used as the single unified interface to Windows—We saw how this would work when we looked at Distributed File Systems in an earlier chapter. The Microsoft Explorer and Internet Explorer interface were being merged in Internet Explorer 4.0.

► Existing Windows technologies would be Web enabled–From the same interface, Microsoft envisaged that a user would be able to invoke Java applets, invoke ActiveX components (objects, controls, or documents) and display pictures or data generated by other applications including Office, Exchange, SQL Server, and so on.

► All Microsoft's client operating systems will be given this same interface. Eventually, Windows NT Workstation and Windows 95 will be browser based.

► HTML would be used as a Windows standard, and Microsoft would extend Windows and provide tools to ensure that this became reality.

► ActiveX (which was announced at this conference) would become the key to component-based development both over the Web and within a company. ActiveX would bring together OLE, OCX, and VBX technologies.

► The Internet Developer's kit was launched.

Microsoft already had a series of initiatives going at the time of the announcement—the code name for the whole spread of technology initiatives being "Sweeper." Sweeper covered ActiveX, unified browsing, Internet protocol support, and so on.

We now explore this approach more by looking in more detail at Microsoft's Web browser and Microsoft's Web server.

Microsoft Internet Explorer

Microsoft Internet Explorer is Microsoft's Web browser. Internet Explorer can support Microsoft's Java Virtual Machine and can run on Windows 3, Windows NT, Windows 95, and the Macintosh.

Internet Explorer started life as a version of NCSA's Mosaic—once the dominant Web browser. It was launched in August 1995. Initially, it was bundled with the Plus add-on pack for Windows 95, but as Netscape started to grow and take a larger slice of the market, Microsoft devoted more effort to its development and Explorers 2 and 3 followed in quick succession.

Internet Explorer version 3 was placed in beta test in June 1996 and was the first truly distinctive/separate version of the product. This version added support for VB Script and ActiveX controls, as well as Java applets. These three points are important:

► With this version of Internet Explorer, the developer could create scripts which could be used to access elements of a page/document and change the elements using VBScript. We will be saying more about this in the next section.

▶ The same version allowed a download of the normal Java applets in the same way we have seen earlier in the description of Java.

▶ It also enabled ActiveX controls to be downloaded. This is especially important.

Microsoft uses the term Active Desktop to describe the resulting client environment. The underlying desktop is browser based, but ActiveX controls can be downloaded and equally important *can operate outside the sandbox.* Thus, ActiveX controls can operate with ActiveX controls within the browser and ActiveX controls outside the browser in the user's desktop environment. Java applets can also communicate with Active X controls on a Web page.

Figure 12.4
ActiveX controls can be downloaded to communicate with ActiveX controls outside the Web browser

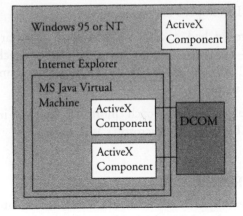

It is possible, for example, to use an ActiveX wrapper (written in Java) around a Java component to download a Java component which is then run using Microsoft's JVM. Visual J++ can be used to create ActiveX wrappers for Java components.

If the machines are capable of running the ActiveX component, a binary version of an ActiveX component in some other language can also be downloaded to run on the client machine. Once the controls have been downloaded, they intercommunicate with each other using DCOM.

Thus, it is possible to have precompiled ActiveX components in different languages from Java. They could be in C++, for example, to be preloaded onto the machine and for them to communicate with wrapped Java applets and downloaded ActiveX controls.

I will have more to say about this in the chapter on security.

Microsoft Internet Information Server

Internet Information Server (IIS) is Microsoft's Web server for Windows NT version 4 (and upwards). IIS was code-named Gibraltar and was launched in February 1996. IIS version 3.0 was released in December 1996. IIS version 4 and Windows NT 5.0 have more code in common than the previous version of IIS—again a precursor to the integration of Internet and Windows technologies now taking place in version 5 of Windows NT.

IIS supports ISAPI—a set of API extensions to the Windows API that developers can use instead of CGI or Perl to access other applications, or ISAPI can be used with Perl/CGI/Rex scripts. IIS can support ordinary "static" pages of information, or it can support Active Server Pages.

Static pages can be the normal HTML text files or images and so on. Pages can be created using any HTML generation tools, but Microsoft has a group of tools called Internet Assistants that can be used to convert documents in Word, Excel, or PowerPoint into HTML versions ready for loading onto a Web site. There is also an Internet Assistant for Access95, which converts data into HTML tables and others for Schedule Plus, Outlook, and SQL Server.

PowerPoint users can also use the ActiveX Animation Player, which shows Powerpoint's animation, sound, and special effects. The presentation then appears in the Browser window.

Microsoft Active Server Pages (code-named Denali)–Support server-side generation of Web pages "on-the-fly." The Web page is thus no longer static, but a dynamically created page of text, images, and data. Perhaps key is the fact that the state can be preserved in the server across pages.

Active Server Pages are the key to Internet support for Microsoft and form the foundation of their distributed application support from the Web. We will see this in a moment.

The developer can use server-side scripting and basic templates to create Active Server pages, generally called "active page generation." Scripting languages that Microsoft supports include JavaScript and VBScript. In fact, Microsoft's version of Java Script is called JScript and is slightly different from JavaScript. Both scripting languages can be used to control Java applets or ActiveX controls written in Visual Basic 5, C++, Borland Delphi, and so on.

Options for distributed application developer

We have seen how DCOM worked on Windows NT and how it worked when it ran on other platforms. Given what we have just learned about Microsoft's strategy and its products, what are the options open to the developer if he or she wants to build distributed applications using DCOM that use the Internet? There are only two approaches that the developer can use, and they depend upon whether the user is a **known user** or an **unknown user:**

Unknown user–In this case, the developer has to use direct communication from a Web browser to the Web server. Where this approach is used, the user uses the Web browser to access a page of information that is downloaded from the Web server. Where communication is directly between Internet Explorer and the Web server (IIS), normal HTTP is used.

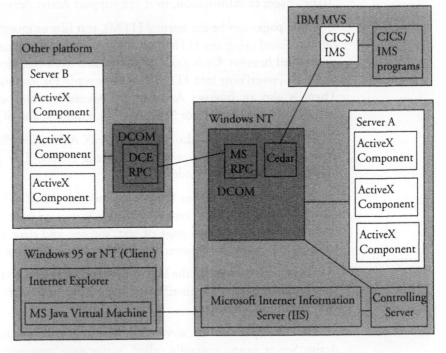

Figure 12.5
Example configuration for an unknown user

This page will be an Active Server Page, which, via a CGI Script or ISAPI, accesses a controlling server program on the Web server host. This program can then use COM to access components on Windows NT machines, other platforms, or on the MVS machine using Cedar. A connection exists between

IIS and DCOM—particularly Microsoft's Transaction Server, which means that server applications can be invoked via IIS and put under transaction control.

As we have seen in our description of other products, HTTP is a limited protocol supporting only a request/reply format and is also unable to sustain the sort of context information which may be needed if transactions are invoked over the Web. It is a useful method of communication, however, if only request/reply communication is needed. Microsoft has extended the capabilities of the Web server by adding Active Server page capability, so even a simple request/reply could produce quite a comprehensive result. But we must still realize the limitations of this approach in comparison with the approach used by other middleware vendors.

Known user–Where the user is known, the Internet may still be in use, but the desktop environment of the end user is under the control of the company and internal to the company. There are two basic assumptions made about the environment in which the user is working:

▶ First, it is assumed the user will be using Windows NT or Windows 95, will have Internet Explorer, and will have a copy of the JVM. COM services will be already available as they are supplied with Windows NT and 95.

▶ Second, a copy of the client application will not be available on the user's machine. Thus the machine is configured for DCOM use but has not been configured with the application.

The user uses the Web browser to access a page of information that is downloaded from the Web server. The page contains Java applets or ActiveX controls (usually the latter) downloaded with the page. Once the controls have been downloaded, they then intercommunicate with each other and via components on server machines using DCOM. In effect, once the ActiveX controls have been downloaded, DCOM takes over, and the Web browser is bypassed. The Web browser has simply been used as a means of downloading Active X components to the user's machine; from the point where communication via DCOM begins, the configuration behaves like an ordinary client server DCOM configuration.

In Summary

In Microsoft's world only two approaches for building distributed applications using the Internet are possible. Microsoft does not provide a Java version of the COM libraries, so DCOM itself cannot be downloaded, primarily

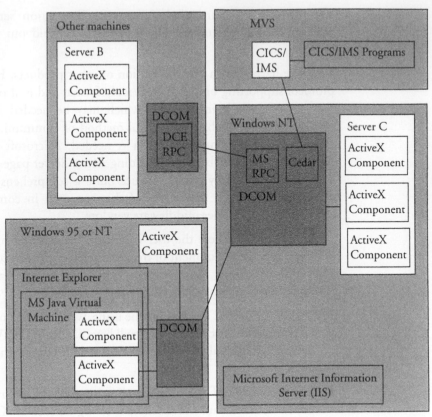

Figure 12.6

*Example
configuration
for a known user*

because Microsoft does not want to encourage the use of Java, which has the potential to seriously undermine their hold on the desktop. This means that Microsoft's first solution for Internet use is based on the normal HTTP and Web server–based model of connectivity. A Windows client accesses Microsoft's Web server from Microsoft's Web browser and through the Web server gains access to DCOM and applications via Active Server Pages.

This approach is limited, as we have seen, because of the use of the HTTP protocol. It means that building applications which run over the Internet is going to be something of a dispiriting experience if you are using DCOM because of the limitations of the technology. Essentially, DCOM is not designed to support distributed applications over the Internet. Alternatively, a known user can use Windows, with DCOM preinstalled, and use the Web browser to download ActiveX components which can then be used to run the application. This approach can be used to ensure that users have an up-to-date version of the software and is very handy if you have thousands of users wanting to use the application. This is where we think DCOM will shine in the future—easy upgrading of software—fat clients—over the *internal network.*

But there are problems even with this approach that we will explore in more detail in the section on security, but that can be summed up by saying that ActiveX components which are allowed free rein of your desktop could be lethal.

In the world of the other middleware vendors the casual user could be running anything, and as such, the use of Java and the Java interface provides the common client interface. Using their approach, the user has no need to use Windows, which is why Microsoft does not support the approach.

The developer can use the Java-based client for access to the system whatever the role of the user—known, unknown, casual, or regular user. The advantages of this approach are that the user always uses a common interface to access that application—or all applications if you are using the same middleware to support all applications—and the developer only has to develop one client. The disadvantages are that another interface has been introduced that the user has to learn (he or she may still be using Motif or Windows for other applications) and the Java Virtual Machine may not be running on every platform.

Microsoft also argues that if the AWT is used, the user is being denied the richness of the normal Windowing environment—more of a Lowest Common Denominator approach. But I'm not sure that this either is true or that this really matters if the interface is simple to learn and use.

The alternative approach is for the developer to build multiple clients—a Java interface and a Web browser for the casual user and other client interfaces for regular company access using Windows or even Motif as the interface. The interface will then not be the same. The advantages with this approach is that the end user keeps the familiar interface to access the application if he or she is a regular user within the company, but an easy-to-use interface is available for use by the casual user—within the company or outside it—via the Web browser and Java. The disadvantage is that the user may end up having to learn more than one interface depending on what *role* he or she is taking anyway (he or she may be classified as a regular user for one application and a casual user for another application). Another disadvantage from the developer's point of view is that he may end up developing several versions of the client.

All this points to the fact that in the future if we use other middleware, we may be developing clients that use this Java virtual machine–based approach for all applications. Where does this leave DCOM and Microsoft? It will be interesting to see.

13

Microsoft Transaction Server

- ▶ Code-named Viper
- ▶ Runs on Windows NT and 95 only
- ▶ Provides number of functions
  - ▶ Admin utilities—monitoring, statistics
  - ▶ Buffer pool
  - ▶ Shared property manager
  - ▶ Automatic multithreading
  - ▶ Just in time activation
  - ▶ Distributed Transaction Processing support

Microsoft Transaction Server is a key component within DCOM. It not only provides distributed transaction processing support, but also a number of additional services aimed at providing the sorts of support found in products like CICS (a TP monitor). MTS is a step towards making DCOM more like the heavy-duty advanced Distributed Transaction Processing Monitors such as Tuxedo or TOP END. In this chapter we will look first at the additional services, and then I will explain in some detail what is meant by distributed trans-action processing and how it works in MTS.

A Bit of Background

Work started on Microsoft Transaction Server—code-named Viper—in early 1995. An early specification of the OLETX transaction protocol was made available to ISVs and database vendors for comment in June 1995 with the

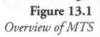

Figure 13.1
Overview of MTS

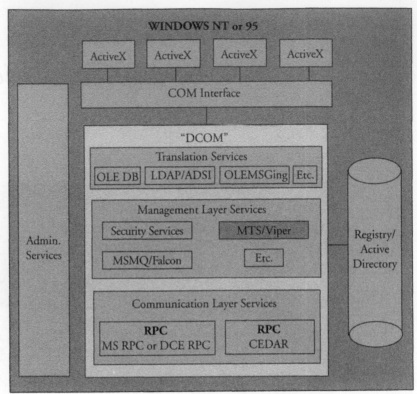

final specification posted on the Internet in March 1996. Nearly 80 companies were involved in the alpha testing of Viper, and it went into beta testing in June 1996.

Microsoft Transaction Server was released in December 1996. At the time, 80 technology vendors committed to the product including test tool vendors such as SQA and NuMega; tool vendors such as PowerSoft and MicroFocus; package vendors such as Software 2000 and Marcam; and DBMS vendors such as Informix, Sybase, and IBM with DB2.

An Overview of the Services Provided with MTS

Overall, the extra services Microsoft Transaction Server provides over and above DCOM services are:

▶ **Additional administration utilities** to help monitor transactions, monitor performance, etc. We won't be covering these in this chapter but will cover them when we talk about administration as a whole in the chapter on administration services.

▶ **Support for resource management and pooling**–The resources which are managed and can be pooled include the threads, memory, and the connections:

   ▶*Buffer pool*–A receiver listens to the network and accepts incoming calls, placing them in a memory buffer pool managed by a queue manager. The buffer is used to queue incoming calls so that they are treated on a first come, first served basis.

   ▶ *The Shared Property Manager* provides shared access to information in main memory by components on one machine.

   ▶*Automatic multithreading of the server* (DCOM's multithreading is not automatic).

▶ **More sophisticated triggering mechanisms**–"Just in time" object activation.

▶ **Support for asynchronous processing**–In addition to the synchronous processing support provided by DCOM.

▶ **Distributed Transaction support**–Support for the update of distributed data.

MTS also provides support for "environment state" for each component, for example, transactions, language, security, etc. Support is planned for load balancing.

Buffer Pool Management

A transaction processing application is different from other types of application. It is characterized not just by the very obvious fact that its purpose is to handle business transactions but usually by high and often unpredictable volumes of data. These high volumes of transaction data must be handled by the system in an efficient way. Thus, one of the key tests of a transaction processing service is whether it can give good performance, even in times when volumes peak to extreme levels.

The buffer pool is there to help with input transaction handling and acts like a queue—storing and smoothing requests, keeping them in sequence so that they are executed in the correct order. The queue or buffer pool used by MTS is invisible to the programmer and certainly inaccessible. This feature is an internal service, something MTS is using to improve performance.

The way the memory pool is handled is remarkably similar to the way CICS works (for those of you familiar with CICS). In CICS, a Listener service handles the communication links on the network and collects requests received from the network software, breaking the requests down into their component parts.

MTS has a component called the Receiver, which performs an identical function—listening to the network and accepting incoming calls. In CICS, as requests are received by the Listeners, they place the requests on a thing called the Schedule queue. Again, MTS acts in the same way; the Listener places the incoming calls into the memory based buffer pool, which is managed by a queue manager. The buffer is used to queue incoming calls so that they are treated on a first come, first served basis. The queue contains the requests from multiple clients and is destined for multiple components or servers. Requests are placed on the queue in the order in which they were received by the Listeners.

Requests are dequeued from the pool in order. MTS passes the request to the server. Clearly, a server thread must be running to handle the request, and MTS ensures that a server thread exists to handle the request as it is removed from the buffer in one of three ways. It:

► activates the server using the underlying DCOM services (triggering), as we saw in a previous chapter

► passes the request to the server thread, if the server is already running and the thread is free

► automatically creates a new thread to handle the request

and this is where the automatic multithreading capability of MTS plays a part.

Automatic Multithreading

We saw in a previous chapter that when just using DCOM without MTS, the programmer has to handle the creation and deletion of threads. If the developer uses Transaction Server, the developer does not have to program the thread management, and the creation, allocation, and termination of threads is automatic. He or she still has to understand locking and apply the necessary locks to data. Thus he or she has to write his program so that it is "threadsafe," but he or she doesn't have to worry about manually creating and deleting the thread.

As we saw in the chapter which described threads, the purpose of multithreading is to improve performance. Threads can be processing in parallel, which means that many more clients can be handled simultaneously than would be the case if no threads were used. Microsoft uses threads because although they are more difficult to program, they are more efficient on memory than tasks and multitasking.

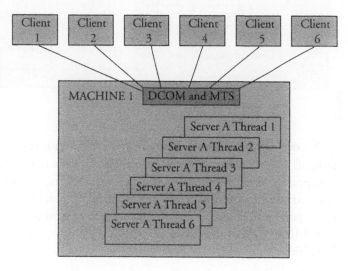

Figure 13.2
Automatic multithreading to handle multiple client requests

It could be the case, however, that you have so many clients that even on the machine you have you cannot handle the sheer volume of clients you may get. How, then, do you spread the load across machines so that client requests are handled by the same server, but on different machines? The answer is load balancing.

Load Balancing

Load balancing is the spreading of the requests for a server across machines that each have a copy of the server on them. Load balancing can be combined with multithreading; a middleware product can be both multithreaded on a single machine and load balance across machines.

There are certain assumptions made about load balancing, which define whether it can be used or not. First and foremost, the component/server must be capable of being placed on more than one machine. Clearly, if the component accesses data in a database that is only accessible from one machine, the component cannot be duplicated. If the database can be accessed from more than one machine, then the component can be duplicated.

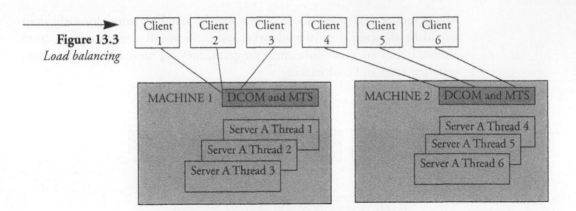

Figure 13.3
Load balancing

Second, the Directory must support the duplication of the component around the network without the programmer's having to know that the component is duplicated. This latter point is important. Many Directory systems enable you to put the server on many machines, but each time you do it you have to give it a different name. This means the client has to use this different name, and true automatic and transparent load balancing isn't possible.

It is worth noting that Microsoft's current Registry service does enable you to duplicate components anywhere on a network (we will see how in the chapter on the Directory services) so load balancing—transparent load balancing—is possible. This contrasts with the approach taken in CORBA, where the Directory/Naming service does not support the duplication of a component around the network. Apart from the obvious dangers of this from a reliability view point—the component then becomes a single point of failure on the network and could cause your whole system to fail—it also means CORBA cannot support load balancing.

Third, load balancing must be an automatic function of the middleware—not a program-controlled service. If we take as an example a sophisticated product like TOP END to show how it operates, you will be able to see how load balancing works when it is automatic.

In TOP END, it is the Directory service which decides which, of a number of server instances on different nodes, are to receive the request. The Directory decides which server instance will receive the request by using one of three methods. The administrator decides which of the three methods are to be used. The options available are:

▶ **Random**–Where the servers and their nodes offer the same level of service and where workload distribution cannot be predicted, random routing may be used. As requests are received they are distributed in random order to the server instances. It is not possible using this method to predict which server will receive the message, but over time, each server will receive approximately the same number of requests.

▶ **Round robin**–In this case the workload is evenly distributed across each of the servers in a defined order. Requests are thus distributed one at a time in a predictable order to each server in turn.

▶ **Enhanced routing**–Achieved by using a load-balancing algorithm.

The load-balancing algorithm is based on three main parameters, which can be used in combination:

▶ **Local/Remote Ratio**–This is a ratio assigned by the administrator to direct workload either locally or remotely based on factors which he knows of, such as communication costs and availability. The ratio describes within a TOP END node what proportion of requests should be processed locally rather than remotely.

▶ **Node Desirability**–This is a weighted value assigned by the administrator to each node. The desirability of a node is based on its size, processor speed, and geographical location on the network, plus other things. In essence, the administrator must decide how desirable that node should appear to other nodes.

▶ **Server Copies/Potential ratio**–This is a ratio assigned by the administrator to influence how TOP END routes messages among multiple server nodes based on how many actual and potential server instances are available. In effect, the ratio describes what potential the node has to start up yet more server instances if the number currently provided is not enough. To make this work, TOP END periodically propagates status information to other server nodes in the configuration, and the frequency with which this status information is propagated can be set by a tuneable value called the "Notification Frequency." This ratio can be used by the administrator to throttle or tune up the sensitivity of server instance startup and shutdown activity

TOP END has perhaps the most sophisticated load balancing capability of any middleware product I know of, and you can see from this description just how well developed the services in these really heavy-duty products actually are.

But what does MTS provide? Despite all this explanation, the answer is currently nothing!! But there are plans to support load balancing via MTS, and, as we have seen, it is potentially feasible given the structure of the Registry. Load balancing is planned for version 3 and will initially be based on a random method of allocation.

Shared Property Manager

We saw in the chapter on Windows NT that the operating system does provide support for shared memory on a single host. Windows NT has a virtual memory system which enables up to 32 processes to read the shared memory area.

The Shared Property Manager service provided with MTS extends this capability and makes it available to components. The Shared Property Manager thus provides shared access to information in main memory by components on *one machine*, but again, *distributed* shared memory is not supported. Microsoft provided the Shared Property Manager so that the programmer had an alternative to the various persistent store mechanisms available via the Active Data Object (of which we will learn more later in the chapter on Data Objects). It effectively provides a mechanism for storing data that does not need to be "durable."

The Shared Property Manager has a built-in locking mechanism, just like Windows NT, but what makes it different is that it is accessed and manipulated using the COM interface. It is accessed via the ISharedProperty interface, which is intended to provide a means of classifying the data from Groups to Properties and down to values. And so, for the first time in this book, I will actually give you a little bit of code from this interface to show you how this might look.

```
ISharedPropertyGroupManager        [to create the property group

    ISharedPropertyGroup

    Create Property                [methods

    Create PropertybyPosition

    get-Property

    get-PropertybyPosition

    ISharedProperty

    get-Value

    put-Value
```

Triggering

In the basic DCOM approach the client has control over the object lifetime; client references are bound to the same object instance for as long as the reference is valid. But Transaction Server incorporates a process called "just in time" activation.

During method execution, a Transaction Server object can use the Set-Complete and SetAbort methods to indicate that the object does not need to maintain state after returning the call.

As a result, the Transaction Server can deactivate the object when returning back to the client. The object remains deactivated until the client makes another call to the object. Only when the object is subsequently called is it reactivated, at which time it reacquires the resources it needs to service the call. From the client's point of view, it thinks it holds the object all the time; in reality it is activated and deactivated many times. Why do this?

As long as the object is deactivated, only limited server resources need to be allocated to it—those required to maintain object context and its association with client references. Other server resources, such as memory for the object's private data, do not need to be allocated to the object and can be used for other purposes. The purpose of this service of MTS is thus to make more efficient use of resources—again, a feature essential in a transaction processing system.

Support for Asynchronous Processing

Normal communication between clients and servers using DCOM is synchronous, with the client sending a request and then waiting with its thread blocked until the reply is received. We saw in an earlier chapter that there were ways in which asynchronous communication can be supported indirectly:

▶ **By using threads**–The client can spawn a new thread to handle any additional processing while the existing thread waits for the reply.

▶ **By using the outgoing interface**–All events sent to outgoing interfaces are by their nature asynchronous, as the event is sent to DCOM and server processing can then proceed.

▶ **By using a call back object**–In this case a special call back object is created to handle any replies.

▶ **By using MSMQ**–When the client sends a message, the message is placed first on the local transmission queue. Once the acknowledgment of receipt has been given, the client can proceed, acting asynchronously.

MTS, however, provides *direct* support for asynchronous processing. A client can issue a number of calls to the various servers under transaction control and not block processing; all the calls can be executed in parallel. Why is this important?

Support for asynchronous processing is absolutely essential in a distributed transaction processing application—not for the end user client part of the application particularly, but the "business logic" transaction part of the application. Let us use an example:

Suppose clients accessed a server process that performed some business transaction that updated three DBMSs and also invoked two components.

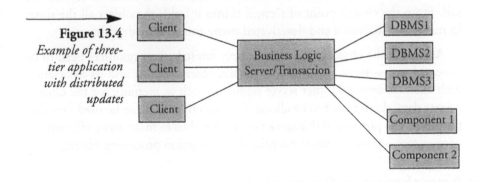

Figure 13.4
Example of three-tier application with distributed updates

If no support was available for asynchronous processing, the transaction would need to pass the updates to DBMS1 and then wait for a reply. Once the reply had been received, it would then send the updates to DBMS2, then wait for a reply. Once that reply had been received, it would send the updates to DBMS3, then wait for its reply. After this reply had been received, it would invoke component 1 and wait for the reply. Once the reply had been received, it would then invoke component 2 and wait for the reply. Once it had replied, it would then do the rounds again to see if the DBMSs were ready to commit, and so on.

The processing would probably take as long as it has taken you to read the previous paragraph—if not longer—hardly the sort of high performance you want in a transaction processing application. By supporting asynchronous processing, all these calls can be executing in parallel; processing time is probably reduced by a fifth in comparison with the equivalent time when synchronous processing is used. Support for asynchronous processing is thus key as a service and actually of real use in other sorts of applications—not just transaction processing ones.

Distributed Transaction Processing Support

This section is going to be quite a long one as it is the main service provided by MTS and also the most difficult one to understand. I will start by giving you an explanation of what distributed transaction processing actually is, how it works, and the standards on which it relies, and then we will look at how MTS actually works.

I will start, however, by getting back to basics.

What is a transaction?

A transaction is a unit of work that, when complete, leaves the computer system and its data in a consistent state, in other words, a sort of integrity unit. For example, a business transaction that records an order might involve the update of customer data, the creation of order and order item data, the update of stock data (to reserve stock to fulfill the order), and the creation of delivery details (so that the order gets delivered). If any part of this business transaction fails, the data will be inconsistent—we may have an order without item details, a stock record which does not reflect the goods reserved from it, a delivery going to the wrong customer address, or an order without delivery details, which, as a consequence, never gets delivered.

Those of us that have done data modeling know that the logic of a transaction is often driven by the structure of the data in the database. For example: A customer may have an order, and the order must specify the customer. The Order must have Order Items, and the Order Items must show the Order and

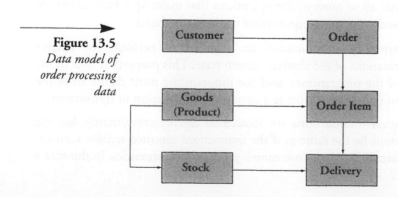

Figure 13.5
Data model of order processing data

the Goods they were for. Order Items are split into Deliveries. Deliveries are reserved against stock. Some Products may not have been ordered.

Some stock items may have no deliveries reserved against them. Stock items each describe what product is in stock. Some products may not be in stock. The database structure thus defines the rules of the transaction and the integrity of the data which must be preserved.

A transaction involves a series of smaller units of work which together make up the transaction as a whole. As we have seen in the example, the transaction may involve the update of data—customer details, create order, create order item, and so on—where the data is in databases or files. It may also involve other sorts of units of work—putting messages on queues, putting print out on a print spooler, and so on.

You may also be in the unfortunate position of having duplicate data in your organization, and, as such, the transaction will then involve units of work which update all of this duplicate data, for example, customer data in one database and customer data in another database. In a transaction, all of these smaller units of work have to be completed for the data to be consistent and for the business unit of work to be deemed "complete."

If any smaller unit of work should fail, the work already completed by the other units of work has to be **rolled back**—in effect undone. The processing within a transaction is thus organized around an "all or nothing approach." It all has to be completed or none of it must appear to have been completed, which leads us to what are termed the ACID properties.

The ACID Properties

The ACID properties define the rules of transaction processing:

▶ **A**—atomicity—if a transaction's work is interrupted by a failure, any partially complete results must be undone. The system must ensure that either all or none of the operations that make up a transaction are performed—the transaction either commits or aborts.

▶ **C**—consistency—transactions are assumed to perform the correct transformations of the abstract system state. This property is thus in the hands of the programmer, and the programmer must define what the operations are that constitute a correct transformation or transaction.

▶ **I**—isolation—transactions are allowed to execute concurrently, but the results must be the same as if the transactions executed serially. Concurrently executing transactions cannot produce inconsistencies. In this way, a programmer can cause temporary inconsistencies during the execution of a transaction, knowing that these partial modifications will never be visible.

▶ **D**—durability—once a transaction commits, its updates must be permanent. The new state of objects updated must be preserved, even in the case of hardware or software failures.

What is a distributed transaction?

Now let us imagine that all these units of processing, instead of residing on the one machine, reside on several machines. Perhaps the data is split across machines so that the Customer file is on one machine, the Order and Order Item on another machine, the Stock is on another machine, and the Product on another machine.

We now have a distributed transaction. The units of work are distributed across machines and the data is distributed across machines.

Now let us make it even more complex and say that the data not only resides on more than one machine but is managed by different DBMSs. Perhaps the Customer database is held in an Oracle DBMS, the Order and Order Item database is held in a Sybase database, and the Stock database is managed by Informix. Maybe we even have duplicate customer data held in a DB2/6000 database.

A distributed transaction in this case not only runs on several possibly heterogeneous machines in a network but is also split across DBMSs. Now, most DBMSs can handle the update of data—distributed transactions—which handle data in their own DBMS, but the update of data in multiple DBMSs is tricky and the DBMSs cannot help you here. So, enter Distributed Transaction Processing middleware.

What is distributed transaction processing middleware?

Distributed Transaction Processing middleware manages transactions in a heterogeneous environment. The transactions themselves may involve:

▶ the execution of distributed processes and/or

▶ the update of distributed data

The DTPM ensures that transactions are completed successfully or that the system is recovered to a consistent state if the transaction is unsuccessful. DCOM with its MTS service can be classified as Distributed Transaction Processing middleware.

To roll back or undo units of work, the software managing the transaction may have to coordinate the undoing of work with other software products that manage resources. These are called Resource managers.

Resource managers

In one of those annoyingly tautological definitions one often finds in textbooks, I will define a Resource Manager as a software product which manages resources. Any the wiser? No? Let us look at this, then, from another point of view.

Resource managers can be queue managers, DBMSs, file managers, even print queue managers. Queue managers manage queues (a resource), DBMSs manage databases (a resource), file managers manage files (a resource), print spool managers manage the print spool (the resource), and so on. Resources are thus any sort of external asset which could be accessed and used by a program.

DTPMs coordinate multiple **resources** and multiple **Resource managers** of different types (DBMS, and other file handling systems, for example), providing end-to-end management of the communication process. If any of these Resource managers fail—DBMS, queuing file, flat file, etc., the DTPM takes the necessary action to recover and put the data and system back into a consistent state. As most of you are probably aware, Resource managers such as DBMSs hold the details of updates in temporary holding files until the programmer issues the command to commit. When this command has been issued, the updates are applied. DTPMs coordinate the commit process; we will see how in the next sub-section.

Let us first look at an example to see how DTPMs and Resource managers work with one another. In the example below, the business transaction A updates data in two different DBMSs and data in a file, puts a message on a queue via a queue manager, and also includes a process, which must return with the reply that the processing was successful for the transaction to be deemed successful.

If, for example, the process didn't complete successfully, one of the updates planned for the DBMS wasn't correct, or the message couldn't be put on the queue, the transaction A would be deemed to have failed in its entirety, and the DTPM would need to work with the Resource managers to ensure none of those updates held in temporary storage was actually committed. In other words, the DTPM would instruct the Resource managers to remove any updates in temporary storage:

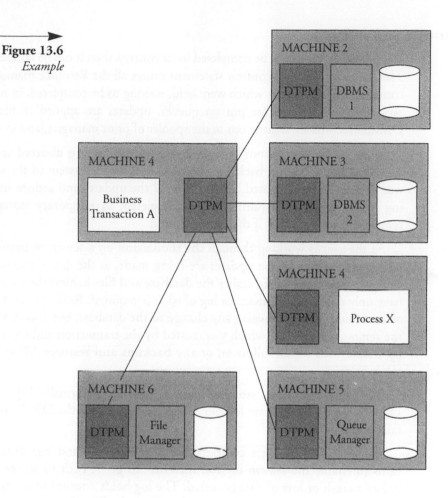

Figure 13.6
Example

▶ the "updates in waiting" that the DBMS was keeping ready for the command to commit would be removed

▶ the "messages in waiting" that the queue manager was keeping ready for the command to commit would not be stored on file

▶ the updates in waiting that the file manager was keeping ready for the command to commit would be discarded

If, on the other hand, all the process X came back with a reply that it had succeeded, the DBMSs all said the updates could be applied OK if need be, and the file manager and queue manager also said that they, too, could update OK, the transaction would be deemed to be a success and the transaction would then be "committed." In this case all the "updates in waiting" would be applied.

Commit and rollback

If a transaction is able to be completed in its entirety, then it can be **committed.** The action of issuing a commit statement causes all the Resource managers to complete the commands which were held, waiting to be completed, in temporary storage—messages are put on queues, updates are applied to files and DBMSs, records are written out to the spooler of print managers, and so on.

If the transaction cannot be completed successfully, it is **aborted** and will be **rolled back.** Rolling back a transaction restores the system to the state it was before any work started. In this case, all the updates and actions in waiting which were held, waiting to be completed, in temporary storage are removed from storage as if they never existed.

As the user is working through the transaction on a screen or monitor, it will appear as though the updates are being made, as the data on screen will be up-to-date data, but in reality the database and files behind the scenes will have only this working image or log of what is required. Rolling back a transaction, thus, does not involve any change to the database, but it does involve the removal of any data which was created by the transaction and could mess up transactions which follow on or any **backups and restores.** What do we mean by this?

Well, this temporary store of data in waiting is normally kept in the DBMSs log file. This same log file is also used to restore the DBMS when it fails entirely.

All good DBMSs use a combination of backup files and logs of transactions to enable the system to "roll forward" to get it back to where it was before a crash or loss of data occurred. The log holds a record of the transactions made against the database, and the effect of rolling forward these transactions against the backup file is to redo all the updates which were lost, bringing it back to the state it was before the failure occurred. The backup file and log thus have to be synchronized. Some DBMSs perform this synchronization automatically; some need the database administrator to control the frequency of backups and the allocation of log files.

If a transaction fails, the updates in waiting need to be removed from the log file so they do not get confused with real updates that have been committed.

Locks

A lock is a preventative measure which stops other processes updating or optionally using the data while the update is being performed. It is there to ensure that the update is consistently applied. It is also there to ensure that users looking at data don't make decisions or do calculations on data that is in the process of changing.

Where you have many concurrent users and you allow one user to update data which another one is also trying to update at the same time, you can get in a real mess without locking. Let's look at an example to demonstrate.

One user may be trying to enter an order at the same time as another. The first user checks the stock and all seems OK. He or she then starts to create the order and the delivery. In the meantime, however, the second user may have started to update an order of massive proportions, which completely removes all the goods in stock.

The first user may think he or she has enough stock to fulfill the order, so this first user creates the order. He or she then tries to create the delivery and can't because there isn't enough stock to fulfill the order. Inconsistency!

You can only get a consistent update if you apply a transaction from beginning to end without any amendments to the data being allowed from other users in the meantime. This is what locks are for; they stop others updating the data while you are doing it.

Resource managers apply locks differently, and it is just one of the ways in which you can see whether they are good products or not. Locks can be applied at the record level, the page level, the file level, or the item level. The lower and more detailed the level at which locks are applied by the Resource manager, the better, as the less likely it is that performance will be degraded.

I think you should be able to see that if your DBMS locked at the file level when you updated data, you could end up stopping the update of hundreds of other users. Whereas, if your DBMS allowed locks at the record level, you are unlikely to lock out many other users at all because the likelihood of two of you working on the same data at the same time is very remote.

Locks are usually applied when the command to commit is given. In other words, when the command to commit is finally given, the DBMS or Resource manager should also apply locks to the data being updated. This deserves some explanation to those of you designing conversational online updates.

Conversational styles of dialogue force a different style to that used in batch, where locks can be employed over the duration of a transaction. A conversational style of update should normally not apply locks until the last exchange in the dialogue—once the user has committed. This is because during the conversation you would be locking out every other user from that data, and if your user sat there for hours trying to complete the transaction, he or she could bring the entire system to a standstill. Worse still, he or she may get bored and walk away, leaving the entire transaction hanging and unresolved with all locks in place.

So locks are applied normally at the end, on the commit, which means that before a commit is issued the validity of the update may be checked then by revalidation, comparison of time stamps, comparison of version numbers, plus other methods, depending on the capabilities of the DBMS.

Distributed two-phase commit

So, we now have all our Resource managers, locks in place ready to update the transaction, and they are told to commit. What happens next? All products that support distributed transactions use a process known as two-phase commit.

In the first phase of the commit, the DTPM asks each Resource manager if it is ready to commit. If the reply from any of the Resource managers is no, the DTPM gives all the Resource managers the command to abort. They then remove the "updates in waiting" from their logs.

If one or more of the Resource managers did not reply because, for example, the line went down, the DTPM holds the instructions to abort in its own log file. Once the line or DBMS is online again, the DTPM gives the instructions to abort, and these remaining Resource managers will remove their updates in waiting.

If the reply is given from all Resource managers that they can commit, the DTPM then enters the second phase of the commit process—hence the expression two-phase commit. In this phase the DTPM tells all Resource managers to finally commit and they apply the updates in waiting to make them permanent. Once made permanent the locks are removed. There are some added complexities to this process, but we will have a look at them in the context of MTS itself, as each DTPM tends to handle the more complex problems differently.

Standards

As we have seen in the above explanation, it is essential that the distributed transaction processing middleware and the Resource manager communicate with one another. The whole success of the two-phase commit and distributed transaction process is dependent, in fact, upon the communication that takes place between the Resource manager and the DTPM.

It is, therefore, not surprising that the protocol between the two types of product is the subject of standardization. What is perhaps especially good news is that the DTPMs agree on the standard and so do most Resource manager vendors.

At last, a standard which vendors agree on. And, even better news, it works!

The standard was defined by the X/Open Group and is called the X/Open DTP (Distributed Transaction Processing) standard. The X/Open DTP standard provides a framework to build heterogeneous distributed transaction processing systems and was developed by X/Open's *Distributed Transaction Processing Working Group* (DTPWG). The standard defines a model used by all the vendors of DTPMs and Resource managers that defines the interfaces between the products.

The diagram they use is the one shown below.

Figure 13.7
X/Open DTP standard

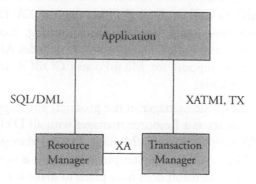

The application communicates with the Resource manager using its normal API—SQL in the case of a relational DBMS such as Oracle or Sybase, some other *Data Manipulation Language* (DML) in the case of file managers, and commands such as GET and PUT in the case of queue managers. The application communicates with the DTPM (the Transaction manager part) using its API. There aren't really any standards here, although X/Open does include XATMI, TX, plus others. This, too, doesn't really matter from your point of view as a developer unless you would like all the products to have a common API you use. Overall, it doesn't actually affect the working of the products.

The key interface is between the Resource manager and the Transaction manager, and this is the one that has to be standard. It is called the *XA interface*. The programmer does not need to know the XA interface exists. All synchronization, commit, and rollback actions are coordinated by the Transaction manager via the XA interface.

The standard is defined as a specification—not source code, so each Resource manager vendor and each DTPM vendor has to build his own implementation of the standard. This does mean that no assumptions can be made by the vendors on whether their product works with other products. One Resource manager vendor may produce an XA implementation that works with DTPM A, but his implementation may not work with DTPM B. The implementations do have to be tested and there may be different versions.

The DBMSs that definitely support the XA standard and also work with all DTPMs that support the standard currently are **Oracle**, **Informix**, **MS SQL Server**, and **DB2/6000**. Gresham also provide a product called **ISAM-XA**, which is an XA-compliant Resource manager for ISAM files. This, too, appears to be able to work with all DTPMs that use XA. ISAM-XA incorporates before and after image logging, checkpointing, record level locking, deadlock detection, and buffer management. It includes APIs for both C and COBOL, as well as support for MicroFocus's COBOL ISAM access verbs. ISAM-XA runs on Unix.

MQSeries (the queue manager in the product) also supports the XA standard so it, too, can act as a Resource manager with all DTPMs. BEA is planning to add XA support in their Message Queue Manager BEAmessageQ. Microsoft's MSMQ is not yet XA compliant, but as it is very new this is probably not surprising. Microsoft does have plans to make it XA compliant in the future.

Gresham also supplies an XA conformant **spooler/printer** product, which we believe all DTPMs that support XA can support. **Sybase** and **Ingres** have XA components, but there seems to be some doubt as to whether these components completely conform to the XA specification. Some of the DTPM vendors stated that they could work with Sybase and Ingres, and others stated that they were still working on providing support for these two DBMSs.

In summary

In this section we have looked at transactions, distributed transactions, Resource managers, locking, distributed two-phase commit, and the XA standard. We will now look at MTS and how distributed transaction processing works in this specific service.

Microsoft Transaction server and the Transaction manager

The specific component within MTS which handles Distributed Transaction Processing is called the Transaction manager or, at one time, *Distributed Transaction Coordinator* (DTC). The Transaction manager is geared towards supporting transaction control of both database updates and object calls. A "transaction" can thus be defined as being a set of both Resource manager calls and object calls.

Platforms

MTS currently runs only on Windows NT and 95, although the services can be invoked from a browser via an Internet Web server as we saw in the chapter on DCOM and the Internet. Clients can be Windows NT Workstation, Windows NT Server, or Windows 95. The servers must run on Windows NT Server.

Architecture

Transaction managers cooperate to manage transactions spanning multiple machines. Resource managers can exist on many nodes. Each local Transaction manager takes responsibility for that node's Resource Manager. When the transaction is initiated, the two Transaction managers establish a relationship. These ingoing and outgoing relationships form a tree of Transaction manager relationships called the "commit tree" with Resource managers being part of the tree. When a distributed transaction commits or aborts, the commands flow outward on the tree. The root Transaction manager of the commit tree is the commit coordinator. It makes the decision whether to commit or abort.

As a consequence of this architecture, the Transaction manager cannot handle nested transactions, but can handle chained transactions (objects calling objects, calling objects).

Database connection pools

The database connection pool capability was added to ODBC 3 and is thus a feature of this component, but it can be used—is used—by Transaction Server. The DCP establishes and manages a set of sessions between the Transaction Server environment and the database. Rather than establishing database connections on a request-by-request basis from the application, ODBC 3 sets up a pool of reusable preconnected sessions. Application components

Figure 13.8
The Commit tree

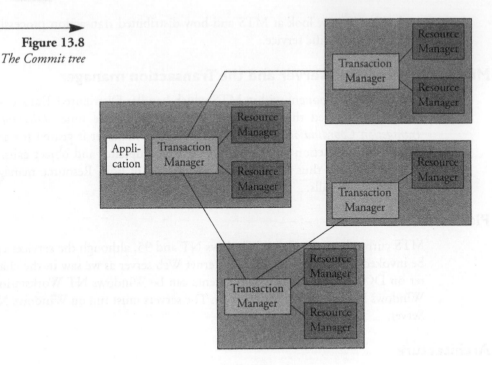

make standard ODBC calls, but the resource dispenser allocates new connections from the shared pool.

The Database connection pool manager avoids the server/client's having to set up connections with the DBMSs and manage them within the server code. It also avoids the overhead of having one connection per server. Furthermore, the processing overhead incurred when connections are created and terminated occurs only once within Transaction server initialization and termination. Thus, the purpose of the Database connection pool is primarily to save the programmer time in coding but also to improve performance and make database access more efficient.

Standards

The Transaction manager of MTS uses the same conceptual model as the X/Open DTP model of distributed transaction processing but is based on Microsoft's own object-based transaction processing protocol they have termed **OLETX.**

XA is a procedural API, based interface and Transaction Server is object based, thus Microsoft decided—much as the OMG did with CORBA—

that an object-based interface was needed between the Resource manager and the Transaction manager (Transaction server). They thus invented OLETX—a different protocol from that used by CORBA (OTS) and different from XA.

Clearly, this is not an entirely satisfactory solution as it stands, as no Resource manager currently works with OLETX, and any move by the Resource manager vendors to produce an implementation for their product that works with OLETX is likely to mean a lot of additional work for them. But this is not the whole picture.

Microsoft has to use an object-based interface internally because its Transaction manager is component based, and it is clear that Microsoft hopes Resource managers will eventually come around to their way of thinking and build implementations of OLETX for their products. In the meantime, however, they have to provide a solution that works with XA, so the solution they use internally is to use a "driver" to map from OLETX to XA within Transaction server. The diagram below shows how this works, by using the original X/Open DTP diagram as the basis, with the additional components Microsoft is using added in.

Thus, as long as the DBMS is XA compliant, Microsoft is able to use the OLETX to XA driver/mapper to map from OLETX to XA internally within

Figure 13.9
OLETX and XA

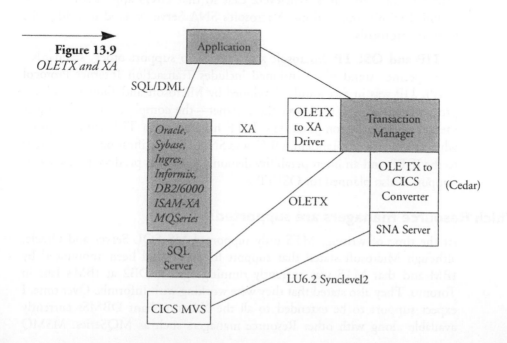

Transaction manager. In fact, Microsoft (Redmond) stated to us that, "The fact we did an OLETX to XA mapper is irrelevant. It is an implementation detail; all the customer needs to know is that we support XA."

Cedar–The diagram also shows Cedar support for CICS on MVS.

A transaction in CICS is a unit of work, but it is also the context in which a program runs, or the "policy" attached to the program. Transactions are defined by the program name, the security level, the users that may use the transaction, the priority, and the hours of the day in which the program may run. If a program has a different security level, for example, or different priority, it is a different transaction. Each transaction in an application is given a transaction identifier (or transaction code)—a four-character code.

Transactions are not explicitly started and terminated using BEGIN TRANS-ACTION and COMMIT or ABORT commands as they are in other products. When a CICS application starts running, it is *automatically* presumed to be within a transaction. When the application terminates and returns control to CICS, CICS itself issues the Commit—a **SYNCPOINT** in CICS terminology. Hence the origins of the protocol, used to handle two-phase commit Synclevel2—the only one of three protocols provided by IBM that supports two-phase commit.

As we saw in the chapter on Cedar, Cedar translates the calls—the OLETX calls—to CICS Synclevel2 calls so that CICS applications can be included within transactions. Microsoft's SNA Server is used to bridge the network protocols.

TIP and OSI TP–Microsoft also intends to support other "standards." One specific "standard" mentioned includes Transaction Internet Protocol (TIP). TIP was in fact jointly developed by Microsoft and Tandem and is a protocol that can be used over the Internet—the complete reference implementation is based on Java. The IETF has formed a TIP working group which includes Bull, Tandem, DEC, and SNI. The specification has been sent to the IETF, and an interoperability demonstration was produced early 1997. Support is also planned for OSI TP.

Which Resource managers are supported?

At the time of writing, MTS only supported MS SQL Server and Oracle, although Microsoft stated that support for MTS had been announced by IBM and that MTS was currently running against DB2 at IBM's labs in Toronto. They also stated that they were working with Informix. Over time, I expect support to be extended to all the XA-compliant DBMSs currently available along with other Resource managers such as MQSeries, MSMQ queues can also be placed under transaction control. A *local* enqueue or dequeue of a message can be part of a transaction.

It should be remembered that because the XA implementations available from each vendor are different (because they were based on a specification), they will all need to be tested separately—thus the uncertain nature of the support and the need for combined lab testing. Longer term, the team working on Transaction server aim to provide support for many other Resource managers—OODBMSs, transaction file systems, queues, and workflow files. One small point. If ODBC and Oracle are being used, the developer needs to change the ODBC Driver to the Microsoft-supplied driver that supports the new protocol.

MTS in operation

Microsoft's Transaction server's model assumes no programming of the start transaction or end transaction commands. Instead, each component is declared to be transactional or not using Transaction Server Explorer—the administration tool.

Applications written in Visual Basic cannot initiate transactions directly. Instead, the application must invoke an object which then invokes the transaction—this could be in a three-tier architecture. In practice, Transaction Server is probably best used within a three-tier architecture, where client calls business logic server (the controlling transactional object/component), which in turn makes calls to the data sources.

When a Resource manager is loaded, it contacts the Transaction manager to declare its presence. The application/component begins the transaction by calling the Transaction manager's BeginTransaction method. This creates a transaction object that represents the transaction. The application then calls Resource managers to do the work of the transaction.

The application's calls to each Resource manager identify the application's current transaction, that is, the transaction object. Thereafter, all calls are associated with the transaction object until the transaction is ended. This is like giving the transaction a unique identifier.

The Resource managers "enlist" in the transaction by calling the Transaction manager as the transaction progresses. The Transaction manager keeps track of each Resource manager and its actions. The Resource manager then performs the transaction requests on behalf of the application, but instead of updating the resource (DBMS, for example) it keeps the updates in a log as we saw earlier in the general description, awaiting further instructions from the Transaction manager.

The application then completes the transaction by calling the COMMIT method on the Transaction manager or alternatively, if it is unable to complete the transaction, by using the ABORT method. The abort command causes the Transaction manager to contact each Resource manager, which is then instructed to discard all updates in waiting for that transaction.

If the application itself fails before completing, the Transaction manager will abort the transaction on behalf of the application. Similarly, if any Resource managers have failed, the Transaction manager stores the abort command and forces an abort once the Resource managers are again active.

Once the application has issued the commit command, however, the Transaction manager takes over and controls the update via the two-phase commit protocol.

Phase 1–The Transaction manager issues the command to each Resource manager to **prepare to commit.**

▶ If all Resource managers reply that they can commit, processing proceeds to Phase 2.

▶ If any of the Resource managers reply that they cannot commit, the Transaction manager contacts all the Resource managers to force an abort, and instructs them to discard all updates in waiting for that transaction.

▶ If any of the Resource managers cannot be contacted, for example, the Resource manager itself has failed or the network has failed, those Resource managers that can be contacted are told to abort. The abort command is then stored in the Transaction manager log awaiting the restart of the Resource managers that could not be contacted. Once the Resource managers are up and running again, the abort is forced.

Phase 2–If all Resource managers confirm they can commit, the commit message is broadcast to each Resource manager by the Transaction manager.

▶ If all the Resource managers are still active, they commit the updates.

▶ If any of the Resource managers fail to respond, it could be for two reasons—either a communication failure or because the Resource manager has failed.

▶ If there is a communication line failure, the commit or abort notification may not arrive for minutes, even hours. During this period the Resource manager is termed to be "in doubt" about the outcome. But it will keep locks on the data until notification is received. Once the line is up and running the Transaction manager will commit the transaction. Although not advisable normally, the administrator can abort in-doubt transactions manually from his console if they are tying up the system.

▶ If the Resource manager fails and then restarts, the Resource manager must reconstruct the committed state of the resources it manages. If it does fail, all of its enlisted transactions are aborted, except those that prepared or committed prior to failure. When the Resource manager restarts, it asks the Transaction manager about the outcome of the "in-doubt" transactions in which it enlisted. The Transaction manager then tells the Resource manager the outcome of each in-doubt transaction, and the Resource manager commits or aborts accordingly.

The Transaction manager thus keeps its own log of transactions so that it can coordinate with Resource managers over in-doubt transactions. This log is disk based and sequential. The Transaction manager records transactions, starts, enlistments, and commit decisions in the log. During normal processing, the Transaction manager only writes to the log. If the Transaction manager itself fails, it is able to reconstruct the transaction's most recent state by reading the log.

When commit trees exist, the Transaction managers cooperate to determine the status of in-doubt transactions, and each Transaction manager on each node is then responsible for handling the transactions on its node. Thus each Transaction manager uses the log to handle both the transactions where it was the coordinator and incoming and outgoing transactions.

In Summary

Microsoft Transaction Server is a very useful additional service within DCOM. We can see that the way the Transaction manager works is extremely well thought through and that useful additional services have been added to help DCOM become better able to support high-volume distributed transaction processing systems.

In fact, it is MTS that Microsoft is using to try to make MS SQL Server scale up to support larger volumes of data and more users. In this case, the database is distributed across many Windows NT servers, and MTS is used to control the distributed update using two-phase commit.

When Microsoft talks about scalability, this is what it means—it achieves scalability by splitting the data across machines and handling the distributed updates using MTS. But it is still the early days when it comes to support for other DBMSs, and if, like many other companies, you have data in Ingres, Sybase, Informix, or DBMSs, then you are going to have to wait a little while before you are supported. Furthermore, if you are running them on platforms other than Windows NT you are also going to have to wait. MTS runs on Windows NT.

14

MSMQ (Falcon)

> ▶ Message queuing service
>
> ▶ Supports message prioritization, guaranteed delivery, deferred delivery, polling, pulling, notification, broadcast/multicast, time expiration of messages
>
> ▶ Primarily Windows NT with Windows 95 client access
>
> ▶ Other client platform access being provided by Level 8—HP-UX, MVS/CICS, AIX, Solaris, possibly OS/2, and OpenVMS

MSMQ is a message queuing service. Message queuing is not the same as mail messaging—a service with which it is often confused. Whereas mail messaging (or just "messaging") is used by people to send mail messages to other people and communication is directly between people, message queuing is a service used to enable messages to be sent between processes. Thus, a client process could send a message, with data in it about an order, to a server process for that process to act on the order.

Message queuing products and services can support **asynchronous processing** of communicating processes. The sending process hands the message to the message-queuing service and can then carry on working; it doesn't have to wait for a reply. In order to achieve this, the products use a store and forward-like approach to handle interprocess communication at runtime. When one process sends another process or processes a message, the middleware stores the message on queues along the route the message takes.

Processes which use message queuing services are actually acting in a peer-to-peer way—process A can send process B a message and in turn, process B can also send process A a message.

Figure 14.1
MSMQ

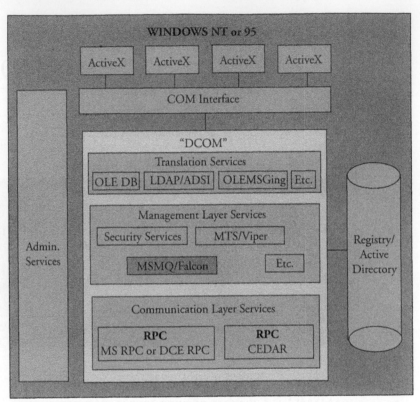

Figure 14.2
*Store and
forward queuing*

Message Passing vs. Message Queuing

You may have heard the terms message queuing and message passing. A *message passing* service or product enables one process to send another process a message by addressing the message directly to the receiving process—SEND MESSAGE nnnn TO PROCESS B. In this case, the sending and receiving process know very little about the existence of the queues; they are there simply to provide a useful storage place to keep messages on the route. The queues are known only to the middleware services—the processes can neither access them nor control them.

In a *message queuing* service or product, the processes do know about the existence of the queues and address the message specifically to a queue— SEND MESSAGE nnnnn TO QUEUE X. By using message queuing, the vendors of these products provide more options to the developer. The vendor can allow a queue to be read by more than one process at the other end— perhaps sharing messages or alternatively taking messages off the queue in a round-robin fashion.

Internal queues may still be used, for example, a transmission queue at the sending end, intermediate receipt/transmission queues en route, and a receipt queue at the receiving end. But the final queue is a known queue—one the processes can access:

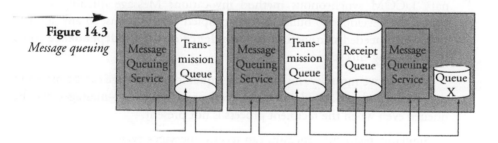

Figure 14.3
Message queuing

Message content

The next obvious question most people ask is what goes in the message— what sort of **data content** can it have? The answer is that, in general, you can put anything you like in the message—blobs, structured data, sound, images, and so on, even instructions such as a list of SQL commands if you really want. The only restriction might be the length (some products do restrict the length of the message).

But there is a down side to this apparently unlimited freedom of data content. We saw that in order to send a message over the network, the middleware has to translate the data formats between machines—ASCII to EBCDIC, little endian to big endian. The way it did this in DCOM was by using the interface definition, which defined the content of the data going across the network. But message middleware does not use an interface to define data content—the message content is defined within the program—all the middleware knows is that a block of data is passed to it with an unknown content, but a defined length. All it does then is add a header to it to give it an address, priority, and so on.

Some message products do not do data format translation because they do not know the contents of the message, but those that do employ several cunning ways of doing it. Some get you to provide a dictionary with the message contents defined; some get you to tag the fields with a name and then hold information about the name and its format in libraries which you set up. Whatever solution is used, the idea is that you, at some stage, will have to give the middleware details about the content of the message so that it can do the data format translation for you.

Uses of the service

Where, then, would you use the message queuing service rather than the ordinary DCOM synchronous method invocation? Message queuing services enable the developer to build "loosely coupled" applications, so any application which needed **connection independence** or **time independence** could be built using this service.

What do we mean by this? In message queuing, a message can be placed in the queue and processed once the receiver is available—messages can be queued even when the recipient process is not present.

Similarly, recipient processes can receive messages even when the originator is not present. But if sender and receiver are both present on the network, messages can be sent and received immediately. It is this feature that makes them different from RPCs, where both processes have to be available on the network before a call can be made. In message queuing products the processes do not both have to be available.

Message services are thus extremely useful for building applications which must run over unreliable lines, or where the processes to be connected are remote from one another—separated by a WAN, for instance, or in different locations. Many existing message queuing products (like MQSeries, VCOM, and BEAmessageQ) are being used today by large organizations with many centers of operation and a large base of legacy systems they need to integrate. Typical applications have not only included end-user applications such as order entry, warehousing, stock control, and so on, but generic applications such as work-flow. Let me provide you with some examples:

Replacing paper–Message queuing middleware can replace paper-based methods of information transfer between computer systems—often with improved reliability of data transfer and reduction in time taken. One user of an MOM product, for example, uses message queuing to connect their order entry system with their warehousing and shipping systems; another uses it to connect shop floor applications with inventory and accounting systems.

Replacing batch transaction systems–Message queuing middleware is also particularly well suited to supporting applications that would otherwise be implemented as traditional batch transaction–based systems. For example, the application on one machine gradually produces transactions during the day that are batched and then transmitted for overnight processing by another machine.

A programmer would normally have to write and design these sorts of systems from scratch, but with message queuing middleware, the transactions can be transmitted over the network as and when they are created to be processed whenever there is free capacity. The messaging middleware can be used to take care of the file control, recovery, guaranteed delivery, and so on. These sorts of applications occur frequently in banks, securities companies, and supermarkets and stores (EPOS data).

Applications needing strictly ordered processing–Some applications employ an architecture where a number of client applications seek the services of one server. The server needs to process the requests for service in the strict order in which they arrived, in order to guarantee fairness to the client and also to ensure the integrity of the data. Examples of this sort of application might be an airline bookings system receiving bookings from travel agents or a car rental company receiving bookings from agents.

Message queuing middleware can be used in these circumstances because its architecture is based on messaging and queues. The queues are sequenced—normally in FIFO order, so the order of processing matches the order in which they were received. We will also be seeing that MSMQ supports message prioritization, which means that urgent messages can be given priority and processed ahead of others in the queue, adding to the flexibility of this form of approach.

What Is MSMQ?

Microsoft Message Queue Server (MSMQ), code-named Falcon, is a Message-Oriented Middleware service that supports message queuing, message prioritization, broadcast and multicast, poll/pull and notification, guaranteed delivery, deferred delivery, and time expiration–based messages. In the following chapter I will be describing what each of these terms means and the functions they provide.

It is administered using MSMQ Explorer. Administration is possible from any computer running MSMQ Enterprise Manager.

MSMQ is based on a foundation of COM and can be accessed by ActiveX components using the normal COM interface together with the additional "commands" provided in MSMQ. The API provided with MSMQ supports components which have been developed in C or C++ or Visual Basic. The MSMQIC (Internet Connector) enables the developer to use a Web page as the interface, or the developer can use MAPI and Exchange as the interface.

A bit of background

Falcon was developed by Microsoft in Israel by the same organization that "owns" NT 5 and the Directory. All these people were led by Moshe Dunie, a VP of engineering based in Redmond. Work started on Falcon towards the end of 1995. It was released in December 1997.

There were two betas of Falcon. Beta 1 of Falcon supported all the features described in this chapter, except encryption and authentication, which were in Beta 2. It ran on Windows NT workstation and server. Beta testing of Falcon 1 began in August 1996, when the beta was shipped to selected customers and developers. The first copies of Falcon were provided to developers on a CD at the Microsoft Developer's conference in Los Angeles towards the end of 1996.

Beta 2 not only supported security but also provided support for transactions (queues were capable of being placed under transaction control), as well as "exactly once delivery and end-to-end confirmation" using DTC. Falcon was released towards the middle to end of 1997 as part of NT, when it was renamed MSMQ.

Platforms

MSMQ runs on Windows NT and 95. Clients can be Windows NT Workstation, Windows NT Server, or Windows 95. The servers must run on Windows NT Server. Level 8 Systems are providing gateways from *clients* running on other machines to the MSMQ services on Windows.

The diagram below shows the platforms supported and the way the gateways will work. The platforms shown in the diagram are the main platforms to be supported initially; other platforms (OS/2, OpenVMS) are planned.

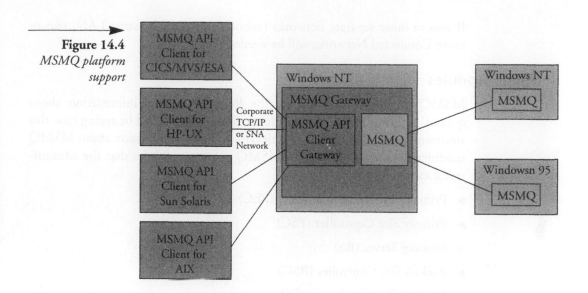

Figure 14.4
MSMQ platform support

Main concepts and modules

MSMQ consists of a set of DLLs and EXEs called the MSMQServices, which, along with the MSMQ Device Drivers, provide the core functionality and run on all machines whether these are acting as clients or servers.

Sites and connected networks

MSMQ uses the concepts of a "site" and a "connected network" in order to configure the queues and MSMQ modules. A site is a physical site with computers linked by communications lines. A connected network is a collection of computers where all the computers in the group can communicate directly using the same protocol. A computer can belong to more than one connected network and a connected network can span sites, for example:

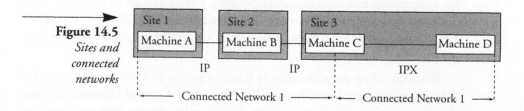

Figure 14.5
Sites and connected networks

If two or more separate networks (subnets) exist on the same LAN, two or more Connected Networks will be needed.

Main modules

MSMQ currently does not use the Registry to store information about queues, etc., but rather its own Information Store. We will be seeing how this store works later, but the store is relevant in the next discussion about MSMQ modules. There are six types of MSMQ software modules that the administrator can deploy:

▶ Primary Enterprise Controller (PEC)

▶ Primary Site Controller (PSC)

▶ Routing Server (RS)

▶ Backup Site Controller (BSC)

▶ MSMQ Client Software (CS)

▶ Site Gates

Primary Enterprise Controller (PEC)–There is one PEC per enterprise network. The PEC holds information about the entire enterprise configuration. It can also function as the PSC for the site, or as a routing server

Primary Site Controller (PSC)–There is one PSC per site in an enterprise, but there is no need for a PSC on a machine which has the PEC because on this machine the PEC fulfils the role of PSC. The PSC holds information about the computers and queues at that site. It also functions as a routing server.

Routing Servers–A Routing server is the prime component in MSMQ supporting asynchronous messaging, store and forward, context bridging between protocols, session concentration, and dynamic routing. It is installed on all machines needing these services.

In-Routing servers act as a gateway for all incoming messages and provide session concentration. Out-Routing servers do the reverse and act as gateways for all outgoing messages to clients. Routing servers can act in the capacity of both in- and out-routing servers. The administrator can allocate more than one Routing server as an in or out server to a group of clients in order to protect against failure.

When deciding the allocation of Routing servers to Connected Networks, at least one Routing server must belong to each Connected Network in order that the two sites can communicate. Where only one machine on a site has been designated a Routing server, messages sent from clients will be channelled through this machine. Where a number of machines have been designated as Routing servers, client messages can be routed through any of these machines to the remote site.

Backup Site Controller (BSC)–The BSC is installed at each site where protection against failure in case of PSC failure is needed. One or more BSCs can be installed per site. The BSC holds a read only replica of the PSC database and also functions as a routing server.

Client Software–MSMQ Client software runs on machines where the applications act only in the capacity of a client. The client software connects to a PSC and also to the BSCs. A special version of the Client Software used in development comes with the MSMQ Software Development Kit.

Site Gate–Intersite session concentration is achieved using Site Gates. If a site is configured to use a Site Gate, every message sent between computers in different sites is routed through the Site Gate. By doing this, the computers within the site do not need to know about routing or the topology of the network beyond the site.

MSMQ Information Store

The MSMQ Information Store holds information about computers, queues, the logical enterprise topology (sites, CNs, inRSs, outRSs, assignments), and logical enterprise settings (enterprise name, PEC name, default replication intervals, etc.).

MSMQ does not use the Registry to hold this information. Instead, it currently uses its own database. This database is maintained by the PECs, PSCs, and BSCs and uses MS SQL Server version 6.5 as the underlying DBMS. In the future, it is likely that this store will be replaced by the Active Directory.

The database is replicated between sites and machines based on the scope of the data held:

▶ *PEC data*–The database maintained by the PEC contains the master copy of enterprise, site, site link, and CN settings. This database is replicated between sites, with the PEC having write access to this information and the PSCs having read access.

▶ *PSC data*–The PSC's database contains a master copy of its site's computers and queues. Queues can have either site or enterprise scope. If the queue has site scope, details of it are replicated within the site. If the queue has enterprise scope, details are replicated between sites. Thus, each PSC database also contains a copy of the information from other sites, if it has enterprise scope. Each PSC has write access to the information it owns and read access to the replicated data.

▶ *BSC data*–BSCs contain a replicated database from the PSC in their site to which they have read access.

Routing servers thus use the PSC data for their site (or BSC data in the event of failure) and PEC data (master or replicated) to obtain information about the enterprise. Routing servers must thus be aware where in the site (on which machine) the PEC data, PSC data, and BSC data reside.

Data is replicated from the owner directly to other sites, that is, from the PEC to the PSCs and from PSCs to other PSCs. But the PSCs replicate to BSCs at their site, not to other sites. By default, intrasite replication occurs every two seconds and intersite replication every 10 seconds; however, replication intervals can be changed, and immediate replication takes place if the topology is changed. MSMQ actually uses its own queues and routing mechanisms to support the replication.

Queues

Types of queue

There are three main types of queue supported by MSMQ—transmission queues, target or receipt queues, and dead letter queues.

Transmission queues are queues used by every Routing server to enable messages to be received from other Routing servers (or a client application) and then either transmitted to another Routing server or sent to the final receipt queue. They provide various points of store and forward capability along the route to the final destination queue. Transmission queues are thus held on each node that has a Routing server—including the initial client and the final server hosts.

Messages created/sent by a client application are passed to the local Routing server, which stores them on its local transmission queue. It looks up the Routing table to find out where the final queue is and also which route should be followed to get there. After this route has been determined the message is passed to the next Routing server on the route, which stores the message in its local transmission queue.

This "hopping" from one Routing server to the next (possibly across multiple sites) continues until the final destination is reached and the message is stored on the final destination's transmission queue. The message is then placed on the final receipt queue from where it can be read by the application(s).

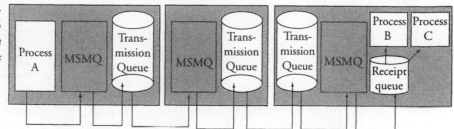

Figure 14.6
Transmission queues

The storage medium used for transmission queues is dependent on the delivery method required for the message. Two delivery methods are supported—recoverable and express. Each message is marked as to the method to be used.

▶ For each recoverable message, the "write" operation to the transmission queue is automatically flushed to disk. Thus, the transmission queues used for recoverable messages are stored on disk.

▶ For each express message, the message stays in memory. These memory-based queues, however, can be the subject of journaling. So, even though the message may be memory based, it may still be logged and therefore recoverable in case of machine failure. Other than any logging which takes place, messages may be written to disk when the computer has physically run out of memory and needs somewhere else to put the message. In other words, the disk is used as an overflow.

Transmission queues can be the subject of *journaling*—the process of logging a message to disk. Two types of journaling are supported. If source journaling is used, the outgoing messages are logged. If this option is used, the logging is configured on a message-by-message basis. If target journaling is used, incoming messages are logged. This form of logging is configured on a per queue basis by the administrator.

Target or receipt queues are the final destination queue for a message before it is read by an application. There are two types of receipt queues—public and private queues.

Public queues–Public queues are queues from which one or more server applications can read. They are thus shared queues. Not only can a public queue be read by more than one process, but a process can read more than one public queue.

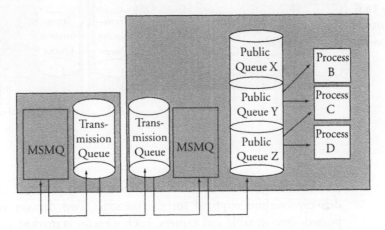

Figure 14.7
Public queues

Not only can the queue be shared, *but messages can be shared as well.* Applications can "peek" at a message or read the message. Applications that peek at the message read without removing the message; applications that read the message cause the message to be removed.

Public queues can have site scope—in which case their contents can be read by anyone on that site, or they can have enterprise scope, in which case their contents can be read by any application in the entire enterprise. Public queues are stored in the MSMQ Information Store along with Directory type information and as such are stored on disk. MSMQ uses MS SQL Server version 6.5 as the underlying DBMS. Because of this, they are automatically replicated along with the rest of the information to the other sites. Queues with *site scope* are replicated to *all BSCs within the site*. Queues with *enterprise scope* are replicated to *all controller servers* (PECs, PSCs, BSCs) within the enterprise.

The replication that takes place across the enterprise ensures the contents are available across sites and avoids a shared queue from having to be read from multiple sites. Because a replicated copy exists on each site, it is this copy that is used, not one centrally stored one. The replication thus serves to both provide a backup mechanism in case of failure and improve performance.

Applications reading the message from an enterprise queue effectively result in the removal of the same message from other copies of the queue. In effect, therefore, even though the message has been duplicated to the other sites, it only remains on the queue until an application reads that message. Once the message has been read by an application, all duplicate messages are removed.

Figure 14.8
Replication of public queues

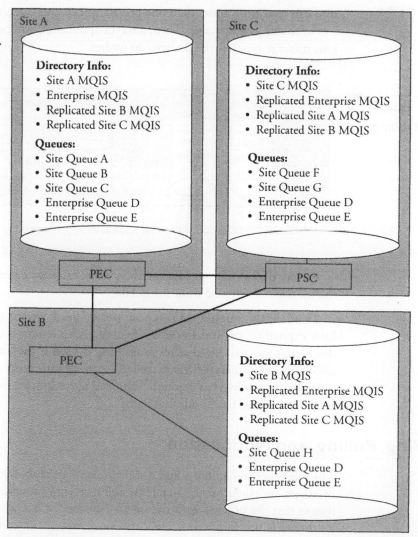

Site A

Directory Info:
• Site A MQIS
• Enterprise MQIS
• Replicated Site B MQIS
• Replicated Site C MQIS

Queues:
• Site Queue A
• Site Queue B
• Site Queue C
• Enterprise Queue D
• Enterprise Queue E

Site C

Directory Info:
• Site C MQIS
• Replicated Enterprise MQIS
• Replicated Site A MQIS
• Replicated Site B MQIS

Queues:
• Site Queue F
• Site Queue G
• Enterprise Queue D
• Enterprise Queue E

PEC

PSC

Site B

PEC

Directory Info:
• Site B MQIS
• Replicated Enterprise MQIS
• Replicated Site A MQIS
• Replicated Site C MQIS

Queues:
• Site Queue H
• Enterprise Queue D
• Enterprise Queue E

If, however, an application peeks at a message, the message simply stays on the queue and, of course, all the duplicate queues. An application is responsible for the removal of messages if they are shared.

Private queues–Private queues cannot be shared—they are used by only one application. Private queues are used for point-to-point communication. One or more clients can place a message on a private queue, but only one application can read from the queue. Private queues are located on the host of the application that will use the queue and are stored in the local Registry of the server host and as such are stored on disk.

Although private queues can only be read by one application, an application can read from more than one private queue and can also read from both a private and public queue. Thus, a server application can be in receipt of various message types, if the designer so wishes.

Figure 14.9
Private queues

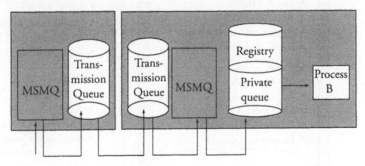

Private queues *do not* support the ability to peek a message—once read, the message is removed from the queue.

Dead letter queues–MSMQ supports "dead lettering"—messages that have expired or are undeliverable are called dead letters and are stored in the dead letter journal. Dead letter journaling is used if the destination queue is not known, the message has exceeded its maximum number of hops, or the message time to live has expired. The dead letter journal can be both viewed and manipulated by the administrator.

Polling, Pulling, and Notification

The terms polling, pulling, and notification are used to describe the ways that messages are taken off the queue by the receiving process. The word *polling* means that the process reads the queue (the receipt queue), but in reading it, its thread is not blocked; it can carry on working. The word *pulling* means that when the receiving process reads the receipt queue, its thread is blocked and it sits and waits until a message arrives.

The word *notification* means that the message queuing middleware actually notifies the process when a message does arrive by triggering it. Thus, notification does not mean the interruption in processing of a running server; it means that a dormant server is activated when the message actually arrives.

MSMQ supports all three methods of removing messages from a queue—polling, pulling, and notification. It is thus possible to devise servers that are dedicated to handling a specific type of message and pull that message from the queue, or a server could be designed that responded to multiple message types and polled various queues in turn to determine the processing it needed to follow.

Message Prioritization

Normally messages are stored in FIFO order in flat files, but MSMQ also supports the prioritization of messages. Priorities of 0 to 5 are supported (5 being the highest priority). Message priorities 6 and 7 are reserved for internal use. Prioritization is used to transmit the message across the network—from transmission queue to transmission queue.

This latter point deserves some explanation. It is possible to use the prioritization at many stages of delivery—as the message is stored on the transmission queue, over the network, as it is removed from the transmission queue and placed on the receipt queue, and so on. What we are seeing in MSMQ is that the priority field is only used for transmission over the network.

Message Content

Whereas DCOM uses a fixed format "message" because the ordering and type of parameters are determined by the interface definition, MSMQ messages can contain any information the developer wants. In principle, there is no restriction on what goes across the network. The developer packs these messages, and MSMQ adds the necessary header information to the message. In principle, there are also no limits to the size of messages used in MSMQ (the beta limited the size to 1 megabyte).

Data format conversion is a little more of a sticky problem, and for the short term, where MSMQ is being run on machines with different formats, you may have to do the data format conversion yourself, as (as far as we are able to make out) MSMQ doesn't support automatic data format conversion of messages. You need to check this yourself, though, when you use the service, as it was such early days in the life of the product when I wrote this that they could have added it by the time you read this.

Session Handling

Sessions are established between Routing servers, and as such from the applications point of view communication is essentially sessionless. MSMQ uses the concept of session concentration to reduce the number of actual sessions between nodes. Intrasite session concentration is used to reduce network bandwidth use and intersite concentration is used to reduce costs—these two approaches employ different methods to achieve their aims.

In addition to the session concentration, the administrator can use site gates as a means of funneling site traffic between two computers, thus providing another form of session concentration. Furthermore, he or she can use In-Routing and Out-Routing servers as a means of funneling request from or to the client via the server.

Broadcasting and Multicasting

We came across the concept of a broadcast or multicast message in the chapter on COM. There we saw how the Outgoing interface could be used to provide a form of broadcast or multicast delivery which was not "reliable" because the messages were not stored en route. If a server process happened not to be available when the event was generated, it wouldn't get the message.

I concluded that the Outgoing Interface was useful when you didn't mind if the event was not delivered—for example, events that only had validity anyway at the time they were generated—but that MSMQ was a better solution if you wanted reliable delivery of events or messages to multiple servers. If you remember, I said that a broadcast of a message was delivery of a message to all the processes on the network where the sender did not need to know the recipients, their name, or address.

Multicast delivery of a message enabled a sender to output a message that was then sent to a selected number of processes on the network that had subscribed to receive the message. Again, the sender does not have to know who has subscribed; its only job is to send the message. It is the recipients that decide whether they need to know about the message or not.

Public queues can be used for simulating a form of "broadcast" or "multicast" of a message. In true broadcast and multicast, the message is placed on a single queue and applications can subscribe to receive the message. That message is then sent in turn to each (running) application registered until the last application registered has received the message.

In the approach used by MSMQ, applications don't subscribe to receive a message; they have to read a specific queue to see if a message is there, but they can share a queue. So, for example, a single message could be sent by a client to a site queue that would then be "peeked at" by one or more applications at that site (thus ensuring the message was not removed when it was looked at). These applications could themselves be situated on different machines on the site.

Similarly, a message could be sent to an enterprise queue that was then duplicated across sites. At each site one or more applications could then peek at the replica copy or the master copy of this queue. The effect of this approach is pretty much identical to that achieved by broadcast or multicast messaging.

Guaranteed Delivery/Delivery Assurance

What do we mean by *guaranteed delivery?* In middleware terminology, guaranteed delivery is a function that ensures that a message is guaranteed to arrive at its destination, despite failures, outages, server failure, client failure, middleware failure, and so on.

It is notoriously hard to achieve, as the more safeguards you build into a message queuing product to ensure it doesn't lose a message—that its queues are protected from failure, that it has a protocol for removing messages from one queue as they are stored on the following queue—the slower the processing gets. The provision of this service thus tends to be something of a compromise—the vendor does the best they can to ensure the message is delivered but without compromising performance. Some of the best middleware products provide you with an option—various levels of service.

DCOM without MSMQ clearly does not support guaranteed delivery in the sense we mean it here, that a message is guaranteed to arrive despite failures. At this basic level, the client receives an error message if the message is not delivered. But MSMQ can support guaranteed delivery; thus, if the developer wanted to ensure a message was always delivered, he or she would use MSMQ.

The safeguards provided within MSMQ are quite extensive. When a client sends a message, the message is first placed on the transmission queue of the client machine. Transmission queues can be memory based (express) or disk based (recoverable), but in both cases they are logged, which means that any sort of machine failure would not result in the loss of a message—the log could be used to reconstitute the queue.

The message is then passed to the next transmission queue in the route in a series of hops, which will take the message to its final destination. A series of acknowledgments takes place between sending MSMQ module and receiving MSMQ module to ensure the message has reached the next stop on the route. Thus, at each stage an acknowledgment system is used to ensure the message has been transferred between transmission queues successfully. The client, however, is not sent acknowledgments—either en route or when the message reaches its final destination.

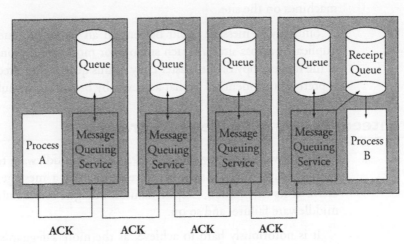

Figure 14.10
Guaranteed as "assured" delivery service

When the message has reached the final receipt queue, MSMQ transfers the message from the transmission queue on that host to the public or private queue. Both queues are disk based and as such protected against machine failure. The public queues are based on SQL Server and can as a consequence be logged as part of the normal DBMS procedures. These queues are also replicated, so even if SQL Server logging is not used, the replicated queue acts as a protection against disk failure.

The only rather remote point of failure in the sequence is the private queue, which is neither logged nor secured using a DBMS. As such, although it is safely stored on disk, if the disk crashes, messages could be lost. As the public queue is stored with the Registry, however, the disk failure could cause more catastrophic failure than just the simple loss of a queue, and as such the administrator may well consider supporting the configuration using disk mirroring and striping on Windows NT.

It is possible to get a situation where some messages are not delivered because they time out, the server doesn't exist, or the queue disappears, but even then the message is not lost. Instead, the dead letter queue is used to store these messages, which can be handled separately under administrator control.

Deferred Delivery

Deferred delivery describes the ability of a message queuing product to (as is implied) defer the delivery of a message until the recipient is there. It does not mean that the message is deliberately held back but refers to the capability of a product to deliver a message even though various components on its route are temporarily unavailable or missing.

The same approach used to support guaranteed delivery in MSMQ also supports deferred delivery. If we use the example below again to explain the features in MSMQ:

Figure 14.11
Deferred delivery

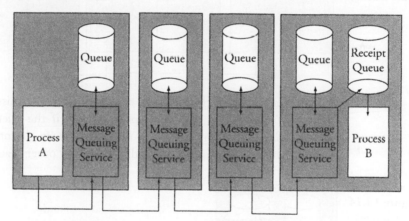

We want to deliver a message from process A to process B. In the first place, the client can deliver the message to MSMQ even if all the machines along the subsequent route are unavailable. MSMQ will safe store the message on the queue.

Figure 14.12
*A client process can
send a message even
if no other nodes
are active*

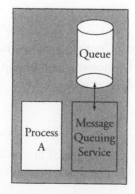

MSMQ can then subsequently move the message along the route, safe storing it as it goes along, even if the client process has shut down and no server process is running.

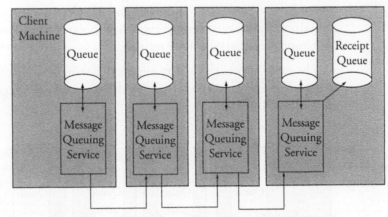

Figure 14.13
*MSMQ can move
the message
between nodes,
even if client and
server applications
are inactive*

Once the server machine has the message on its transmission queue, it can deliver the message to the server process even if the client process, client machine, and all the machines en route have been disconnected from the server machine or the line between the server and other machines had failed.

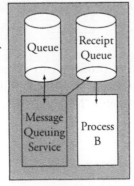

Figure 14.14
*A server can receive
a message even if
all other nodes are
inactive*

The server process can be triggered (notified) when the message arrives, but even if this method is not used, the message will wait on the receipt queue until the server process was loaded or restarted.

Message Routing

We have already seen that messages can be routed across multiple machines and that MSMQ supports routing of messages across multiple nodes. In fact, routing occurs when a session cannot be directly established between sender and receiver, or when in-routing or out-routing servers are being used, or when site gates are being used. So how does MSMQ do its routing?

MSMQ uses two type of routing—**intrasite** routing and **intersite** routing.

Intrasite routing–MSMQ makes the assumption that intrasite routing is fast and inexpensive and bases its routing algorithms on this. MSMQ measures intrasite routing in "hops"—the number of routing servers a message must pass through before it reaches its destination. The route is then chosen to minimize the hops.

Figure 14.15
Intrasite routing

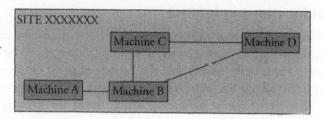

For example, a message going from Machine A to Machine D would go from Machine A to Machine B and on to Machine D.

Intersite routing–MSMQ makes the assumption that intersite routing is slow and expensive and bases its routing algorithms on this. Where intersite routing is being used, the routing is based on the concept of a SiteLink. SiteLinks are (as the name implies) communication links between two sites and the administrator assigns relative numbers (representing cost and speed) to the SiteLinks, which are used at runtime by the routing module to decide which route to take.

Numbers between 0 and 999,999 can be allocated, and it is entirely up to the administrator how he or she allocates the numbers. High value numbers are used to denote undesirable links (slow or expensive); low value numbers are the more desirable links (less expensive and faster).

The administrator might typically balance the cost with the delay (the speed of one link versus another). The administrator sets up the SiteLink values when he or she installs new sites. Thus, for example, if he or she had only two sites, any value above zero could be chosen (zero means not connected). Once three or more sites existed he or she would need to start thinking about using different numbers. An example is provided below.

A message needing to go from Site A to Site C would go first to Site B, then Site D, then site C. The SiteLink concept thus not only defines the

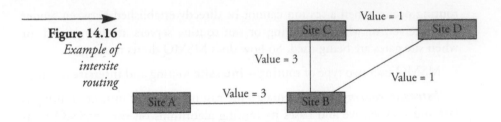

Figure 14.16
*Example of
intersite
routing*

topology of the network but priority routes. But the information is clearly "static," not based on traffic or line availability.

Other useful functions in MSMQ

It is worth noting that MSMQ does have some additional useful functions to help the developer during program testing. Messages can be tracked to keep a record of the route taken, and the tracking can be done at the application level or for all applications. As messages pass the Routing server, a message is sent to a report queue indicating which server the message passed through, the source address, destination address, a hop count, and the times. Where application level reporting is required, the application sets a message property to indicate tracing is to take place. Where all applications are to be traced, the administrator enables monitoring; tracing does not have to be set by the application. MSMQ Explorer can then be used to view the report queues.

MSMQ also has some debugging capabilities. MSMQ can be used with Visual C++. The developer gets two debug windows—one showing the debug messages for the MSMQ process and the other showing debug messages for the application. Only errors are displayed in the windows, but the developer can trace other information by changing defaults during setup. It is also possible to dump the entire contents of the MSMQ database to detect problems.

In Summary

What an interesting and useful service MSMQ is. For a new release it has some quite advanced features—features only found currently on the more mature MOM products such as BEAmessageQ, MQSeries, and VCOM.

It is chock full of functions—guaranteed delivery, deferred delivery, broadcast, multicast, notification, polling and pulling, message prioritisation, and so on. I think most developers can see that potentially it has an enormous number of uses.

But it is worth noting two small notes of warning. The first note is about platform support. Remember that MSMQ is essentially a Windows NT-based product with client access from other platforms. The other MOM products on the market cover many more platforms and are not restricted to client only access from those platforms. A product like BEAmessageQ can link SunOS, Solaris, AIX, HP-UX, Digital UNIX, OS/2, Windows NT, OpenVMS, Ultrix, 88000 Delta, DG-UX, and NCR Unix. It can also provide access from OpenVMS to MVS/CICS and MVS/IMS via LU6.2 services.

The second note of warning concerns the change to the Active Directory. MSMQ may need to undergo some quite extensive adaptation when Windows NT version 5 is released, as this release should include the move to the Active Directory. At the moment MSMQ uses its own Directory. But in the future, MSMQ's Information Store will probably be replaced by the Active Directory.

Furthermore, MSMQ's Information Store is also used to store its public queues, so the move to the Active Directory is not just going to affect the Information Store itself but also the queues themselves. Finally, MSMQ's private queues are stored in the old Registry used by Windows NT 4.0, so the move to the Active Directory will affect the private queues too. I don't expect the functionality of MSMQ to change, but I would be prepared for the fact that the changes needed will affect its stability for a while.

15

OLE DB and Active Data Objects

- OLE DB and Active Data Objects used to gain access to stored data in non-object-based format
- Thor is special product for DB2 access from OLE DB
- Outgoing interfaces can be used with Active Data Objects
- Storage Objects provided as part of DCOM—own file system

One of the key things that developers have always found is that computing consists of a combination of the execution of functions and the manipulation of data. Some functions only need data stored in the computer's memory, but the majority of functions need data that is stored safely on a secure storage medium—a storage medium that can maintain a record of the data even after the computer has been switched off. All simple and obvious stuff, of course, but object-based computing is based on the idea that data is stored with function, which makes any data access that much more complex. In this chapter, we will find that OLE DB is just one of a number of features within DCOM that enable a developer to access data—data in a variety of formats.

Back to Basics–Storing Data

There are four main methods that can be used to store data generated or used by a program:

- Memory
- Shared memory
- Distributed shared memory
- File systems and DBMSs

Figure 15.1
*OLE DB and
Active Data
Objects*

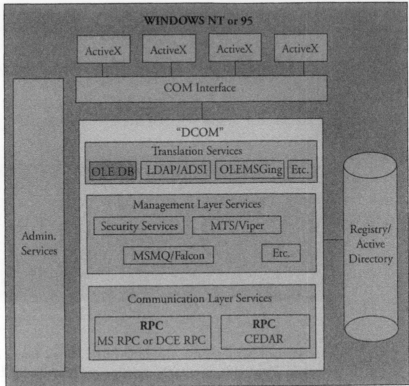

A single program can store temporary data in its memory, two or more programs on a single machine can store their shared data in shared memory, two or more programs on different machines can store their data in distributed shared memory, and one or more programs can store its data in a file system or DBMS.

As we saw in chapter ten, DCOM supports the storage of data in memory and shared memory via Windows NT. Windows NT provides a virtual memory system that enables up to 32 processes to read shared memory on that host as long as the manufacturer's HAL drives are installed. MTS also provides shared memory support. Neither DCOM nor Windows NT supports distributed shared memory.

Memory provides a mechanism of storing temporary data—data that is needed only for the duration of the execution of the program. But practically all programs need to store data permanently so that it can be used again by different programs at different times. This permanent storage mechanism must preserve the state of the data even if the machine is switched off. All very obvious, but the proponents of object-oriented methods have coined a phrase for this—persistent data.

Over the years we have seen an extraordinary multiplicity of different types of persistent data mechanisms emerge. The start, of course, was the early file systems with products like ISAM and VSAM. But over the years we have seen all sorts of "models" for data storage emerge. I will first take a look at the types of persistent storage system there are now to understand something of the reasons why products such as ODBC and OLE DB exist.

A brief history of DBMSs

The first DBMSs started to appear in the late '60s and early '70s. Since then, the IT industry has seen a plethora of different "types" of DBMS, in other words, products conforming to some basic set of principles. The main types of DBMS are:

▶ two-level networks

▶ hierarchical

▶ network (Codasyl)

▶ relational

▶ object oriented

▶ extended relational

The very first types of DBMS were based on "two-level networks" and included DBMSs such as TOTAL or IMAGE. IBM then produced a DBMS based on what is now referred to as a "hierarchical" model and which we now know as IMS or DL1. Other more esoteric DBMSs used at this time were based on transposition and inverted lists, for example, ROBOT.

Even in the late 1960s, DBMS vendors and end users started to realize the benefits of standardization, and the first standards work to be undertaken was initiated by the *Codasyl* (Conference on Data System Languages) committees, a group established in 1959 and responsible for the language COBOL. Two subcommittees—the Database Task Group and the Data Description Language Committee—produced a specification for the *DML* (Data Manipulation Languages) and *DDL* (Data Definition Languages) for what were to be called "network databases."

Products conforming to this specification include IDMS/X and CA-IDMS, IDS, VAX DBMS (from Digital), DMS 1100, MDBS, and so on. These DBMSs proved to be high performance, reliable, and excellent transaction processing machines, and large numbers of firms bought and developed strategic systems using them.

IBM rejected the Codasyl proposals (primarily from a marketing standpoint, as it had no DBMS conforming to the standard) and started to promote the relational model proposed by Ted Codd via a number of papers produced in the early 1970s.

IBM, along with many new startups, realized they could leapfrog to the new relational paradigm by using the work of the exploratory System R* research project and consequently bypass the competition. The combination of IBM, Ted Codd, and the publicity that surrounded him and the emergence of companies like Oracle with equally good marketing muscle tolled the death knell for the Codasyl proposals, and, by the early to mid-1980s, Codasyl DBMSs ceased to be developed.

Oracle was released in 1979 and represented the first commercialised version of SQL. In 1981, IBM produced SQL/DS, a commercial version of System R* for VM/370. This was followed in 1983 by SQL/DS, rewritten for MVS and known as DB2. The release of DB2 created considerable publicity for IBM and the relational approach in general.

A flood of products has since appeared conforming to the relational model. They included Ingres, Sybase, Informix, Rdb, Interbase, SQLBase, Rbase, CA-DB, Non Stop SQL, and so on. End users have bought and developed large numbers of systems using them.

SQL (Structured Query Language), upon which many of today's products and standards are based, was originally called SEQUEL and was conceived as a query language for databases aimed at the end user. Not surprisingly, the end user didn't show the slightest interest in the language, so SQL was then developed to be a programming language.

Most developers found that to be useful, SQL had to be embedded in another language (using either embedded code or the call level interface) and that the nonprocedural nature of SQL was at times highly confusing and difficult to program. Vendors such as Oracle provided P*SQL (procedural SQL) to get around the deficiencies of the language.

In the early 1980s, ANSI and ISO initiated efforts to standardize the language resulting in the 1986 and 1989 SQL standards. During 1992, a more comprehensive standard (previously called SQL-2 and now known as SQL-92) emerged. The standardization process has tended to lag the vendors' efforts at extending the language. For example, data type definitions in the ANSI 89 standard covered only a very basic set—INTEGER, SMALLINT, CHAR, VARCHAR—and did not cover such other important types such as date, time, float, decimal, character set, and conversions, or "blob" type data such as images or sound.

During the late '80s and early '90s, yet another paradigm for DBMSs was proposed—the Object model. The interest sprang from the need by the CAD/CAM community for a DBMS that could support the complex data and structures that their applications used.

Early OODBMSs were developed as extensions of object-oriented programming languages such as C++ and Smalltalk, but later work has produced special purpose languages capable of supporting inheritance, locking, recovery, and so on. The main standards-making body for Object-Oriented Databases is the OMG, and perhaps the most influential description of OODBMSs is the "Object Database Standard" produced by the ODMG in 1993 and supported by most of the major OODBMS suppliers—Object Design, Ontos, O2 Technology, Versant, and Objectivity. Take-up of OODBMSs has not been large. Most end users have bought them to support specialized applications.

The final development in the ongoing saga of DBMS development is the emergence of the "Extended Relational Model," a hybrid of a relational model with object-oriented extensions. This approach is proving to be more popular with end users than the pure OODBMS, simply because it represents a more evolutionary path—one which does not require them to discard yet another DBMS. ISO has been working on a standard in this area—SQL3—but many of the relational DBMS vendors have added object-oriented extensions to their products ahead of the standard.

So what is the point of this? What it does mean is that a typical company could be using anything up to six different sorts of DBMS, each with their own paradigm, data manipulation language, and data definition language.

Most large IT departments have at least two DBMS and sometimes far more. The DBMSs straddle the entire range of types of DBMS—many companies have relational DBMSs, Network DBMSs, hierarchical DBMSs, some even have Object-Oriented DBMSs as well. Recent surveys of DBMS use show that large numbers of users still have a vast investment in IMS, CA-IDMS, and IDMS/X, even DBMSs such as Image (from HP).

Furthermore, they often have several relational DBMSs—Oracle, Sybase, Access, DB2 on the mainframe, Unix midrange, and PC. Most of the databases based on these DBMSs contain vital strategic data, essential to the everyday operations of the company. But many end users are discovering that to develop new applications they require access to all the data in all the DBMSs wherever it resides.

To exacerbate the problem further, companies are also introducing *data warehouses*—databases of data culled from production files with the duplication removed and data cleaned up. These data warehouses often reside on specialized file systems rather than normal DBMSs.

The ideal for many companies would be to replace the old databases with a well-designed integrated database based on a single DBMS, especially as there is often considerable data duplication between the databases and the designs often leave much to be desired. But most companies can only justify replacement of these databases as part of some much wider business-led initiative—and even then, there may be no good business reason why the data and database itself should be replaced; it may only be the functions and underlying technology which require updating.

It is worth noting that the argument often used by the DBMS vendors that you need different DBMSs for different applications is also a valid one, but for different reasons from those they tend to use. You only need different DBMSs when the one you have isn't up to the job. A DBMS should be capable of supporting all types of application. All they are admitting is that their DBMSs aren't very good!

So the user is stuck. He or she needs to access all these different databases, but they lie on different machines and are often supported by different DBMSs. Existing databases can't be merged and integrated, partly because there is often no good business reason to do so and partly because the DBMS vendors themselves admit their products don't cover all the application uses. So the only solution is to find a way of accessing them all as they are.

We have already seen that one service provided by Microsoft within DCOM supports the update of data in different DBMSs—MTS. But this does not solve one fundamental residual problem with all this data in all these DBMSs.

If a company wants to access this data, its developers will probably have to use many different data manipulation languages and versions of languages. In addition, these same developers will also have to understand the different underlying philosophies used by each DBMS in order to be able to understand the data structures.

Data access without help is potentially a time-consuming, painful, costly, and unproductive task—prone to error. And so, we see the emergence of a new class of middleware onto the scene to solve the problem—database connectivity middleware.

Database Connectivity Middleware

Database connectivity middleware provides an insulating layer between the application and the DBMS. The database programmer uses one standard language to access all the DBMSs, whether these are relational, object oriented, hierarchical, network, or some other type. The middleware converts this standard language to the various flavors, versions or other languages of the target DBMS. Thus, for example, the middleware may convert ANSI standard SQL to the version of SQL used by Oracle, or the version of SQL used by Sybase.

This is a nice idea in theory but it does have some limitations. To understand this we need to take a brief look at how these products actually work in practice.

How does translation actually work?

There are two parts to the process of translation of instructions to the DBMS, the translation of the DML and the translation of the names used for records, data items, and so on.

Name translation

The translation of names is an optional component of the database connectivity software, but it adds further transparency if it is available and can be used to simplify names which may be obscure or may have been restricted by bizarre DBMS rules (TOTAL, for example, only allowed data item names to be eight characters long).

The translation of names is usually handled via a Directory/Dictionary, which contains the names the developer can use to access the data and the names that are actually used in the DBMSs themselves. The creation of this Directory is a one-off job, but it must of course be kept up-to-date as the database designs change.

Translation of the DML

The translation between the DMLs of various DBMSs may seem a simple enough concept at first, but the complexities involved in true translation only start to emerge once one examines the differences between the DBMSs. In essence, a translation tool has to be able to smooth out and provide one interface which covers:

▶ The differences between the basic underlying models used by the DBMS vendors

▶ The differences in DML

▶ The differences in dialect between supposed standard DMLs

Translation of the underlying models–We have seen what the main types of DBMS are. Each of these types of DBMS uses different concepts, and the database connectivity software has to translate first and foremost between concepts before it can translate the DML itself, for example:

▶ Two-level networks–Two-level network DBMSs use Master Data records and Detail Data records with Elements, synonym chains, link paths, Manual Masters, and Automatic Masters (indexes).

▶ Hierarchical–Hierarchical DBMSs use segments, links, root segments, indexes, and data items or fields.

▶ Network (Codasyl)–Codasyl (network) databases are based on the concept of records (types), data items, sets, and areas. Sets can be ordered, indexes are allowed on records, and sets can be one or more record types

▶ Relational–Relational DBMSs are based on tables, columns, and foreign keys, and tables can be indexed. The link between tables is implemented implicitly using foreign keys, not explicitly using sets.

Although it is possible to provide some correlation between concepts such as the record (table, segment, Data Record, etc.), data item (column, element, field), and set (link, link path, embedded foreign key), not all concepts do translate. If the developer has used an ordered set, for example, in IDMS, no direct equivalent exists in the relational world. The closest concept might be an index on a specific key of the relational DBMS, which is itself ordered. One area of particular complexity is the use of the concepts themselves to record integrity rules.

Codasyl DBMSs can be designed to incorporate many of the rules of data integrity within their design (the use of mandatory and optional sets, for example); only recently have relational databases incorporated similar checks by using stored procedures, and some types of DBMS have no built-in integrity checking mechanism. There are thus basic differences in the way integrity is handled by each DBMS—automatically by using the design, automatically by using stored procedures, or not at all.

Equally important is the fact that even DBMSs within the same family may not support all the concepts. Stored procedures, for example, are a feature of relational DBMSs. They can be used to not only implement integrity rules and validation procedures (e.g., validate date) but to perform calculations (e.g., calculate age from date of birth). But not all relational DBMSs support stored procedures.

The different DMLs (Data Manipulation Languages)–Each of the different types of DBMS uses a different DML. The Relational language includes update commands such as INSERT, UPDATE, and DELETE, and similar commands exist in other DBMS types. The correspondence between update commands in the various DBMS types is thus reasonably clear cut, although DBMSs based on nonrelational DBMSs often contain more explicit references to the locking to be used and the creation of indexes.

The main differences are to be found in the commands used for "navigation" around the data in the database. Relational language queries are what is called nonprocedural in that they do not require the programmer to navigate his way around the database. Codasyl and two-level network databases, for example, do require navigation, and the programmer defines the query by traversing sets or links, by direct access, or by access using indexes. Whereas a programmer using a relational database may use command such as SELECT*FROM and SELECT statements that join tables—SELECT C1, C2, C3 FROM T1, T2 WHERE T1.C4 T2.C5—a programmer using a Codasyl database would use commands such as :

FIND CUSTOMER DB_KEY IS CUSTOMER_NO

FIND NEXT ORDER WITHIN CUST-HAS-ORDER

FIND OWNER WITHIN PROD-HAS-ORDLINE

If the Codasyl-based DML being input to the translation process requires a traversal of a set, the relational DML being output from the translation process has to provide the equivalent, for example, access to a table via an index or specific foreign key.

There are two essentially different approaches being used to get at data.

The dialects of each DML (Data Manipulation Language)–Not only have DBMS developers produced many types of DBMS, they have also produced many "flavors" of the same original standard DML. Codasyl databases and Relational databases both suffer from this problem. As DBMS developers developed their own implementations, they "adapted" the standard. Many of the additions were added to provide missing functionality and some were added to provide some form of obviously discriminating feature.

What has resulted, however, is a large collection of both Codasyl and Relational DBMSs that do not adhere to the original single standard. The problem is probably more severe in the Relational DBMS area, simply because this class of DBMS has had longer to evolve and there are more products on the market to exacerbate the problem. In the following paragraphs, some of the differences that can occur between the various versions of SQL are explored in more detail.

▶ **Variations in syntax and semantics of commands**–Although the SQL standards have provided some degree of commonality in statements such as SELECT, INSERT, UPDATE, DELETE, and so on, there are still some significant differences in the vendors' implementations of these commands. SQL Server, for example, used to assume that certain keywords were optional—such as the INTO keyword in the INSERT statement. DBM, on the other hand, used to assume such keywords were required.

▶ **Data types**–Although every relational DBMS supports the simple data types for integer and character, there are big differences in the way and the extent to which other data types are supported. Varying character strings, date, time, decimal, binary data, floating point, and so on may or may not be supported. Even if the data type is supported, the format used may be different; for example, DBM used to support DATE and TIME with two constructs, whereas SQL Server had one DATETIME construct

▶ **Status codes and messages**–Every database system must return a status code upon the completion of each SQL operation. Even successful operations generate status codes. Clearly, the operation of most programs is likely to depend on these status codes, whether they indicate a successful conclusion to a request or an unsuccessful one. In practically all the DBMSs, not only are the status codes themselves different for the same errors and conditions but the method in which the errors are handled is also different. For example, DBM used to return status codes as binary values in a field called SQLCODE in the SQL Communication Area. SQL Server, on the other hand, handled error conditions through two call-back procedures that received an integer identifying the error condition. Furthermore, some error conditions in DBM did not exist in SQL server and vice versa.

So What Does Database Connectivity Middleware Really Do?

It can handle dialects of the DML–In general, the majority of database connectivity middleware smoothes out the differences in the dialects between products of the same type. So, for example, a developer can use one standard version of SQL and the middleware will translate this to the dialect used by Oracle, the dialect used by Sybase, the dialect used by Informix, and so on.

These products can handle the differences in semantics and syntax, can potentially handle the difference in status codes and error messages (though not all translation products do), and can occasionally handle name translation. They have problems with data types. Where a developer wants to access a table or record containing data types that the standard API doesn't recognize as a data type, he or she has to use "pass thru," meaning an instruction in the native dialect that is simply passed through to the DBMS.

A small number can handle different DMLs–Only a few specialized products can translate the DML of different DBMS types. So, for example, only a few products can translate from one standard version of SQL to the DML used in IDMS. The translation performed by these products is almost entirely limited to translation of query functions, not update functions. So, products such as EDA/SQL, for example, are able to translate from an SQL dialect to the IDMS dialect, but only if the DML is for a query.

Some of these specialized translation products can also help a little with security privilege translation. As you are probably aware, the database administrator can set privileges and passwords for access to data, and for each DBMS this information has to be repeated. This information is often set up differently with different names and passwords. The translation software keeps its own "translation files" to show the mapping between all the ids. Some products also automatically synchronize their central security database with those of the DBMSs, meaning that an administrator has even less work to do.

So what doesn't it do?–The one thing database connectivity middleware cannot do is protect the developer from having to know he or she is accessing a certain DBMS or from having to know how that DBMS works. He or she may be able to use a single API, but the developer still has to understand the *effect* of that API within that DBMS—how it affects performance, how it affects the integrity of the data, and so on. Runtime services such as locking, deadlock detection, optimization, and so on all work differently in each DBMS, and all affect the workings of the DBMS differently. You could write a single line of common SQL code for Oracle and the performance could be fine, but in Sybase it could be awful, simply because the locking levels are different.

The developer also has to understand the database design, understand the meaning of the fields, and handle all the problems of data duplication, incompatible formats, incompatible coding systems, and so on. This is really the crux of the problem with database connectivity products—they don't tackle the main problem. What makes access of all these DBMSs so difficult and time consuming is not the differences in the DML, but the awful designs, the lack of documentation, the duplication, and the misuse of data fields by endusers and programmers alike. The real problem isn't actually solved by database connectivity middleware at all.

So, database connectivity middleware looks like promising stuff on the face of it, but in practice it doesn't bring the total transparency it promises and doesn't deliver the levels of productivity improvement often claimed. Nevertheless, one shouldn't knock it. It simplifies things considerably for low- to medium-volume queries as long as the data is reasonably well documented and does not contain too much duplication and too many incompatibilities. I'm not sure I would recommend it for high-volume queries or any form of update.

Why? Well, we have seen that you really need to know what you are doing for an update (locking, commit actions, deadlock detection, etc.), and in this case you might just as well use native DML to ensure you get the right result. Similarly, you also need to know what you are doing with high-volume queries to get the best performance, so again it might be better to use native DML where you understand the effect of the command.

Another reason is simply that translation is performed at runtime, which of itself is bound to slow processing down. In fact, most developers know that updates and high-volume queries are often better compiled (as static SQL, for example) as the compiled code provides better performance.

Microsoft and Database Connectivity

So, all of this lengthy introduction to the world of database connectivity eventually brings us to Microsoft and how it provides access to stored "persistent" data. There are in fact two methods which Microsoft now supports to access data—**ODBC** and **OLE DB.**

Microsoft's standard answer to the approach of database connectivity is *ODBC* (Open Database Connectivity)—a de facto standard that provides a standard SQL dialect with which to access files and databases. *OLE DB* is for use with DCOM and provides an interface and method-based approach to accessing data. OLE DB provides a means for the developer to access data in all sorts of different file types and DBMSs from a component possibly written in an object-oriented language.

Whereas ODBC is "procedurally" constructed with commands that are based on functions—READ, SELECT, etc.—OLE DB is interface based and includes a set of interfaces and methods which can be invoked from components. Let us first examine ODBC; then we can look at OLE DB and how it works.

ODBC (Open Database Connectivity)

Microsoft's standard answer to the approach of database connectivity is ODBC (Open Database Connectivity)—a de facto standard that provides a standard SQL dialect that can be used to access many *Relational DBMSs*. Microsoft, together with many third-party vendors, have produced "drivers" (translation products), which converted the ODBC dialect to other dialects of SQL.

Some specialized vendors such as Information Builders (with EDA/SQL) and Platinum Software (with InfoHub) can convert from ODBC to the DML of other types of DBMSs. ODBC is based on the Call Level Interface (CLI) specification of the SQL Access Group (SAG). The importance of the Call Level Interface as opposed to the use of an Embedded API is that in general terms, the SQL is not static SQL (compiled and bound to the program prior to execution), but dynamic SQL—processed during program execution.

ODBC comes in two parts—the core functionality and the extended SQL functions. The **core grammar** and functions are based on the SAG CLI, and these functions enable a developer to:

▶ Establish a connection with a data source, execute SQL statements, and retrieve results

▶ Receive standard error messages

▶ Provide a standard logon interface to the end user

▶ Use a standard set of data types

▶ Use a standard SQL grammar defined by ODBC

The **extended SQL grammar** provides developers with a way of exploiting the more advanced capabilities of DBMSs, those that are not covered in the SAG CLI. The extended set of functions is split into **Level 1** and **Level 2**.

The tables overleaf list some of the commands which are core, level 1, and level 2.

The extensions include support for:

▶ Data types such as date, time timestamp, and binary

▶ Scrollable cursors

▶ A standard SQL grammar for scalar functions, outer joins, and procedures

▶ Asynchronous execution

▶ A standard way for programs to find out what capabilities a driver and data source provide

ODBC can also support the use of DBMS specific SQL grammar (native code), allowing applications to add "pass thru" code when necessary.

Table 15.1 *Core and Level 1 functions*

Level of function	Type of function	Function/command
Core	Connecting to a data source	SQLAllocEnv
		SQLAllocConnect
		SQLConnect
	Preparing SQL requests	SQLAllocStmt
		SQLPrepare
		SQLSetParam
		SQLGetCursorName
		SQLSetCursorName
	Submitting requests	SQLExecute
		SQLExecDirect
	Retrieving results and info about results	SQLRowCount
		SQLNumResultCols
		SQLDescribeCol
		SQLColAttributes
		SQLBindCol
		SQLFetch
		SQLError
	Terminating a statement	SQLFreeStmt
		SQLCancel
		SQLTransact
	Terminating a connection	SQLDisconnect
		SQLFreeConnect
		SQLFreeEnv
Level 1	Connecting to a data source	SQLDriverConnect
	Obtain info about a driver and data source	SQLGetInfo
		SQLGetFunctions
		SQLGetTypeInfo

Table 15.1   *Core and Level 1 functions (Continued)*

Level of function	Type of function	Function/command
	Setting and retrieving driver options	SQLSetConnectOption
		SQLGetConnectOption
		SQLSetStmtOption
		SQLGetStmtOption
	Submitting requests	SQLParamData
		SQLPutData
	Retrieving results and Info about results	SQLGetData
	Obtaining information from System Catalog tables	SQLColumns
		SQLSpecialColumns
		SQLStatistics
		SQLTables

The architecture of the ODBC software is shown in Figure 15.2. The client application communicates with the ODBC Driver Manager, a Microsoft supplied product, which establishes which driver to use and routes the instructions to the correct driver. Client applications use the Application Programming Interface.

The driver translates the SQL calls into the syntax expected by the target DBMS and routes the call to the DBMS. The DBMS sends the results of the call to the driver, which are in turn sent to the application. The driver handles connection to and disconnection from the DBMS.

Microsoft supplied their own ODBC Desktop Driver pack for communicating with Access, FoxPro, Excel, Btrieve, Dbase, Paradox, and formatted text. A very large number (hundreds) of third parties also supply drivers, and these suppliers can be specialized middleware suppliers or the DBMS vendors may also provide drivers for their own products. Drivers are generally supplied by third parties such as DLLs. The Driver Manager communicates with the Drivers using a different interface—the Service Providers Interface (SPI).

Notice the existence of the communication software from the DBMS vendors themselves (or it could be a third-party communication middleware

Table 15.2 *Level 2 functions*

Level of function	Type of function	Function/command
Level 2	Connecting to a data source	SQLBrowseConnect
	Obtain info about a driver and data source	SQLDataSources
	Preparing SQL requests	SQLParamOptions
		SQLSetScrollOptions
	Submitting requests	SQLNativesql
		SQLDescribeParam
		SQLNumParams
	Retrieving results and info about results	SQLExtendedFetch
		SQLSetPos
		SQLMoreResults
	Obtaining information from System Catalog tables	SQLColumnPrivileges
		SQLForeignKeys
		SQLPrimaryKeys
		SQLProcedure Columns
		SQLProcedures
		SQLTablePrivileges

product). Oracle, Informix, and Sybase, for example, all provide their own communications middleware to enable processes to communicate with remote DBMSs. You will have heard of SQL*Net, I-Net, and OpenClient/ Open Server. These products are all middleware products, but highly specialized ones providing connectivity to the DBMS vendor's own DBMS.

If local DBMSs are used, the driver communicates with the local DBMS engine. If the driver needs to communicate with a remote DBMS, the communications software provided with the DBMS is used; for example, a developer using Oracle would use SQL*Net, a developer using Ingres would use Ingres*Net, and so on.

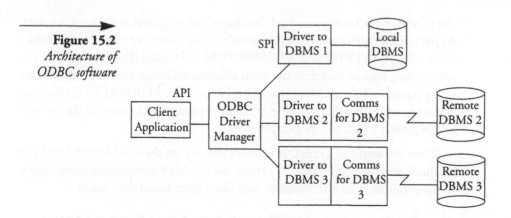

Figure 15.2
Architecture of ODBC software

If you want to access a remote DBMS you are still going to need the DBMS vendor's connectivity product, and if you want to access a number of DBMSs you are going to have to have a copy of each of the connectivity middleware products of those DBMSs on the machine you are using as the "client"—a very compelling reason to use three-tier architectures instead of a two-tier architecture. In other words, all your drivers and connectivity software goes on the "business server," not on the "presentation layer."

OLE DB

OLE DB is a set of interfaces and methods conforming to the COM model that provide the developer with access to data stores (persistent data stores) of different types from components. OLE DB is thus not a replacement for ODBC but an alternative to it. Whereas ODBC can be used with normal procedural languages and function-based programs, OLE DB has been specifically designed for use in DCOM and for use with object-oriented languages.

OLE DB is intended to be more far reaching in its coverage of persistent data than ODBC. Through OLE DB many different sorts of data—text, graphics, relational data, geographic data, e-mail messages, and so on—is intended to be accessible. In effect, data from many sources and of many types will be accessible using component-oriented method invocations based on a set of defined interfaces. What sorts of methods can this interface(s) support? Let me provide an example.

Where data transfer is between a Data Object and a component, special facilities are provided to enable both Data Object and Component to find out or specify the format of the data and the medium of transfer. The client uses the IDataObject Interface, which has functions to get/set and query the data. As part of the functionality of this interface, the client can use two data structures—FORMATETC and STGMEDIUM. STGMEDIUM is used by clients or data sources to define the most efficient exchange medium for the data being passed—disk, global memory, and so on. The FORMATETC structure is used to indicate either the type of data the client wants from the data source or the format a data source can provide.

Thus the world of OLE DB is based entirely on the COM model and has methods specifically devised to handle the world of component-based access to data sources, which themselves look like object-based data stores.

How can the developer access different data types from a component interface?

As we have seen, the paradigm used by object-oriented applications is fundamentally different from that used in normal function-based applications. Most data sources are accessed by an API that is function based—SELECT, DELETE, INSERT, and so on.

Clearly, when an object-based application is being used to access object-oriented databases, the mapping between concepts used in languages such as C++ or Smalltalk is relatively simple as the concepts and paradigm being used are the same. As long as OLE DB is accessing a persistent store of some kind that was built to be accessed via interfaces and methods, then the mapping is quite straightforward, but in all other cases—relational DBMSs, hierarchical DBMSs, network DBMSs, spreadsheets, file systems—practically all our "legacy" or heritage file systems—something has to be done to "map" the interface/method invocations to API calls. The answer would seem to be translation of the commands at runtime, but in fact there are four possible solutions open to the developer:

▶ **Database Object Using DML**–If this approach is used, the *developer* creates a special "database object" in a language (such as C) that directly supports the DBMS API. In effect, the developer creates a component in a non-object-oriented language from which normal DML commands can be issued. The developer then does the mapping of data structures from within the object. The advantages of this approach are that the developer can use the DML directly and therefore can be sure of the overall effect of the command.

Furthermore, the commands can be compiled with the component, so the access is likely to be more efficient. The disadvantage is that the mapping of the data structures from the database component to the calling client can be tedious and may be difficult to achieve. Microsoft does not use this approach although there is nothing to stop the developer using it.

▶ **Database Object Using ODBC**–If this approach is used, a special "database object" is used that directly supports ODBC. In effect, the developer uses a special component that can support ODBC commands. The advantages of this approach are that the developer can use ODBC to access numerous DBMSs and file systems—hundreds of drivers exist for these systems and one dialect of SQL can be used. The disadvantages are the ones we have already seen in all translation products—performance may not be very good as translation is at runtime and the developer still has to understand the DBMSs and how they work to get the best from them. There is an additional problem as the mapping of the data structures from the database component to the calling client can be tedious and may be difficult to achieve. Microsoft can support this approach using the Active Data Object—we will see how shortly.

▶ **Relational Mapping**–If this approach is used, the software translates at runtime between the commands and concepts used in the component and the commands and concepts used in the DBMS. I will take two example companies that supply this sort of software to demonstrate how the products work—Persistence Software's products and the ONTOS Integration Server. Both work in a similar way.

A table is set up that describes the mapping between concepts, for example, objects to tables, aggregations to foreign keys, etc., and then the programmer writes code to read, write, and update data using normal object-based invocations on methods. The software then translates at runtime between the commands and concepts used in the object and the commands and concepts used in the DBMS.

Now, we saw in an earlier section that this form of translation or database connectivity could be classified as "different DML translation." Persistence Software and ONTOS thus provide products that compare in specialized functionality to those from Information Builders or Platinum Software because they provide specialized mapping from an object-based "DML" to a relational DML (or similar). They will also suffer from the same limitations. The administrator will need to ensure the tables are always up-to-date as the databases change, the developer may have to limit himself to only certain sorts of access (probably only queries—certainly not updates), and because translation is at runtime, performance may suffer. Microsoft does not use this approach.

▶ **Interface Language Mapping**–In this approach the entire database engine is mapped into components, which are then accessed through interfaces. Microsoft does support this approach, so it deserves more explanation. We will examine this solution in more depth below.

What makes this solution different is that no translation takes place, but the vendors of the DBMSs, or file systems have all the work to do. They have to provide components that conform to the interfaces. Thus it is not up to third-party "driver" companies to provide simple translation engines; the DBMS vendors themselves have to actually provide components that implement the functions of the interface!

The functionality of the database is partitioned into components, each accessible via an interface. Thus there are components to manipulate this data, handle the caching, store the data, delete the data, and so on. Database or data source providers/vendors or third-party providers then implement one or more of the actual components that access the data source.

Perhaps the important point to make here is that the same interface is used to access multiple data sources, and behind the scenes different components from each data source vendor will actually be used to implement the functionality—real polymorphism in practice.

Figure 15.3
Interface language mapping

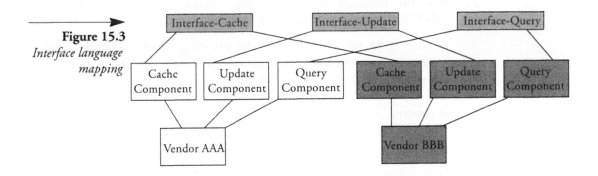

The developer thus gets a common interface to access all data sources; all the data will appear to the developer as though it was a simple table.

Microsoft has provided DBMS vendors and file system vendors with a sort of "kick start." The OLE DB SDK provides one component that implements common functionality associated with managing a rowset. This component can be used by data providers to expose the rowset interfaces on top of their data; however, Microsoft is encouraging both the vendors and third-party service providers to develop their own components to implement the interfaces, with components for query processing, cursor engines, and so on. Each is intended to be a stand-alone component with a defined interface that can be integrated with other components where need be.

One advantage with this approach is that the components can use the same interfaces and functions themselves as ordinary components. One useful example of this is the use of the Outgoing Interface.

Outgoing Interfaces and Data Objects

In the description above, we saw how the OLE DB COM interface can be used to access data and how the components can be built to provide the functionality of OLE DB. But Microsoft has also provided an interface by which **Data Objects** can inform **clients** of events, and this is called the IAdviseSink.

This is a special implementation of the Outgoing Interface, as it allows a "server" component to inform a client of an event. If data in the Data Object/ source changes, for example, the data source itself can asynchronously notify the clients connected to it of the data change event. DCOM refers to this as "notification"and achieves the notification via an object called an "Advise Sink," which is placed in the client.

Figure 15.4
*AdviseSinks and
DataObjects*

The client contacts the Data Object through the generic interface called IDataObject. The client then provides a pointer to the Advise Sink that can be used by COM to communicate with the AdviseSink. At the same time, the client also registers its interest in a specific data change. It is then the Data Object's responsibility to detect that data change.

Data Objects can send notifications to multiple Advise Sinks, but the Data Object itself does not have to know which clients are interested in the data change. COM itself manages the pointers to each of the clients on the Data Object's behalf, and it is COM that actually does the notification.

What does all this mean? Well, it means that a database or file of data managed by a DBMS or file system can act like a connectable object. If the value of a data item, for example, changes, one or more clients can be informed. So, for example, if the share price was held on a database and the share price rose to astronomic heights, the "Data Object" could be used to inform all the clients (shareholders, customers, stockbrokers, the share company) of the change.

How it all works in practice

We have seen that Microsoft effectively provide two solutions to the problem of data access of existing file systems and data sources—via vendor provided components or via ODBC. So how does all this work behind the scenes? The diagram below shows how.

From the developer's point of view, he or she will access all OLE DB data through a new version of ActiveX Data Objects—ADO. OLE DB data consumers use the OLE DB SDK to access data. A new OLE DB Driver Manager directs calls either to the OLE DB components I have described or to ODBC Drivers.

Where the calls are directed to the ODBC Drivers, the consumer communicates with ODBC-compliant data providers through existing ODBC drivers. In this case, the data is usually relational and accessed using SQL commands.

If the data source provider has provided a component to implement the methods and interfaces in OLE DB, however, the calls will be directed to these components. In the diagram you will also see a box marked **Thor.** Thor provides OLE DB to DB2 data access. In the diagram I have also included the last piece in this puzzle—stream and storage objects.

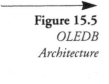

Figure 15.5
OLEDB
Architecture

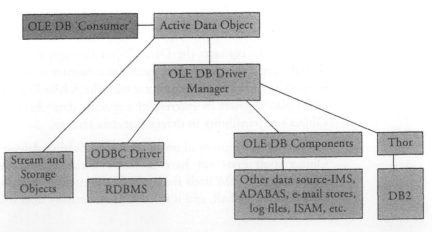

Stream and storage objects

Up to now I have assumed that the developer is accessing existing data sources—data sources from third-party vendors or from Microsoft themselves. But what if the developer wants to use a purpose-built object-oriented storage mechanism to store data—one that is supplied with DCOM.

The Active Data Object provides direct access to a **Persistent (object oriented)** storage mechanism used by COM and DCOM itself. Two types of storage element are supported—stream objects and storage objects:

▶ **Stream objects** are the conceptual equivalent of a single disk file—the basic file system in which data lives. Each stream can contain any sort of data, and data in stream objects can itself be manipulated using objects geared to the data type, for example, text objects, bit map objects, drawing objects. A stream is named using a text string, has access rights, and a single seek pointer. Through the IStream interface, the stream can be told to read, write, seek, and perform other operations on its underlying data. Functions in IStream map nearly one to one with file handling functions.

▶ **Storage Object** is the conceptual equivalent of a file directory. Each storage, like a directory, can contain any number of substorages and any number of streams (files). Each storage has its own access rights. The IStorage Interface is used to move, copy, rename, create, destroy, etc., storage objects. Storage objects cannot store data.

Every "data item" in effect becomes a stream. Although the objects themselves manipulate the streams, COM handles storage (physically) on disk and manages unused space, overflow, etc. As long as the data type of the stream is known, any application can look at data in storage—not just the application that created it.

Every storage and stream object has a character-based name that is not dependent on the underlying file system, but the name of the root storage object is the name of the underlying file system. In effect, the persistent data storage mechanism supported by COM is a little like a hierarchical file system, except that the "data items" aren't stored as a group in records, but stored singly within a storage object representing that record.

Clients can browse directory and data using the IStorage Interface and DCOM. Clients can also update data. As objects have direct incremented access to their bit of data, objects can also make incremental changes to data or do incremental reads.

Two modes of update are allowed—direct and transacted. Direct mode provides immediate and permanent update of data. Transacted updates are

Figure 15.6
*Storage and
stream objects*

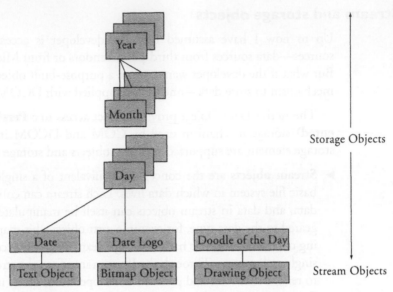

buffered so that they can be saved/committed. The client, however, has to keep the update changes separate from the old version of data itself; DCOM does not do this for it. It then issues a commit/save or close/revert. Only when the client commits is the storage updated and two-phase commit is built in to ensure the update is successful.

Clients, as is the case with all of DCOM, use interfaces and calls on methods in those interfaces to tell DCOM what it wishes to do with storage:

▶ IPersistStorage–This interface enables the component to read and write its persistent state to a storage object.

▶ IPersistStream–This interface enables the component to read and write its persistent state to a stream object.

▶ IPersistFile–This interface enables a component to read and write its persistent state to a file on the underlying system directly.

In Summary

Developers need to be able to store and access data in permanent data stores—stores which in object-oriented terminology are called "persistent data stores." Two main types of store are supported in DCOM:

▶ existing DBMSs and file systems, any file in fact which is accessed currently via a non-DCOM interface

▶ a purpose-built data store supporting stream and storage objects

Access to both is via OLE DB and the Active Data Object, with added support for ODBC for existing, primarily relational, DBMSs. OLE DB is an interface/method-based means of accessing data in data stores, based on the COM model. Where access is to existing DBMSs or files via OLE DB, the vendors of these products will be expected to build components that implement the method in the OLE DB DCOM interfaces.

There are clearly advantages to using a COM-based interface to access data. Commonality of interface from the developer's point of view does help to simplify things, and we saw that many interfaces used in COM to achieve development actions—for example, the Outgoing Interface—could be used to good effect by the Data Objects.

It does remain to be seen, however, whether this will really work in practice first, whether DBMS vendors will bother to produce components (it does seem a lot of work for them with only Microsoft to gain from it) and second, whether a standard interface to the sort of complex often duplicated data companies actually have in practice will work. As I explained, it may not be a good idea to hide the complexity anyway, given that it can affect the accuracy of the results and can also affect performance. This is the one area of DCOM, in fact, where I have misgivings about the whole approach being taken.

I'm not sure it isn't just better to get dedicated developers to write components destined to be resident on each DBMS host, which use a language like C and native DML to access the data. By using this approach the components with their DML can also be compiled.

The developer will have the job of mapping the data structures in the database with those destined to be passed across the interface, but in doing so may also be able to do some basic format translation, coding system conversions, or data cleaning. Where the data is collected from many different data sources to be merged, it could then be merged on a middle tier using the stream and storage objects as a working store.

The result is likely to give far better performance and more reliable results than the somewhat complex translation solution offered by OLE DB or ODBC. It may be better to limit the use of OLE DB to low- to medium-volume ad hoc queries, for example, on straightforward, well-documented data structures.

16

Security

▶ Currently Windows NT specific service

▶ No end-to-end security across operating systems

▶ CryptoAPI can link with third-party services—BBN, Cylink, Spyrus, RSA

▶ Accessible from Windows NT and Internet Explorer

One of the more difficult aspects associated with designing and implementing distributed applications is ensuring the resulting application is secure against theft or malicious damage. Distributed applications are particularly vulnerable to attack, as by their very nature they provide a means of navigating the network—getting into the nooks and crannies of every machine connected to it. With the increasing use of the Internet as a means of gaining access to systems, the threat becomes even greater. At least 47% of U.S.-based companies using the Internet have suffered attack; 75% of them suffered financial loss.

So, security is a big issue and a service we would expect our middleware supplier to take very seriously. In fact, it is only the middleware supplier that can provide an integrated security mechanism as only middleware works across heterogeneous networks and machines—no other software is capable of providing "end to end" security.

What Are the Risks?

We can't take any action to protect ourselves from theft or malicious damage unless we first understand the risks associated with distributed applications.

Figure 16.1
Security services

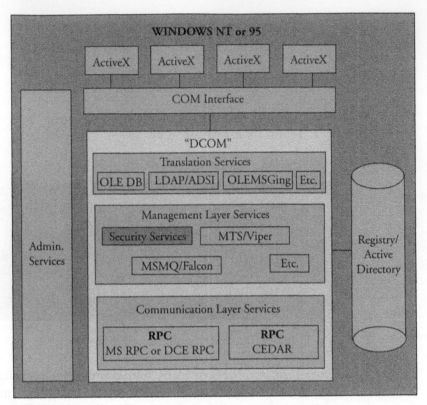

Whenever we build a distributed application we are not only vulnerable to the normal risks associated with functions and data resident on machines, but to these a new set of risks is added—those associated with data passing over the network. We can thus classify the threats under two main headings:

Risks associated with the data going across the network

▶ Removal of the message en route (theft or malicious damage)

▶ Corruption of the data en route (accidental damage)

▶ Tampering of the data en route (malicious damage or theft)

▶ Loss of the data en route (accidental damage)

▶ Diversion of the message en route (theft or simply malicious tampering)

Risks associated with data and functions on machines

▶ Unauthorized access of data on a machine to look, copy, add, delete, remove, or amend it (theft or malicious damage)

- ▶ Unauthorized use of applications on a machine (theft or malicious damage)

- ▶ Unauthorized removal of applications from a machine (theft or malicious damage)

- ▶ Unauthorized copying of applications on a machine (theft)

- ▶ Unauthorized addition of applications on a machine (theft or malicious damage)

- ▶ Unauthorized change to an application on a machine (theft or malicious damage)

These threats/risks actually apply to whatever the type of distributed application you are using.

If you are using an e-mail application as opposed to building a distributed application, for example, the removal of your e-mail message is still at risk from theft (say you had spilled out all the company secrets in a message) or tampering (a competitor changes the information you had provided on financial results to make them look worse than they actually were), loss (your invoice to a customer gets lost), or diversion (a competitor diverts the message destined for you from a potential customer so that he can compete for the business). However, when you want to build a distributed application these risks apply to the data you have stored in the databases and files you use, in the programs and components you have built in the application, and in the messages you send across the network.

Why the fuss?

In the first place, it is the nature of distributed applications of whatever sort that they are that much more vulnerable to attack than, for example, postal services, the telephone, or even fax, simply because computers can be used to automate the process of message interception. Nobody is going to intercept the thousands of letters a company sends every day, open them all, and then sift through them in the hope that in there is some nugget of useful information. (Although it has been done).

The process is generally too time consuming, too difficult to do without being spotted, and too labor intensive. It is also not very cost effective—you'd probably need hundreds of people to do it who would all cost money— probably more money than you would ever make from the exercise. The committed thief or malicious prankster, however, can set a computer to monitor the output from machines, intercepting messages from key users (remember that no one knows who a letter is from until they open it, but everyone knows who an e-mail message or application message is from).

One of the ways of doing this is by using packet sniffing. Ethernet LANs work by sending packet information to all the hosts on the same circuit. Only the machine with a matching address is meant to accept the packet; however, a machine in "promiscuous mode" will accept all packets, no matter what the packet header says.

By using automation ourselves, we have opened up the possibility of automation in attack.

In the second place, the "rewards" of computer crime are potentially much greater than the rewards of conventional crime. Criminals can gain access to not one credit card (the reward of conventional theft of a wallet) but thousands of credit card numbers (the reward of computer-based crime). If you find this difficult to believe it is worth mentioning that in 1997, FBI Agents arrested a man at San Francisco Airport who had a diskette with 100,000 credit card numbers he was attempting to sell. A Visa International database with 300,000 credit card numbers has also been stolen (ref. Risks Forum).

In the third place, by storing data on machines connected by a network, we have provided a totally different route to get to the assets of the company. In effect, all the tedious work of the criminal—the long distance journeys to the victim, the break-ins, the safe cracking, the hitting of the security guard over the head—are all now unnecessary as we have provided our criminal with an electronic route to the assets instead.

We can, of course, feel pleased for the security guard, but the company is at great risk. It is as if every locked door, security guard, closed filing cabinet, safe, and secure store had suddenly been opened to anyone with the wherewithal to take advantage of the fact. From the comfort of his own home the criminal can now send down unauthorized applications which do all the work—transferring money between bank accounts, for example, or corrupting key application data in a database (for example, your customer database).

One of the ways used to do this is by using "spoofing." Spoofing is the alteration of a packet to make it appear that it originated from a different part of the network. This method has been used to steal credit card numbers. The criminal changes the IP address to make it appear as though the request came from within the organization's network.

The Internet makes us that much more vulnerable because it was designed to be an open system from the very start—it has absolutely no security built into it. This wouldn't be a problem if the Internet was a nice, closed network separated from us by a huge barrier, but it isn't. The Internet has provided a handy little open door for anyone everywhere in the world with a modem, a PC, and a telephone line to come strolling around our networks and machines, as if they owned them. They can do it in the time it had taken me to type this—crime or malicious damage is far, far easier—no traveling, no security guards, no locked doors, no safes.

So it is worth making a fuss because there is a lot at stake here.

And are the risks real?

It is in the nature of human beings that they are absurdly optimistic. In the first place, most people assume it isn't going to happen. When it does happen it is treated as an isolated incident. Only when it happens over and over again is action taken. By this time, of course, the company could be on its knees financially or a dead duck.

Take it from me, all the risks I've identified are happening—a lot.

Since 1988, there has been an increase in the USA of 2000% in the number of just Internet security-related attacks. In recent surveys over 47% of the companies asked have been attacked—again over the Internet. Three quarters of these companies suffered financial loss; the rest suffered malicious damage.

There have been reports of large numbers of credit card numbers being downloaded from computers, for example, and in one case handled by the FBI in 1995, the cards were used to purchase $50 million of goods. So we need to take these things seriously.

Policy Setting

We have seen what risks there are and how serious those risks can be. How, then, does a company decide what needs to be protected? The answer is that it must task a security administrator to define the company policy. All companies need to have a security policy. The aim of the policy is to list a set of rules that precisely defines:

▶ which users or groups of users (who)

▶ are allowed access to which applications and data (what)

▶ together with the dates, times, days, and so on when they are allowed to access them (when)

▶ where they are allowed that access (from where and to where)

▶ as well as how they are allowed to do it (equipment, lines, and so on)

For example:

▶ All users are allowed to access the Web Server XXX to look at pages A, B, C, D, E, F, G, at any time, from any location.

▶ John Smith is allowed access to Web Server XXX to amend pages A, B, C, D, from 9 to 5, Monday to Friday, from Machine XXXX in Building SSS.

▶ Alan Jones is allowed to use Payroll Function "Enter Bonus Payments" to access Manchester's Payroll data, Monday to Friday from 8.00 a.m. to 6.00 p.m., from terminal CCCCC in Payroll Room AQSRT.

▶ Annie Oakley is allowed to use DBMS ZZZ administrator's utility TTTT to reconfigure, reorganize, and repair Manchester Payroll database, Ealing Payroll Database, Boston Payroll Database, and Chicago payroll database at any time, from Machines X, Y, Z, in Building DBA1.

It is only by having a policy that you can decide when to employ the safeguards and decide which safeguards to employ. The combination of policy and risk provides us with the means of starting to define the mechanisms of protection. What, therefore, are the main mechanisms we can use to protect ourselves against these risks?

The Functions of Protection

To decide which mechanisms we should use to protect ourselves, we need to take a first step and decide which services or functions we need. There are six main functions used to protect the distributed application from the risks I have described.

▶ Authorization

▶ Authentication

▶ Privacy

▶ Integrity checking

▶ Nonrepudiation

▶ Audit

Two further services do exist—the guaranteed delivery service we described earlier in the chapter on MSMQ and the error reporting services we looked at in an earlier chapter on Communication services. I will add a small note on these to show how they are relevant to the security area.

Authentication–This mechanism ensures that the process or user requesting access to a system is the process/user it claims to be. Authentication is thus a test of "proof of identity," a particularly difficult service to implement in distributed applications—especially if they also operate across the Internet. The principals in a transaction must be able to prove who they are, whether they are outside or inside the organization. Ideally, authorization should be bilateral—the client should know who the server is and the server must know the client.

Theoretically, the user should be authenticated each time a new message is sent from that same user, but in practice once the process has been authenticated, most authentication services issue the user or process with a code or "ticket" that can be used for the duration of processing. The ticket is "attached" to the messages within the conversation so that authentication does not have to be repeated over and over again. This "ticket" has a lifetime—to avoid other users, attaching themselves to the network on the same ticket.

Authorization–Is a service which ensures that the user or process, once it has proved it is authentic, is allowed to request the specific service or resource it has requested. Thus, authorization establishes whether an authenticated principal is entitled to use a service (application) or access defined information.

Privacy–This service aims to protect the confidentiality of data en route or on file. The way this is achieved in practice is by using encryption. Encryption is a way of encoding data that makes it unintelligible to any casual browser of the system using normal tools. The data is encrypted and decrypted by special purpose secure routines. Encryption methods include:

► **symmetric or secret key encryption**–Where a single secret key is used to encrypt and decrypt a message.

► **asymmetric or public key encryption**–Where one key is used to encrypt a message and a different but related key used to decrypt it. Two keys are used—the public and private key. The keys are mathematically related so that something encrypted with one can only be decrypted by the other.

Integrity checking–Where a message has to be divided into blocks for transmission, or even when only one block is sent, a check is needed to ensure the information has not been changed in transmission. It is important to understand that network software does not necessarily do this for you (it does depend on the network software). Since distributed applications are designed to run across many network protocols, the developer has to assume the worst—that at least one of the network software products being used won't do integrity checking.

Nonrepudiation—Works at the level of an individual message, once the principal has been authorized and authenticated. Nonrepudiation provides a means of authenticating each message—protecting against the forging of a message or denial of transmission or receipt of a message. This capability is especially important for electronic commerce. It ensures, for example, that a user does not deny the transmission of a commercial transaction—an order, for example, or receipt of goods.

Audit—Whereas the other functions in this list are preventative measures designed to stop abuse before it actually happens, audit is aimed at detecting any abuse if it has slipped through the net. Audit is thus a monitoring activity. The subfunctions of audit include the collection of all transmission data—not just alarms—the storage of the data, functions to help in analysis, and functions to help in archival of the data.

Guaranteed delivery and error reporting—We saw that, in general, a middleware product can either report on the nondelivery of a message by using error reporting, or it can provide services which actually help to guarantee delivery. What I did not explain is why these services are needed at all. Most network software provides a "best effort" delivery service. TCP/IP and the IP protocol is not designed, for example, to guarantee quality of service. It will do its best to deliver the packet, but if the packet is lost en route, it is lost en route. There is a reason for this in a product like TCP/IP.

TCP/IP divides the message the sender gives it into packets, which then follow logical rather than physical paths through the network. The service is connectionless—in other words, the network ignores which pairs of end systems have entered into the communication. Each machine forwards the packet on using information in the packet's header until it reaches its final destination. No acknowledgments of receipt are sent to the sender when a packet is received. It is relatively easy to intercept packets as they pass through a machine en route to their destination and remove them, alter their address (all it needs is a change of the header), alter their contents, and so on. Network software therefore does not provide any protection for the sorts of risks we saw were associated with data en route—hence the need for services in the middleware.

Functions and risks

Which functions protect against which risks? In the table below I have provided a chart to suggest which services are used to protect against which risks.

Table 16.1 *Functions and risks*

Risk	Authentication	Authorization	Encryption	Integrity	Nonrepudiation	Audit	Error Reporting & Guaranteed Delivery
Data going across the network							
Removal of the message en route	-	-	X	-	-	-	X
Corruption of the data en route	-	-	-	X	-	-	-
Tampering of the data en route	-	-	X	X	-	-	-
Loss of the data en route	-	-	-	-	-	X	X
Diversion of the message en route	-	-	-	-	-	X	X
Denial of the message	-	-	-	-	X	-	-
Data and functions on machines							
Unauthorized access of data	X	X	X	-	-	X	-
Unauthorized use of application	X	X	-	-	-	X	-
Unauthorized removal of application	X	X	X	-	-	X	-
Unauthorized copying of application	X	X	X	-	-	X	-
Unauthorized addition of application	X	X	-	-	-	X	-
Unauthorized change to application	X	X	-	-	-	X	-

As you can see, authentication and authorization services are always used together to protect against unauthorized access to services or data on a machine. Whereas encryption and integrity checking are the primary services for ensuring the message is transported across the network without interference, coupled with the error checking and guaranteed delivery services we have already described.

Remember that the "application" and data I include in this table could be not only business applications but systems software and vendor-provided software. So, for example, we could have protection for Web servers (an application) and the pages on the Web server (data) probably defined at the page level.

The Mechanisms of Protection

We have seen that there are six main services that can be provided to help protect distributed applications from the risks I've described. Each of these services can be implemented by more than one mechanism of support; in other words, a service such as authorization can be achieved using a number of alternative mechanisms, for example, user/password combinations, Digital certificates, and Smart cards. In the next few paragraphs I will explain some of the more important mechanisms—especially the ones Microsoft is supporting or is aiming to support.

Authentication

One of the most frequently used and better known mechanisms of authentication is the user/group and password approach to checking the identity of someone, but this is not the only mechanism available. Authentication can be based on what you know (for example, a password), what you have (for example, a smart card or other physical device), or who you are (for example, biometric authentication using voice recognition, fingerprint readers, retinal scanners, etc.).

User names and passwords–Despite their widespread use, user names and passwords, as a means of establishing identity, are open to abuse. They can be forgotten, passwords, can be easy to guess, users often leave passwords accessible (on Post-it notes stuck on their machine, for example), and they are not necessarily unique across the organization or across companies. Despite this, the user/password approach is one of the most commonly used within most organizations.

Checking is usually only performed when a user requests a service from a server. The server is not generally asked for its name and password.

A secure file (it must be a secure file as there is no point in having it) containing the user names, groups, and passwords is set up manually by the administrator. This file can be a:

▶ Globally relevant file containing all the users, groups, and passwords—this file may occur just once on the network but be accessible to all in the network, or a better option for performance reasons is an automatically replicated file, which is stored on each machine.

▶ File which just has the users, groups, and passwords of the users connected to that server machine.

The first option, especially if it uses replication, is probably the best solution, as it saves the administrator effort and is more easy to keep secure.

Digital certificates–Provide electronic proof of identity using *cryptographic keys,* which are then used to "sign" or "seal" the message. They have the advantage that both sender (client) and recipient (server) can be asked to prove their identity, thus providing some assurance to the client that the server is also who/what it says it is.

Digital certificates in this case are issued by a third party—often called a Trusted Third Party (TTP) or Digital Certificate Authority.

TTPs have the responsibility of revoking certificates when they are no longer valid, publishing a list of revoked certificates in the Directory, and revalidating and reissuing certificates that have expired. There is no reason why a company cannot be its own TTP if it wants to set up a network of registered authenticated users (internal and external). In fact, this may be the best way, as each company then has a vested interest in ensuring its users are properly authenticated physically before being given certificates, can issue Smart Cards to people in person, and are more likely to keep certificate information up-to-date. So how are certificates issued?

The TTP first generates a key pair—one public and one private key for the person requesting the certificate. The public key is placed in a Directory. This Directory must be accessible by any process or user the person needs to communicate with. The private key is given to the person.

When the person wants to request a service from a remote server, the message is encrypted with the private key. This acts like a signature—as only the person knows the private key, it can only be that person who sent the message. At the other end, the recipient "unlocks" the message—in reality decrypts it—using the public key that it obtains from the Directory.

A standard exists—the X509 Authentication Framework—which covers Digital Certificates and PKCS (Public Key Certificate Standard) to cover the various formats for the requests for certificates. Under this standard, the Digital Certificate Authority receives an initial request from a user and then assigns a unique name to each user, together with the keys. This standard also covers subsequent requests for the public keys of third-party recipients from a sender.

Smart Cards—Care must obviously be taken that the private key does not fall into the wrong hands, and as such as a general rule it should not be stored on a machine accessible by others. One way of ensuring the key is safely stored is to keep the private key routine on a floppy disk, for example, or some other storage mechanism that can be safely kept with the person.

One of the major new ways in which private keys are being stored, however, is via the Smart Card. These have the added advantage that to use them, the person must also have the PIN number of the card, so even if the card is lost or stolen, the data—the private key of the individual—should be protected.

A Personal Computer/SmartCard Workgroup (PC/SC Workgroup) was founded in 1996, of which Microsoft is a founding member, along with Groupe Bull, Hewlett Packard, Schlumberger, and Siemens Nixdorf, to address smart card interoperability issues and to create specifications in the areas of interfacing smart card readers and cards with PCs. It is also looking at ways of providing device-independent APIs to encourage the development of smart card aware applications. Some more details of the public and private key mechanism are provided in the paragraph below on encryption.

Authorization

Most authorization is implemented in practice using *Access Control Lists* (ACLs). But Access Control Lists can differ quite markedly in their levels of sophistication—from exceptionally weak to pretty near foolproof.

We saw in the section on policy that the security administrator sets policy by stating:

- ▶ the users allowed to access the system
- ▶ the applications and data they can access and the types of access allowed
- ▶ the equipment and other hardware they can use to gain access
- ▶ the times of the day, week, and so on they are allowed access
- ▶ and the locations to which and from which they are allowed access

Ideally, and at its best, the Access Control List should be able to record every one of the criteria and rules stated in the policy, and the Access Control service should moreover be able to check all these things too. Authentication establishes the identity of the user and is the key entry point to an Access Control List. Each user will have a whole list of allowed accesses he or she is allowed to perform.

When a user requests a service, for example, the Authentication service will first check the identity of the user. Once this has been established, the Access Control Service should take over using the authenticated identity as the key (more than one key may be permissible here to cater for multiple identities). Access Control services should not only check that the user is allowed to request the service but should check that the user is accessing the service from the right location, from the designated machine, is accessing the service on the machine he or she is allowed to, and at the times of the day he or she is allowed access.

It has to be said that most middleware products—most security products for that matter—fall very far short of this ideal. Some are very poor and only check the service itself—no times of day, no machine restrictions—nothing else at all. Some are a little better with times and machines allowed, but overall, don't expect too much from any of the products—something I feel needs to be urgently addressed.

Access Control Lists must be secure files subject to Access Control (it must be a secure file as there is no point in having it). The contents of the file are set up manually by the administrator using the security policy document. This file can be a:

▶ Globally relevant file containing all the policy rules for all users—this file may occur just once on the network but be accessible to all in the network, or a better option for performance reasons is an automatically (but secure) replicated file which is stored on each machine.

▶ File which just has the policy rules of the users connected to that server machine.

As we saw with the user/password approach, the first option, especially if it uses replication, is probably the best solution, as it saves the administrator effort and is more easy to keep secure.

One further means of implementing authorization rules is to issue the policy rules with Digital Certificates. Policies recorded in this way are called *Digital Certificate Privileges*. Clearly, for this to work well, the policy rules must be exceptionally stable, and the user themselves should not be able to gain access to the rules. I feel that this is actually a less satisfactory solution altogether, requiring far more administrative work and liable to error. I won't therefore be covering it further.

Encryption

We saw that there were essentially two methods of encryption—public and secret key.

Public–Public key encryption is based on the Digital Certificates we saw in the previous section. Where a message from one process to another is to be encrypted, however, the sender uses the public key of the *recipient* to encrypt the message. By doing this only the recipient is able to decrypt the message as only the recipient has the private key. The sender first gets the public key of the recipient from the Directory of public keys. The public key is then used by the sender to encrypt the message. It is then sent and decrypted by the recipient using its private key.

But how can the person sending the message be sure that the public key they are about to use is really that of the recipient? If they use the wrong key—are fooled into thinking another key is the public key—they could encrypt the message and it is then diverted by the interloper and decrypted with his private key.

The key is in the way the Directory sends the public key to the sender. The sender applies to the Trusted Third Party/Digital Certificate Authority and requests the public key of the recipient, using some identifier of the recipient. The Digital Certificate Authority encrypts the public key with its own private key. The sender has a permanent record of the public key of the Digital Certificate Authority and can then decrypt the message and extract the public key of the recipient.

What does this actually achieve? By doing this, the message could only have come from the Digital Certificate Authority, as only the Digital Certificate Authority has the private key to encrypt the message, so the sender can be confident that an interloper has not butted into the conversation and substituted some other public key for the recipient's. In essence, the sender can be confident that only the *intended* recipient can read the message.

These messages containing the public key of some process encrypted using the DCA's private key are known as "*Public Key Certificates.*" Public key encryption is an especially useful form of encryption method because it can be used over the Internet as long as the Directory of public keys is accessible to the sender. It means that any user, wherever they are located, can encrypt a message before it is sent across the line without having to prestore any encryption routines on the machine he or she is using.

Clearly, this last point is important. The last thing you want to do is have the secret keys themselves downloaded over the line to the person, as you have no way of protecting them while you are doing this. By using public key encryption, you avoid having to do this and are able to open up access to previously unknown users—if this is what you want to do. This means that a company can, for example, accept orders from customers who have not registered as users with it (but who can be authenticated using a TTP and the person's public key), and those orders can be encrypted as they pass over the network. This means that the person can place credit card information or other sensitive data on the order and know it is being transported confidentially.

There are, however, some problems with public keys. Public key algorithms are slow—at least a thousand times slower than the symmetric algorithms used in secret key cryptography and, as we saw, are quite difficult to administer, needing a secure up-to-date Directory accessible by the sender and recipient.

Some well-known public key algorithms in use today include:

▶ RSA–Invented by Ron Rivest, Adi Shamar, and Leonard Adleman at MIT. The algorithm is now in widespread use under license. Export of products containing RSA for authentication purposes is allowed, but export for encryption purposes is restricted to a key size of 512 bits or less. Both keys used are functions of a pair of very large prime numbers.

▶ DSA (Digital Signature Algorithm)–Developed by David Kravitz at the NSA. It has been selected by NIST for the U.S. Government's Digital Signature Standard (DSS).

▶ Diffie-Hellman–This algorithm can be used for key distribution but not for encryption. It was invented by Whitfield Diffie and Martin Hellman in the mid-'70s.

Secret key–In this approach each party to the conversation has access to the same secret key, which is used to both encrypt and decrypt the message. A message from a sender is encrypted using the secret key and the encryption algorithm. The message is then decrypted by the receiver using the decryption algorithm and the same secret key. The algorithms are freely available, in that they can be obtained from third-party vendors or standards bodies.

The secret key is thus the most important part of the process, as it is the secret key that the two parties have agreed upon that determines how secure the message actually is. Usually, what determines the degree of security offered is the length of the key. The longer the key, the more difficult it is to crack by an intruder—hence the arguments over 40 bit and 56 bit keys. The main symmetric algorithms used today in security products include:

- ▶ DES (Data Encryption Standard)–a block cipher of 64 bit blocks with a 56 bit key length (depending on where you are in the world this may be less—because of the export rules).

- ▶ Triple DES–the DES algorithm is applied three times in succession.

- ▶ RC5–a block cipher invented by Ron Rivest, cofounder of RSA Data Security. It has variable parameters.

- ▶ IDEA–a block cipher of 64 bit blocks with a 128 bit key (again this may change depending on location). It was invented by Xuejia Lai and James Massey.

- ▶ RC4–a variable key size stream cipher developed by Ron Rivest for RSA Data Security. It was granted a special export status when the key length was limited to 40 bits or under.

Work is also underway in the U.S. Department of Commerce to produce, through NIST, an Advanced Encryption Standard (AES), which will be a publicly available symmetric block cipher with a key length that can be increased when needed. One of the more interesting pieces of information is that the RC5 algorithm used with a key length of 40 bits has been broken in 3.5 hours, whereas RC5 with a key length of 48 bits was broken after only 13 days. Size in this case clearly matters!

Integrity checking

One of the most frequently used methods of checking integrity is the check sum—the contents are summed using a specific algorithm on sending the message and the check sum is added to the message. On receipt, the message is again summed using the same algorithm to see if the check sum on the message and that obtained is the same.

Another way of checking integrity is to apply a hash function. In this case, a variable length input string (the message) is converted by the hashing algorithm to a fixed length (and smaller!) output string. Both sender and receiver create the hash value. The check on integrity value can be achieved either by sending the hash value with the message (the normal approach) or by the sender and receiver comparing hash values.

You will notice in the table that straightforward integrity checking using these two approaches can be used to ensure the message has not been inadvertently corrupted en route, but to ensure it is not tampered with, both integrity checking and encryption may need to be used. If the hashing total or check sum are passed over the network with the message and the interloper has access to the hashing or check sum algorithm, he or she can tamper with the message and then recompute the check sum or hash figure. If, however, both message and check sum are encrypted, the interloper cannot tamper with the message—as he or she is unable to decipher it.

Two commonly used hashing algorithms are MD4 and MD5 (Message Digest), which produce 128 bit hashes of the input message. These are supplied by RSA Data security. Another well-known hashing algorithm is SHA (Secure Hashing Algorithm), which comes in various versions. SHA-1, for example, uses 160 bit hashes of data.

Nonrepudiation

At the moment, there is only one well-used mechanism to implement nonrepudiation, and this uses the public and private key encryption methods we saw in the section on authorization. In this case, the person uses their private key to encrypt every message. This is then proof that the message could only have come from that person and acts like a signature on that message. The receiver then decrypts the message using the person's public key.

Because the person sending the message can also ask for authentication of the server, the person can also treat any message from the server as though it was signed. For example:

A person wishes to place an order with a company. The person first sends a message asking for the service to place the order. The message is signed with the person's private key. The person is authenticated by the server and the server then sends back a message encrypted with its private key to indicate it is willing to accept the order. The person authenticates the server by accessing the Directory to decrypt the server's message using its public key. If the message decrypts OK, the server is the right one; if not, then the server is, for example, an impostor.

Both the person and the server have established each other's identity. From then on each message can be treated in the same way—the order can be signed by the person placing it with the private key and any confirmation of receipt can also be signed by the server. Both parties therefore have then employed the means of preventing repudiation.

Audit

Audit mechanisms tend to be specific to each middleware vendor, if they are provided at all. Many middleware vendors, for example, use an audit log to provide a means of logging all security-related activity, producing an audit trail of security events recording information such as date, time, user, object, and event. The log itself must also be protected from tampering.

Third-Party Security Products (Which Microsoft Uses)

Microsoft not only provides its own security products, but also uses third-party products. Before I examine Microsoft's own security services, therefore, I will describe the links it has to third-party products, how it provides those links, and what these products support—which mechanisms in the list above. The main third-party products that Microsoft includes within its security framework are:

▶ **SSL (Secure Sockets Layer)**–from Netscape

▶ **Products from Cryptographic Service Providers** (CSPs)

▶ **Kerberos**

SSL–SSL was introduced by Netscape and it has submitted the current version to an IETF (Internet Engineering Task Force) working group as an Internet Draft standard. SSL provides security services that are a combination of public key encryption, symmetric key encryption, and data integrity checking. It also includes authentication of the server and, optionally, the client's using both a user id/password approach and using the new public/private key encryption services.

Internet Explorer and Internet Information Server support SSL, which Microsoft has called Secure Channel services. Developers must use the Win32 APIs part of the ActiveX developer's kit to add secure channel support using this product.

Although Microsoft does support SSL, they also provide their own version of SSL called PCT (Private Communication Technology), which is supported in Explorer. PCT is based on SSL but separates the authentication mechanisms from the encryption mechanisms so that it is easier to export the technology.

CSPs–The main CSP with which Microsoft is working is RSA Data Security, but it does have links with others, notably BBN, Cylink, Atalla, Trusted Information Systems, Nortel Secure Networks, HP, and Spyrus. As we saw in the description of the encryption mechanisms, many of the mechanisms available can be freely licensed and thus supplied by a number of third-party companies. The products covered by this umbrella approach include those which support mechanisms such as DES, RC4, and so on and provide public and secret key encryption. They are thus able to cover Digital Certification, Confidentiality checking, and nonrepudiation.

Microsoft provides an API called the CryptoAPI, which connects applications to third-party security encryption services. CryptoAPI is designed to insulate applications from common cryptographic functions. The API is being built into the products of the CSPs; in other words, each service provider is adding a CryptoAPI interface to their product.

Although considered to be part of the Windows NT operating system, the API will also be available on Windows 95 and scaled-down versions of Windows for handheld machines. CryptoAPI can be called from Java, Visual Basic, and C++ as a Win32 API, and version 1.0 was part of the Software Developer's toolkit. The CryptoAPI version 2 ships with both Windows NT 4 and Internet Explorer 3 with planned support for the Macintosh.

Kerberos–Kerberos is an authentication service that uses user/passwords and tokens. It was developed at the Massachusetts Institute of Technology in a project called Athena during the 1980s. As a government-funded project, much of the work is in the public domain for U.S. organizations and has been adopted by a number of suppliers.

Every user, computer, server, and so on (known as principals) in the network is given a secret key with which it can prove its identity. Human users can use passwords, which are then converted to the secret key. The user's secret key is never passed over the network and is deleted from the host once it has served its purpose. Authenticated users receive conversation keys to communicate with the server.

When the user logs in, Kerberos accesses a Registry database to check the user's password and get the user's secret key. These security services also provide the user's process with specially encrypted data structures called *tickets*. Tickets can be cached and used a number of times, although each ticket has a limited life span to prevent unauthorized users from getting access to tickets via the network.

Clients present the tickets to other principals as proof that they are authentic. When the user starts an actual application, the client process inherits the user's identity and its tickets and privileges. In highly secure environments, the client can also be made to provide proof on every call. Each application server also has a secret key and can acquire tickets from the Security services. It is therefore possible to add mutual authentication checking to an application.

Microsoft is intending to incorporate support for Kerberos authentication in Windows NT version 5.0 for the local environment. Certificates from Certificate server (of which more later) will be passed to Kerberos domains and used as validation in Kerberos tokens. The mapping will be held in the new Active Directory.

Table 16.2 *Microsoft-supported third-party mechanisms*

Function/Mechanism	SSL	CSPs	Kerberos
Authentication			
User/password	YES	NO	YES
Digital certificate	YES	YES	NO
Smart card	NO	NO	NO
Authorization			
ACLs	NO	NO	NO
Digital certs	NO	NO	NO
Confidentiality			
Public key	YES	YES	NO
Secret key	YES—RC4, DES	YES	NO
Integrity checking	YES—MD5, SHA-1	YES	NO
Nonrepudiation	YES	YES	NO
Audit	NO	NO	NO

Microsoft's Products and Services

As we saw in Chapter 10, Microsoft's own security services are currently provided primarily by Windows NT although this may change in the future. In the following paragraphs I will describe each of these services in relation to the functions of security we looked at earlier in this chapter.

Authentication

User ID–Authentication in Windows NT is based on a user id and a password. The password is encrypted. A user can be an individual or a group, and roles and aliases are also supported.

The table of users, passwords, and public keys is stored with the Registry on each host, and as such must be set up on every machine. Each table holds host-specific information—the users allowed to access that host. This is likely to change in the future with the introduction of the Active Directory, a service I describe in the next chapter, as the Active Directory is to hold security data and will be a central store for information, replicated around the network.

When a client calls a method or creates an instance of a component, DCOM obtains the client's username and checks to see if the username is valid and the password correct. Only if the username is authentic is the name passed to the machine or process where the component is actually running. DCOM on the component's machine then checks the authorization.

Microsoft Certificate Server–Microsoft Certificate Server is a service used for the management of Digital Certificates (which conform to the X509 standard). Thus, Microsoft has provided the software for a company to set themselves up as a TTP (Trusted Third Party) or Digital Certificate Authority.

It, too, runs as a service of Windows NT and can handle certificate requests, the issue of certificates, and revocation lists. It also logs all transactions for auditing purposes.

The Server consists of four main components:

▶ **The Entry Module**–Used to handle the requests for certificates. It can be customized to take in client requests for certificates in a number of different formats. Once the request has been handled it is sent to the Certificate server Policy Module for processing.

▶ **The Policy Module**–Used to decide whether to grant a certificate according to its trust policy. The module can be adapted to add user policies and can also look up information in external databases as part of the process of checking identity. Where manual checks are required, an alert is sent to the appropriate personnel.

▶ **The Certificate Engine**–These modules are responsible for creating digital certificates, storing published certificates, generating the key pair, and also logging. The log tracks all requests and their status and stores published certificates and certificate revocation lists for auditing purposes.

▶ **The Exit Module**–Packages certificates in the format required by the application. The module can send the certificates by e-mail or publish them in either an LDAP-compliant directory service or an ODBC-compliant database. It is also responsible for delivering Certificate Revocation Lists.

Smart cards–Microsoft has decided that smartcards are a critical component of its security strategy, particularly its public key infrastructure. They intend to use the cards to store private keys, account names, passwords, and other forms of personal information, thus providing not only access via public key authentication and encryption but access via user name/password authentication, for example. The card is intended to provide a form of "single sign-on" mechanism.

Microsoft is also smart card enabling its development tools, including Visual C++, Visual Basic, and Visual J++, in addition to the integration with Windows NT and other Windows platforms. Smart card support has been added to the NetPC and PC98 design specifications. Microsoft has also released an implementation of the PC/SC specifications for Windows NT 4, which has been released to Workgroup members and a limited number of third-party smartcard providers.

Authenticode–We saw in the section on authentication that a sender can encrypt a message using its private key, which the receiver then decrypts using the sender's public key, as a means of checking the authentication of the sender. Authenticode is a specialized application of this approach used to authenticate that executable code sent from a sender to a recipient does indeed come from that sender.

The approach used is identical to the approach we described in the earlier section. The sender encrypts the executable code using its private key and then sends it to the recipient. The recipient may already have the public key of the sender. If it doesn't, it requests the key from the Digital Certificate Authority (perhaps running under Microsoft Certificate Server), which then sends the key.

If the public key successfully decrypts the executable code in the message, the user knows the code came from the sender. If it doesn't, the down loaded component should be discarded—as it is a rogue component or a component from an unrecognized third party (and, as such, potentially harmful).

Authenticode can be used internally by companies needing to distribute software to their end users. But this approach has particular importance in the application of Microsoft's Web technology.

We saw in the introduction that Microsoft can support the downloading of ActiveX components to its own Internet Explorer Web Browser. The downloading of ActiveX components over the Internet, however, does raise the potential of security problems.

As we saw in an earlier chapter, the approach taken by Sun's JavaSoft division with Java applets is simply to restrict the applet. They call the approach the Java Sandbox (where it can play!), and the sandbox defines the set of disk files, network addresses, and system properties that applets are permitted to access from a browser. The restrictions imposed at the moment are fairly severe. Java applets are restricted by the JVM from modifying any sort of file by any means and can only access the network address from which they came.

Microsoft's strategy, as we saw earlier, revolves around the idea that downloaded ActiveX controls can do far more than simply communicate with the original Web server. In their strategy, the controls can:

▶ communicate with other ActiveX controls on the same machine

▶ access data on that machine

▶ and, if the client happens to be part of an internal network with a DCOM registered client, communicate via DCOM to gain access to a whole host of other ActiveX components on servers elsewhere in the network

A user could inadvertently download a page from a browser with an ActiveX control embedded within it, which subsequently wreaked havoc with their machine. The potential for destruction is appalling.

Thousands, hundreds of thousands of users—computer developers and end users—browse the Web. They often innocently access sites out of sheer curiosity—interesting name, or something which looks interesting. With ActiveX technology, the user could download a page with an ActiveX control in it, and he or she would be completely unaware that he had even downloaded it. The ActiveX component could be a virus, malicious bug, or "spy" component—it could roam about the machine unhindered; it could use the client's machine to gain access all over the network.

It is a prime cause of one of our risks—unauthorized addition of an application on a machine.

Does Authenticode help? Even if Authenticode is used, the approach is not without its limitations.

▶ First, the user's machine has to be enabled so that checking of the digital signature is actually performed *automatically* (preferably via the Web browser), as it is unlikely any user would build these capabilities.

▶ Second, to work well, the user will have to have cached the public keys of all the senders of ActiveX components in which he or she is interested and no others.

▶ Third, the Web Browser or other software doing the checking will need to automatically reject all other ActiveX components, deleting them from the machine.

In fact, Microsoft's Internet Explorer Web Browser has been enabled so that it can be made to perform these checks. Furthermore, the checks can also be applied to Java applets and Navigator plug-ins. Microsoft provides a software development kit called the Internet Explorer Administration Kit, which can be used to set the options for acceptance or rejection of components. The settings are:

▶ download everything/accept anything

▶ download nothing/reject everything

▶ download only trusted controls—this is the default setting

The last setting can be further refined, for example, to accept only trusted components from a specific distribution list. Code signing tools are provided in the ActiveX SDK and are used with the WinVerifyTrustAPI.

So, let us examine how this would work in practice. First, everyone would need to ensure their Web browser was set to the default setting that accepted only trusted components. Next, any company wanting to send the user an ActiveX component then has two routes to follow:

▶ The company could send all its potential users its public key. The users would then need to decide if it did trust the company. This is a big if, of course, but at least they are now made aware of the choice they have, and if anything went wrong they could always sue.

▶ Alternatively, the company could use a Trusted Third Party to act as a guarantor and issuer of the private key. This is a slightly more tricky issue, as the end user now has to decide whether the Trusted Third Party is a reliable checker of components. In fact, Trusted Third Parties aren't there to test to see whether components are valid; their job is simply to hand out private and public keys, so this route may not be the safest one from the recipient's point of view.

The approach doesn't work at all for ad hoc users of a company's services. Thus, if a person was browsing the Web and saw a bookshop with some really good books in it, he or she could not be sent catalogs and components to help him or her choose the books. Instead, he or she would have to contact the company and first ask for its public key.

It should also be noted that the Web browser is the point of failure in this whole scenario. If developers find a way via an uploaded ActiveX control or Java applet of changing the setting of the Web Browser to accept any ActiveX controls, then all of this elaborate protection falls apart.

Authorization

Authorization is controlled via Access Control Lists (ACLs). The basic list simply lists the objects and which users are allowed to access them. Control is not allocated at the method level. A user can be granted access to:

▶ any object on any machine

▶ a single class or set of classes on that machine

▶ or any classes on that machine

An object calling another object can pass the privileges it has obtained to the child, but that child cannot pass the security privileges it obtains from the calling object on to any other objects it calls. As such there are no "inherited" permissions.

The lists are set up using a DCOM configuration tool, DCOMCNFG, or can be set up programatically using the Windows NT Registry and Win32 Security functions. ACLs are also stored with the Registry and as such must be set up on *every machine* by the administrator. Each ACL list is unique and pertains to the components on that machine—it is not replicated. Again, this may change when the Active Directory is introduced.

Security checking is automatically applied upon activation. In other words, where the object is being requested for the first time and an instance has to be requested, the checks are performed as part of the normal Directory processes for finding the object and creating an instance of it.

When multiple users require the services of a single nonsecurity aware server, a separate instance is created for each user, so that clients cannot access each other's data. Where more than one client is the same user, the server is shared between clients—of course the server could then be multithreaded. All nonsecurity aware servers are run as the security principal that caused them to run.

Once the connection has been made between a client and an object, further checking at the method level or, for example, to recheck authorization has to be done by the server.

MSMQ's security is an extension of the basic security provided with Windows NT and DCOM. Clearly, there are far more things that need to be placed under security control within MSMQ—sites, CNs, computers, queues, and so on. These are all treated as "objects" within MSMQ, and for each object, security permissions are set up in separate access control lists—these are not part of the Registry.

The administrator can define at queue level which applications can send messages to a queue, which applications can get messages from a queue, peek at messages, or get properties of a queue. The administrator is granted his own special access rights to enable him to set up the security—in other words, the ACL is itself subject to security controls. The special access permission the administrator obtains then enables him to set up sites, enterprise controls, connected networks, and so on. MSMQ also supports an auditing capability.

Encryption

Where encryption is required, the developer must use third-party software such as DES, although Windows NT does encrypt the password. It is now why we see that Microsoft has provided the CryptoAPI—to enable developers to use other products to provide encryption capability.

Integrity checking

Authenticode has 128 bit or 160 bit hash functions in it to help in integrity checking.

Audit

Auditing is provided through Windows NT Event logs. Each NT workstation or server has three event logs—a system log which is used to record configuration problems, state of services, and use of peripherals; a security log; and an application log. Clearly, it is the security log which is of interest here.

Security events cover successful accesses and failures—cases where access was denied. The audit policy has to be set for each server to specify which actions to audit—objects, users, which types (success, failure, both). The messages sent to the log then all have the type of message, the date, time, source, user, eventid, and computer. Although problems are logged, serious problems are also written to the console.

Event logs can be viewed using SNMP links to SMS tools—Netview, etc., by using the System Event Viewer or by using tools provided with each service. MSMQ events, for example, can be viewed from MSMQ Explorer; however, MSMQ Explorer displays events only of type MSMQ. The Event Viewer covers all events but supports sorting, filtering, and searching of events.

Event logs are kept for each machine. In other words, there is no centralized event log for the entire system (although links can be built using SNMP to Systems Management Software if you want).

In Summary

Microsoft provides extensive security services through a variety of third-party software. The table below summarizes the support provided.

Table 16.3 *Summary of security functions*

Function/Mechanism	Windows NT	SSL	CSPs	Kerberos
Authentication				
User/password	YES	YES	NO	YES
Digital certificate	YES	YES	YES	NO
Smart card	YES	NO	NO	NO
Authorization				
ACLs	YES	NO	NO	NO
[Digital certs]	NO	NO	NO	NO
Confidentiality				
Public key	YES	YES	YES	NO
Secret key	NO	YES	YES	NO
Integrity checking	Some	YES	YES	NO
Nonrepudiation	YES	YES	YES	NO
Audit	YES	NO	NO	NO

But as I have done in every chapter, I will end on a cautionary note. These services are to be found in Windows NT. Although third-party services such as Kerberos and DES are implemented on numerous platforms, they are only part of the picture. This means that DCOM on other platforms will not enjoy the same level of support as DCOM on Windows NT, and as we saw in the chapter on DCOM on other platforms, the main problems lie in the area of authorization—a serious problem if it cannot be supported. Be prepared to have to supplement DCOM on other platforms with third-party products to fill the holes, and also be prepared to have to do some juggling around to enable different ACLs to work with one another.

17

Directory Services

- ▶ Directory services are key to the operation of all middleware, not just DCOM
- ▶ Types of Directory include the single file, host-based file, replicated file, replicated file with publish/subscribe, and the "no Directory" approach
- ▶ Microsoft's current offering is the Registry—a host-based file
- ▶ Future plans are for the Active Directory—a replicated file
- ▶ The Active Directory should provide a secure, reliable, available, and moderately high performance base on which to build applications

A Directory is a key service provided by all middleware, but one the developer rarely sees or uses directly. In fact, although the developer may never actually see the Directory, its design and the way it is configured is key to the reliability, availability, and performance of the application he or she builds. A poor Directory can result in system downtime, slow response, and may involve the administrator in a considerable amount of work. We will be looking at the Directory service in general in this chapter and then comparing the approaches that could be used with that used by Microsoft in DCOM.

What Is a Directory?

Most developers are familiar with the concept of databases. A database is an organized file of structured data that contains information used by an application at runtime. Thus, for example, an Order Processing application may use

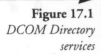

Figure 17.1
DCOM Directory services

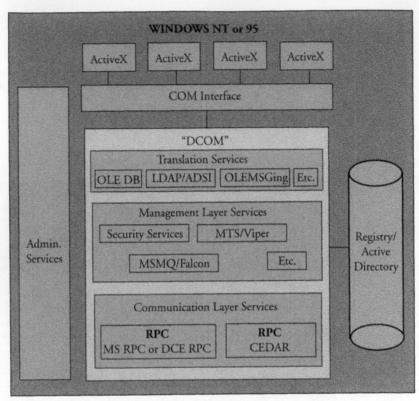

a database with information about Orders, Products, Customers, Deliveries, Stock, and so on.

A Directory is the developer's runtime database. It contains (or should contain) all the information the *system software* that his application uses (network software, middleware, DBMS, System Management Software, e-mail, and so on) and needs at runtime. Thus it could contain information on users, the user groups, their security information (passwords, access control lists), network addresses, processes/components found at each address, mail addresses, data found at the address, queues found at each address and their characteristics, performance data and statistics collected at runtime on the applications and data usage, machines, lines and their characteristics, data used in load balancing such as queue length and current loading at nodes, and so on.

A Directory *should be* a database shared by all the system software. There should be no need to set up one database for the middleware, yet another for the SMS, another for the network management software, another for the e-mail, yet another for the network software, and so on. As we all know, however, what should happen and what does happen in practice are somewhat different. Overall we find that each product, because each tends to be supplied by different vendors, has its own "database," requiring extra effort on the part of the administrator to set up, incurring extra storage costs as information is duplicated, and, in addition, adding to the risk that the information in each one is inconsistent.

Just like application development where data sharing has rarely been achieved in practice, the software providers have also not learned how to share data.

Interestingly, tool vendors have not managed to share data during development either. Remember the Repository concept? A Repository was to be a single shared database of data used and created by the developer when he or she actually built the application. It was to contain data on screens/windows, data models, database designs, system designs, programs, tests and test data, project plans, machines and their configuration, users, and their organization.

Whereas a Directory is the database used at runtime by the system software used to run the applications, a Repository was to contain information used by developers while they were building the applications. Of course, much of the information generated during development is used during runtime, so in reality the distinction between Directory and Repository is a bit blurred, but the thinking was that the two should be kept separate for performance reasons. But no one could agree on what should go into a Repository, so initiatives like AD/Cycle from IBM failed.

In the same way, no one seems to be able to agree on what should go into a Directory, and many of the standards initiatives to define a Directory service specification and content description have failed. Instead, single vendors—such as Computer Associates and Platinum Technology with multiple system software products that use Directories—have taken steps to merge the Directories of their products.

Platinum Technologies, for example, has a strategy called POEMS (PLATINUM Open Enterprise Management System), the key feature of which is the PLATINUM repository. PLATINUM acquired not just one but two repository companies—Reltech and Brownstone—to provide the basis of its repository.

PLATINUM wants to integrate the tools they have acquired via the repository, *not* by building interfaces between the tools. Not only will the repository hold information from the application development tools, but it will also be used to hold systems management type data, events, policies to handle events, escalation procedures, and so on.

So, the ideal of a single Directory and Repository that can be used to store the data of multiple tools and system software products is a feature we are more likely to see being delivered by a vendor of multiple products—and one with the money to develop what is essentially a very complex piece of technology. Microsoft is clearly in this position, and we will be seeing whether their Directory service matches this ideal later in this chapter.

Directory services and middleware

We have seen that a Directory service is a database used at runtime by network software, system management software, DBMSs, and so on. More particularly, it is the store of information used by middleware to drive the inner workings of the software at runtime.

When security is checked, for example, the middleware should look up the Directory to see if the user is a valid registered user, check the password to ensure the user is authentic, and check the access control lists to ensure that user is entitled/authorized to access the process it has requested. When a client process wants to invoke a method on a component, it will use the component name or interface name, and the middleware will look up its Directory to determine the actual physical location (the machine and possibly file location) of the process requested. Similarly, when a process sends a message to a queue, the middleware will look up the Directory to determine the location of the queue.

The middleware may also use the Directory to store performance data on queue sizes, response times, message frequency, loading on processes, number of threads, and so on. It may access the Directory to find out the information it needs to balance the load between processes on multiple machines.

In essence, the Directory service is a fundamentally important part of the inner workings of middleware. A considerable amount of information needed to handle distributed computing and generated as a result of the actual running of the applications is stored in the Directory.

All middleware needs a Directory of some sort to make it work. So the next fundamental question we might ask is "what makes a good Directory?"

What makes a good Directory service?

A Directory service should be reliable, provide high availability, and provide extremely good performance if it is to give the sort of support needed to run a distributed application. But how do you build reliability, availability, and good performance into the design of a Directory service? The easiest way to show what makes a good Directory service is to describe some of the solutions used in middleware products and highlight their advantages and disadvantages.

The single file approach–Directory services of many of the CORBA products and some RPC products are based on a design where the Directory is stored on a single node. The file is not replicated or partitioned in any way. The administrator simply sets up the single file of data on that machine and then provides a configuration file on all the other machines that give the location of the Directory for use by the middleware.

Whenever a service is requested or process invoked, the middleware first looks up the local configuration file and then, using this, makes a call across the network to the Directory service to get the information it needs. The Directory itself is usually stored on disk. Only rarely is it copied into memory at system startup.

The advantages of this approach are that the administrator has only one file to create, along with the configuration files, so administrative overheads are quite low. It is also easier to restrict access to the file, thus ensuring only the administrator can change the information in it or look at its contents. The disadvantages, however are quite extensive.

First, a single file on a single node means that there is a single point of failure. If the node itself goes down, the file the Directory is stored on fails, or any of the lines to that node fail, the entire application fails.

Second, performance even of modest-sized applications and for any large applications could be severely affected, as every request from a client for a service requires the middleware to access the file across the network, incurring both the overheads of network communication and the additional overhead that results from shared access from multiple nodes and processes to the one Directory resource. Where the Directory is on disk, rather than in memory, further performance degradation may occur. Thus the single file approach does not provide a reliable, available, or high performance solution to the Directory service requirements.

File per machine–Many of the MOM products use this approach, and we will see that Microsoft's current Directory service is also based on this approach. In this approach, the Directory is a *host-specific file* containing information on objects and their IDs, users, groups, applications, and preferences plus other information relevant *to that host*. Thus each node contains the information that host and all its clients needs to operate.

The administrator generally has to set up each of these files manually. The setup may be possible via the network from a single remote console, which does ease the burden somewhat, although every file still has to be set up specifically. The alternative is for the administrator to have to actually physically go around to each node to set up the file—a really tedious task.

Overall, whichever method of setup is supported, this design option is an administratively complex and time-consuming one and one very prone to error. Much can change in a distributed application over time, and the administrator has to remember to make those changes on every node, every time the configuration changes. If he gets it wrong, the applications will fail, so this solution is not geared to high reliability.

It is also a solution that is more difficult to keep secure. By having data distributed over many nodes, the problems of restricting access to the data to only the administrator become much harder to achieve. But by having the information the node needs on the node, availability and performance are likely to be satisfactory.

Thus, this solution provides reasonably good availability and performance, but has the potential to provide poor reliability, is less secure, and also incurs a high administrative overhead.

Replicated file–In this approach, a single file of data is set up by the administrator containing all the information needed by the entire application or applications, and the middleware itself replicates this file on each node on the network. If the administrator changes the data, he or she changes the master copy on the main node, and the middleware then replicates the changes to all the other nodes.

Security is usually as easy to maintain as it is with the single file approach. In effect, no one can look at or change the data in the replicates as these are managed by the middleware itself. For all purposes, the replicated files are invisible to both the developer and administrator. Restrictions on access are then applied to the master copy in much the same way as with the single file approach.

Generally speaking, the data is held in memory—loaded upon system start-up—with backup of the data on disk. This solution provides excellent performance and availability, as all the information needed for an application is stored on the node—no network access is needed to obtain the data and contention for the shared Directory resource is lessened.

Performance is further improved as the data is loaded into memory upon system startup. Furthermore, the likelihood of the data's being incorrect is reduced, as the administrator has only to set up and create one file; he does not have to set up numerous files on each node manually.

There is a small price to be paid for this as the duplication of data and resulting storage needed is an additional cost. Generally speaking, however, this is a minor overhead.

A slightly larger problem may be caused if the configuration is an extremely large one with thousands of nodes. In this case, the memory needed to hold the entire configuration may actually be too great for smaller machines, and alternative solutions may have to be used. These often rely on the single file solution approach—a set of clients is given a configuration file that shows where their nearest Directory service node or nodes (for availability) is based. The clients then access this node to get Directory information with the overheads we saw in the description of the single file solution.

There are also other minor problems with this solution. If the master node fails, although all the other nodes can continue working on the replicated copies of the Directory, the administrator cannot update the master with the correct information until the master has been restored. Furthermore, the administrator still has to create the file and keep it up-to-date as the applications and their configuration change— incurring the slight risk that the information may not be up-to-date or correct, affecting reliability.

Replication with "publish/subscribe"–The solution to the above problems is achieved using the concept of a "publish and subscribe" Directory service.

The Directory is similar in principle to the replicated file but with some important differences. A single database of information is replicated across all nodes. This database contains all the information needed by all the applications being run using the middleware. But no single file is the master. Instead, each process registers all its resources—queues, methods, components, and so on—with the local Directory service. The Directory service on that node then replicates the information to all the other nodes.

By using this self-registering approach, coupled with replication, the Directory service is highly available (no single point of failure), reliable (the data is bound to be up-to-date), and the design provides excellent performance (all access can be from the node). Furthermore, it requires no administrative effort—saving time and reducing if not eliminating errors.

One additional advantage with this design of Directory service is that since all the processes must be running permanently in memory, and the Directory service knows the information it has is always up-to-date (that is, the server processes have registered themselves so the details of where they are is correct) the Directory service itself can monitor the processes to ensure they are still running and if any fail, restart them automatically. Thus this form of Directory service helps in automatic fault handling.

The directory is stored in memory on each machine. If a machine fails and is then restored or booted up, the directory "self-configures."

Because the Directory information is memory based, however, it suffers from the same limitations as those we saw for the simple replicated Directory—small machines may have difficulty holding the data on very large configurations in memory, requiring a compromise solution. Thus, although performance is potentially excellent, smaller client machines may suffer from slightly reduced performance because of the need to access another node to get Directory data. The use of "proxy Directory" services, as they are known, however, need not affect availability or reliability, which will continue to be excellent.

Another small disadvantage with this approach is that the developer may have to add code to his program to register the process and its resources. On the whole, this is a minor irritation to the developer rather than a major problem as he or she may have to write perhaps a single line of code to perform the registration. In the better products even this is not needed; the middleware performs the registration for the developer.

It should also be recognized that some of the information in the Directory—users, groups, access control lists, and so on—will still need to be set up manually by the administrator. This aspect of administration is not removed.

Another disadvantage with this approach is that it cannot be used with triggering. Why do I say this? In order for the processes to register themselves with the Directory service, they must be loaded into memory and be running permanently in memory. Where triggering is used, the processes are stored in files or libraries on disk and only loaded when they are needed. As such, they cannot register themselves as they are not executing processes.

This point is a rather interesting one as, generally speaking, the replicated/ publish/ subscribe type of Directory service is provided with heavy-duty enterprise-oriented products such as DCE and the DTPMs (Distributed Transaction Processing Monitors) like TOP END and Tuxedo. Enterprise-oriented middleware is geared towards high performance, availability, and reliability as key design goals of the entire product, and the concept of triggering is simply not one which is compatible with the idea of high performance applications. To trigger a process, the process has to be loaded. This degrades performance significantly, and the whole aim of transaction processing systems is that they should be high performance.

Thus, a publish/subscribe Directory service may provide a highly available, reliable, and high-performance Directory service, but the developer must remember that all the processes he needs must be permanently running in memory for the Directory to work. It also means that the nodes that store the components must have enough memory to be able to support permanently running server processes.

No Directory–This heading may totally confuse you, but it is worth describing one other solution that has been used to provide the equivalent of a Directory service, but where no Directory—database of information—is ever actually used.

It is a solution provided in the Visigenic VisiBroker product—an ORB based on CORBA but which uses its own unique way of providing Directory services. It is worth pointing out from the start that VisiBroker's Directory services are entirely geared towards finding objects—they provide none of the facilities for handling security, storing statistics, and so on, so the solution is limited. It is, however, quite a fascinating one.

CORBA does not include within its *core* specification any description of how objects should be found—in other words, a Directory service. The CORBA Naming service (their Directory service) is an additional COS (CORBA Object Services) component and one which does not have to be provided for an ORB to be deemed CORBA compliant. Consequently, the implementors of the early CORBA specifications could choose to provide any internal service they wanted to enable objects to be found on the network. This gave Visigenic the flexibility to design their own service and they used a technology they had already developed called SMART Agents.

VisiBroker as it stands without the Naming Service does not have a "Directory" or Naming file. Instead, the SMART Agent does all the work of finding objects. There need be only one copy of the Smart Agent on the network, or the administrator may decide to have more than one copy (for fault tolerance and performance reasons).

A server within VisiBroker contains one or more objects. It can be continuously running—that is, loaded up and running on a continual basis—or it can be installed in a library and then triggered when required. Where a server is continuously running and as such loaded into memory as an executing process, the skeleton within the server (libraries provided with the ORB) perform a UDP broadcast to find a Smart Agent. Once the server has found an agent (it could be any agent on the network; it doesn't matter which one), the server and agent are then aware of each other's existence. No connection, however, is established as UDP is a connectionless protocol.

The Agent and the server monitor each other using the ping protocol and UDP. If the Smart Agent crashes, the server recognizes that the connection has been broken and performs another UDP broadcast to find another Agent with which to connect. No Directory files or persistent information is kept in memory. If the Agent crashes or is removed, no trace is left that the Agent ever existed on that machine.

Where a server is kept in the library to be triggered, the administrator must set up an Implementation Repository on each machine that provides the names of the Servers on that machine and the file name (path name) of their location in the filing system on disk. A component of VisiBroker called the Object Activation Daemon then monitors the Implementation Repository and acts on behalf of the servers. In this case, the administrator must manually add and remove servers if he or she adds them to a library, removes them from the library, or changes their library name.

Instead of the servers establishing a communication link with the Smart Agent, the Object Activation Daemon establishes the communication. It also performs a UDP broadcast to find a Smart Agent. This time the Agent and the Object Activation Daemon monitor each other using the ping protocol and UDP. If the Smart Agent crashes, the Object Activation Daemon recognizes that the connection has been broken and performs another UDP broadcast to find another Agent with which to connect.

When the client wishes to communicate with a server, it first issues a UDP broadcast to find the nearest Smart Agent. This broadcast need only be issued once in the life of the client; from then on the client and Agent monitor each other using the ping protocol.

If the client wants to invoke an object, it can use the specific name of the object, or it can use a "type" name. Where the type name is used, the Smart Agent will pick an instance of the object on the network.

To find an object, the Smart Agent will examine the communications "links" it has (the pings). If it has established communication with the Object Activation Daemons, it will request the daemons to examine their Implementation Repositories. If the communication is direct with servers, the servers will be examined. Where the Smart Agent cannot find the object, it will perform a UDP broadcast to other Smart Agents requesting that they perform a search.

If the object is found through the Object Activation Daemon, it will load a copy of the server into memory. Once the server has been loaded, or where the server was already loaded, a direct connection is then established between the client and the server. Once the connection between client and server has been established, a direct TCP/IP connection is made rather than one based on UDP.

This solution is quite unique and novel, but it does have its limitations. From the availability viewpoint, the solution has the potential to provide good availability. By duplicating Smart Agents around the network, a Smart Agent should always be available to handle requests.

Reliability should also be good where the processes are not triggered, as the information is always going to be up-to-date. This solution incorporates the concepts of publish and subscribe, but in a different and novel way, and, as such, problems of out-of-date or inconsistent Directory information will not arise. Where triggering is used there is the possibility that errors are introduced, and there is also the additional administrative overhead associated with setting up all the Implementation Repositories.

But where I do see problems is in performance. A tremendous amount of network accesses are needed to find the agents, provide pinging to ensure the agent and servers are still in existence, and provide searches where local agents cannot find the object. It is not just the amount of network traffic that this solution incurs that is the problem, but the fact that most of the Directory type searches have to be made over the network—they are not local searches. So overall, this solution is not geared to high performance, although it is one providing reliability and availability.

In summary–Overall I believe the best solution is the replicated publish and subscribe Directory service, despite the limitations it imposes on triggering. It provides excellent availability and reliability, is geared towards extremely high performance, and incurs only a small overhead in the additional disk space needed to store replicated data. It can be made secure—the administrator can control who has access to the data and even where very large configurations are being used will scale well.

Even the problems caused by the use of memory to store the replicated directory information need not incur any significant overheads with only a possible slight degradation in performance caused by the need to access a proxy server Directory.

Microsoft's Directory Services

Microsoft's current Directory services are provided by the **Registry service**. Microsoft, however, plans to replace the Registry with a more sophisticated

Directory service in Windows NT version 5.0 (due 1998). This Directory is known as **Active Directory**.

In the next few sections, I will be describing the current Registry service and how it works, and then in the last sections of this chapter I will provide a little more detail of the Active Directory.

Microsoft's Registry service

The Registry that Microsoft uses now is a *host-specific file* containing information on objects and their IDs, users, groups, applications, and preferences plus other information relevant *to that host*. It also contains security information user password and ACLs. It is supported on the NT and 95 platforms.

Thus, the current Registry is of the type file per machine that we saw above. The Registry is stored on disk and not in memory. If the disk on which the Registry is based fails, the contents are lost unless the administrator has set up backup procedures using striped or mirrored disks.

The Registry contains the server name, the classID, the type, and the address. We saw earlier that within DCOM, servers are programs which can be the container for a number of components. The server is thus the name of the Server containing that component, the ClassID is the identifier of the component, the type simply describes what sort of component it is—proxy, EXE, or DLL—and the Address is one of the following:

▶ the pathname of the server DLL

▶ the pathname of the server EXE

▶ or the pathname to the object handle/proxy object's DLL

Proxy objects were described in detail in the chapter on COM; however, one proxy object exists for every remote component that a client could invoke. It thus serves as a special client side component acting on behalf of the server side component (thus the name proxy—it is the server component's proxy).

The Registry thus only contains information about components on that particular host. But, because of the existence of the proxy object, a sort of "index" exists to components on remote hosts. The proxy is a means of showing that that component does exist elsewhere (without actually giving its remote address).

One proxy exists per remote component, but there is nothing to stop a developer duplicating/copying the remote component and placing it on more than one host. Thus, because each Registry contains local data, it is possible using the current Registry architecture to place a component on more than one machine. In theory, it could also be placed in more than one server on the same machine. Thus, there is the *potential* for DCOM to support load balancing, as we saw in the chapter on MTS, as a request could be channeled to one or perhaps many copies of the same component scattered over the network.

When the server is installed, an application set up program for the server ensures the server itself creates entries in the Registry that point to the components. Components are thus generally registered when they are installed as part of the application setup program. Proxy objects also register themselves.

It is, however, possible to have a self-registering server. Where DLLs are used, the developer uses a special feature (HRESULT DllRegisterServer), which updates the Registry with all the classes implemented. Where EXEs are used, the developer uses special command line flags. Clearly, in either case, the code has to be written so that the server doesn't register itself over and over again, but even if it does, the only problem is the waste of processing; the Registry doesn't end up with duplicate entries.

In effect, there are two ways in which entries are created in the Registry. The first way is used when the server is loaded as an executable and executing process. In this case, the server registers itself and its components using commands the programmer must add to his program. The second way is for the administrator to provide a setup program that registers the server, which, in turn, registers its components. In both cases some support is thus given for publish and subscribe type services, but this time applied to a file per machine type of Directory.

But, DCOM's Registry is not self healing. If the component fails or is inadvertently removed, the administrator has to physically remove the entry from the Registry. So, although some features to help with reliability are built in, some problems with reliability may ensue, if the administrator forgets to keep the information up to date.

Either way, the administrator does not have to set up the Implementation Repository used in CORBA ORB types of products. Even where triggering is used, the setup program can be used to set up the information in the Registry.

All security information must be set up manually on each host.

The Registry contains information about what servers exist on the machine—but these will be servers in the library, not running instances of the server. The table used to hold details of the running servers is called the *Class Table* or *Running Object Table*.

A client can create an instance of a server in one of two ways. It can call the COM function CoCreateInstance, which creates an object with the given Class ID, or it can use a special COM class called the *Class Factory*, which is responsible for creating instances of the server. If the Class Factory is used, the client calls CoGetClassObject which obtains the interface pointer to the class factory object (IClassFactory) then uses this interface to ask the class factory to manufacture an object on its behalf. In fact, the more direct CoCreate-Instance function internally calls the CoGetClassObject anyway. It is at this point that the Vtable is populated with the pointers to the relevant objects and functions.

Once the Class factory has created the instance, the Class Table is updated to show that a new instance has been created on the machine. The Class Table thus provides a list of the Class IDs (identifiers of the components), together with Class Factory pointers to the currently running COM servers on that machine.

So how does DCOM find components at runtime? The DCOM component responsible for handling this is called the *Service Control Manager* (SCM).

When the client wants to find a component it uses the *Class Identifier* (CLSID)— the unique identifier of the component. The COM library contacts the local SCM and requests that the appropriate server be located.

The SCM then looks up its local Class Table to see if a server is already running on that host with that ID. If a server is already running, the client is simply given the pointer to the running server.

If no such server is running, the SCM then looks up the local Registry to see if the server can be found on that host. As we saw, COM servers can be DLLs or EXEs on the local machine or could be remotely located. If they are remotely located, they will be described as a "proxy" entry in the Registry.

If the server is an "in-process" DLL, the SCM returns the path name of the DLL and the COM library then uses the Class Factory to create an instance of the DLL. Once the Class factory has created the instance, the Class Table is updated to show that a new instance has been created on the machine.

If the server is not "in-process"—an EXE—the SCM uses the Class factory to create an instance of the EXE. Again, once the Class factory has created the instance, the Class Table is updated to show that a new instance has been created on the machine.

Where the server is remote, in other words, a proxy object exists for the component, the SCM contacts the SCMs running on all the machines to which it is connected. These SCMs search their host's Class Table and Registry in the same way that the local SCM operated. This searching process continues across machines until the component is either found, or the SCMs return with a message that the component cannot be found. At the moment, the first SCM to find the server is the one that is then used to invoke the component, but clearly there is the potential here for more sophisticated load-balancing algorithms to be employed if Microsoft wanted to.

Where the component can be found, the remote SCM establishes a connection with its Class Factory. It passes the pointer to this remote Class Factory back to the local SCM, which invokes (via an RPC) the remote Class Factory. The remote Class Factory then creates an instance of the remote component and updates the remote Class Table. The local SCM, meanwhile, uses the local Class Factory to create an instance of the proxy object. The proxy object is given a pointer to the remote component and communication can proceed—proxy and remote component communicate rather than client and remote component.

So how does Microsoft's current Registry stand up in our assessment of the design goals of available, secure, reliable, and high performance Directory services? Although some features are built into the Directory services that help in the registration of servers and components, the security information has to be set up manually on each machine, and the information on servers and components has to be kept up-to-date manually once it has been registered. There is thus a fairly high administrative overhead involved in maintaining the Registry information, and as a consequence, errors may creep in and reliability suffer.

Furthermore, although security checks can be applied to the Registry to prevent unauthorized access, the fact that these have to be set up on each node for each Registry is tedious, prone to error, and prone to abuse. As we all know, whenever anything starts to get tedious to perform, we tend not to do it, meaning that our administrator could well decide not to bother to set up all the restrictions on access to save himself some effort.

Availability should not be a problem. Each node has the information it needs to access components, and as such the applications will not be reliant on a single node.

But performance may not be so hot. Despite the fact that the file is a local one, each Registry only contains the addresses of the local processes. Where remote processes are to be accessed, the address has to be found by searching the Registries of other nodes—a process that both increases network traffic (and thus leads to performance degradation) and that itself incurs a performance overhead. A further overhead is incurred because accesses are disk not memory based. Overall, then, not an ideal solution— available maybe but not high performance, secure, and not giving the sort of full reliability we would want.

Active Directory

Microsoft fully realizes that the current Registry is limited, and as such their plans are for the Active Directory—a far more ambitious and extensive Directory service. The Active Directory is to be provided with Windows NT version 5.0; however, it is worth mentioning that many of the new features to be released as part of Windows NT 5.0 were provided to developers on a CD at the Microsoft Developer's conference in Los Angeles towards the end of 1996.

Replication–Active Directory will be based on replicated files. A master copy will contain the information, and this information will then be replicated across all the nodes in the network. This contrasts with the approach used now for the Registry, where each host has its own unique table of data relevant to that host. This master file is planned to support "10 million entries."

Active Directory is due to be based on a "high performance storage engine." Note that Active Directory will *initially* only cover Windows systems; it will not be extended to other Unix or mainframe hosts, but other companies are planning to support it.

Contents–The Active Directory will contain far more information than the Registry—networks, users, devices, domain names, database files, security information, e-mail addresses, and so on. It will also support versioning of information and is due to be extensible. It will act as the master database for runtime information for most of Microsoft's products.

Microsoft is merging the functions of the numerous directories they now have—the ones used in Back Office, Exchange, the Registry, and so on. In effect, all these products will be adapted to support the one Active Directory, including DCOM.

Perhaps equally interesting is that Microsoft has started to gain support from a number of third-party vendors, all of whom look like they will use the Active Directory to store the data they need for their products, or reuse the data already stored on it. Bay Networks and Cisco Systems have both expressed support for the Active Directory. Bay Networks already had a close relationship with Microsoft, and their routing software was included in Steelhead—the project that places routing functionality within Windows NT.

Cisco has licensed Microsoft's Active Directory and intends to port it to other Unix platforms as well as use it in its router software.

ADSI–In the future, Active Directory will be accessed by an interface—known as the Active Directory Server Interface (ADSI) and formerly known as ODSI (Open Directory Service Interface). ADSI has already been released with an SDK as an add-on to Windows NT Server version 4.0. ADSI not only provides the interface to Active Directory, it also provides the interface to the Registry in Windows NT 4, and is intended to support NetWare DS and 3x binderies, LDAP 2.0, HTTP, and DNS Internet services as well as X.500.

This is where the Translation service in the diagram marked "Directory" comes in. Microsoft in effect is providing or intending to provide drivers/translation software, which converts the ADSI calls into the native calls of these other Directory services—providing support for "legacy" or existing directories. Note that ADSI does not remove the administration nightmare that comes from having this number of Directories, nor does it solve the problem caused by the fact that all these directories may contain different information, but it does ease things a little from a developer's viewpoint and also makes it possible for the administrator to gradually ease away (where possible) from using third-party directory services towards using just Active Directory. By using ADSI, the developer should be able to provide users with single logon across multiple directories, as well as products such as RACF.

LDAP–Lightweight Directory Access Protocol is an important part to this interface because by supporting LDAP Microsoft also provides the developer with access to any Directory system that itself supports LDAP as well as access to its own Directory over the Web. Netscape, Novell, Lotus, and Banyan have all pledged support for the protocol, and DCE is also getting an LDAP interface. LDAP is complementary to and a strict subset of the DAP (Directory Access protocol) developed for access to X.500 directory systems.

LDAP also provides access to X.500 Directories but reduces the resource requirements typically associated with DAP. LDAP is targeted at simple applications or tools such as Web browsers. It is carried directly over TCP (reliable transport), uses a lightweight BER encoding scheme, and supports asynchronous communication.

Again, it is important to emphasise the difference between the protocol, used to access the directory and the content of the directory, which remains the preserve of each vendor. Harmonization of the protocol for accessing a directory doesn't prevent the developer's having to know its contents.

Microsoft plans to support a number of leading naming conventions in Active Directory:

▶ HTTP URLs (universal resource locators)

▶ X.500 naming conventions

▶ LDAP URLs

▶ RFC833 names

▶ RFC1779 distinguished names

▶ UNCs

Active Directory and the Repository–In a wider context, it is interesting to note that with the arrival of Active Directory, Microsoft will have two "repositories."

Active Directory is effectively Microsoft's runtime repository containing information about things used at runtime by its software products and the applications. Microsoft's other "repository," called the *Microsoft Repository*, is the repository used to store development information. Given that a considerable amount of information about "things" used during development is often used at runtime—objects, versions, users, groups, programs, machines/devices, and so on—I wonder why they didn't combine the two from the start. If the administrator decides to use these repositories, he or she still has the problem of duplication to contend with. Microsoft did state, however, that the intention was to combine the two long term.

Microsoft's repository was released towards the end of 1996. It was a joint development with Texas Instruments and uses Unified Modeling Language (a language developed by Rational) to access the contents. Microsoft's repository is now part of Visual Studio, and a tool called Visual Modeler is used to generate data for the repository. Source Safe is used for management of the contents.

Thus, the tools supporting DCOM that we mention in the development section—Professional and Enterprise Editions of Visual Basic 5, as well as Visual Studio—use or are planning to use the repository. Popkin, Rational, Select, TI, and LogicWorks are also committed to supporting UML and the repository.

In Summary

So overall are Microsoft's Directory services available, secure, reliable, and high performance? As we saw, I believe the current Registry service has its failings. Availability should not be a problem, but security, reliability, and performance may be.

There is a fairly high administrative overhead involved in maintaining the Registry information, and as a consequence, errors may creep in and reliability suffer. Furthermore, although security checks can be applied to the Registry to prevent unauthorized access, the fact that these have to be set up on each node for each Registry is tedious and prone to error.

We also saw that performance may not be that good because where remote processes are to be accessed, the address has to be found by searching the Registries of other nodes. A further overhead is incurred because accesses are disk, not memory, based.

Given that the current Registry has these weaknesses, the Active Directory is a most important development and one that will be key to whether DCOM can provide enterprise level support or not.

Overall, the initial plans look promising. Active Directory has the potential to provide good performance and availability, as all the information needed for an application will be stored on the node—no network access is needed to obtain the data and contention because the shared Directory resource is lessened. At the time of writing, there were no plans for the data to be held in memory and loaded upon system startup from disk, so performance may suffer slightly here, but there may be good reasons for this approach.

We saw that if the configuration is an extremely large one with thousands of nodes, the memory needed to hold the entire configuration may actually be too great for smaller machines. On the whole, Microsoft is geared towards support for smaller machines, and as such a solution is needed to cover this problem. The alternative solution—that reliant on the single file solution approach (a set of clients is given a configuration file that shows where their nearest Directory service node or nodes is based)—may have been deemed unsatisfactory. In this case, a directory based solely on disk is an attractive alternative, even though it has performance implications.

Active Directory looks as though it will also be reliable. The administrator will only have to set up and create one master file; he or she will not have to set up numerous files on each node manually. If publish and subscribe is added to the services, reliability will further improve.

Security should also be easy to maintain as, in effect, no one will be able to look or change the data in the replicates as these are managed by the middleware itself. Restrictions on access can be applied to the master copy—and are more likely to be applied.

Altogether then, Active Directory looks to be a very promising development. Its failings?

One failing is that a question mark hangs over the Directory's ability to handle load balancing. If each component/class is allowed only one address, then load balancing will not be possible as the component will only be capable of being stored once on the network (as it can only have one address). As the new Active Directory evolves it will be important to see how the final architecture copes with this problem.

Another more obvious failing is that its introduction is likely to cause considerable disruption, affecting as it does not only DCOM services such as MSMQ, SCM, and the Administration routines but many of Microsoft's other products. It is worth remembering, for example, that at the moment, MSMQ has its own Directory and uses the Registry to store queues, so considerable adaptation may be needed to merge MSMQ's Directory with Active Directory and devise a new way of supporting queues.

Similarly, all the developments I have described are currently plans, not a product, so we are all going to have to wait for it to appear. This is no simple development that Microsoft has undertaken, and time scales could also well slip.

18

Administration

► Currently Windows NT specific service

► Support given to installation, performance monitoring, problem monitoring, configuration, and some problem resolution

► Management Console in future will greatly improve administrator's interface

► Zero Administration Initiative will also help to ease installation

Administration services are, as their name suggests, used by the administrator to install applications and middleware, to configure the applications and middleware itself, to resolve errors, to monitor performance, and to handle faults. DCOM's administration services are part of Windows NT and accessed from the NT menu. The tools available to the administrator cover far more than those associated specifically with DCOM and include Backup facilities (for saving to local tape drives, for example) and a Disk administration utility (to enable the administrator to view and configure partitions on the hard drive). In this chapter, however, we will be looking at those administration services specific to support of DCOM, and we will (as we have done in the other chapters) be looking at the current offerings and the future plans.

The Range of Tools

Transaction Server, Windows NT, and MSMQ are currently administered using their own **Explorer** tools. These tools provide cross-platform administration, but not cross-operating system administration. All the tools, as one would expect, are GUI based and include a point-and-click interface with wizards and help.

Figure 18.1
Administration
services

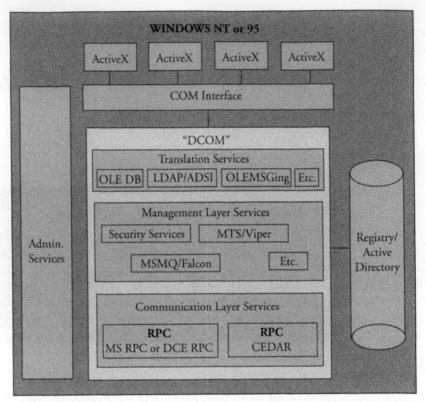

At the moment, the tools are somewhat fragmented. The administrator must go to one set of products to administer one set of software and another set for another type of software. All this is due to change, however, with the introduction of the **Microsoft Management Console**. In fact, by the time you read this MMC should be released. The Microsoft Management Console is just one of a number of enhancements Microsoft is adding to ease the administrative burden (and incidentally improve scaleability, as ease of administration improves scaleability) with enhancements to be added to Windows NT version 5.0.

The Microsoft Management Console will provide a single central point of access to the tools for administration and the resources on the network. The Console will use the familiar Windows 95 style of interface, or plans are afoot to include a Web-based style of access to the tools and resources.

Through the Console the administrator will be able to access all remote processes and machines—the console thus provides a means of administration from a single point in the network of all other resources on the network.

Resources include printers, drives as well as machines themselves, and the software on them.

Tools for centralized administration will, in the future, be available from both Microsoft themselves and from third-party suppliers. These tools will "snap-in" to the console, providing a customized toolset to undertake the tasks the administrator needs to perform.

The tools currently provided with Windows NT that can be used specifically to support distributed applications include the Performance Monitor, User Manager, Event Viewer, Windows NT Diagnostics, and the Task Manager. SNMP links with other tools either already provided or planned to be provided.

The administrator has a number of very specific tasks to perform. These include installation of the software (applications and middleware), configuring of this software (including the set up of security and Directory information), event and problem monitoring (we looked a little a this in the chapter on security), problem resolution, and performance monitoring. We will now look at how the tools provided with Windows NT, Transaction Server, and MSMQ help in supporting these tasks.

Installation

Installation is the task of actually installing the software on the target machines including any distribution of the software to its destination. Installation is not a particularly well-supported function at the moment in Windows NT, Transaction Server, or MSMQ.

Installation of Transaction server, for example, is via a scripted setup in the SDK. It is not achieved remotely—each host must be set up separately. On installation of MSMQ, the administrator uses SQL Enterprise Manager to install SQL Server, but uses separate tools to configure the PECs, PSCs, BSCs, queues, and so on. In this case, the installation can be achieved remotely from a Windows NT machine.

But the installation process is not applied in a uniform way across all types of software. All this is due to change in part with the introduction of the Management Console and *Zero Administration Initiative*.

The Zero Administration Initiative is a set of technologies designed to support centralized administration and control of multiple desktops. It aims to include mobile computers as well as office-based systems. The aim is to remove the guesswork from technical support work, by providing the administrator with a way of controlling what is on the desktop.

The administrator will be able to "lock" the desktop configurations and then automatically install software updates to the operating system and applications. The installation will either be directly controlled by the administrator from a remote centralized console, or the updates may be automatically applied from an automated server.

When a user "signs on" to the server, a conversation between host and client will take place to determine the "state" of the software on the client machine. As a result of the conversation, new DLLs and EXEs will then be installed automatically. The intention is to use existing information on Profiles to aid in the installation process.

Thus, the addition of the Zero Administration Initiative does look as though it will greatly help in the burden of installation, although clearly it can only be applied to desktops and may not cover some of the more complex tasks associated with the installation of middleware.

Configuration

Configuration is defined as the setting up of all the parameters, data, queues, files, and other configuration data needed to run the applications at runtime using the middleware. It can include setting the parameters needed for load balancing, deciding how many threads to include in the thread pool, deciding how many and how big the queues will be and how overflow will be handled, and setting global timeout and retry parameters. It will also include the setup of the Directory information and security data (e.g., users, passwords, ACLs, and so on).

Setting up the Directory–As we saw in the last chapter, there are two ways in which entries are created in the Registry. The first way is used when the server is loaded as an executable and executing process. In this case, the server registers itself, and its components using commands the programmer must add to his program. The second way is for the administrator to provide a setup program that registers the server, which in turn registers its components. In this latter case, work is required by the administrator.

The administrator must also maintain the Registry once it is set up. If the component dies or is removed, the administrator has to physically remove the entry from the Registry.

Configuring transaction data–Transaction Server Explorer can be used to configure and administer components, packages, servers, clients, transactions, and security. The administrator can manage transactions from the interface as well as change display parameters, reset the log, and start and stop the DTC.

MSMQ–MSMQ Enterprise Explorer is used to administer MSMQ. It provides a tree view of the logical configuration of the enterprise and by using the tool the administrator can view and modify properties of the enterprise, sites, computers, queues, and connected networks. Sites, CNs, and PECs are all displayed from the root of the enterprise, and each site contains a view of the available servers, routing servers, and computers, each of which can have one or more queues. MSMQ Explorer also displays all replicated site information.

Setting up the security data–We have already seen how the Security information is created using primarily the User Manager. The table of users, passwords, and public keys is stored with the Registry on each host, and as such must be set up on every machine by the administrator using this utility. Each table holds host-specific information—the users allowed to access that host. This is likely to change in the future with the introduction of the Active Directory, a service I described in the last chapter, as the Active Directory is to hold security data and will be a central store for information, replicated around the network.

Event/Problem Monitoring, Capture, and Diagnosis

Event or problem monitoring is the monitoring of the application, machines, network, and system software in order to capture "events" things that have happened in the system whether these are errors/faults or simply things needing a warning message or information message. The term event is intended to cover all sorts of events—security events, application events, operating system events, middleware events, DBMS events, and so on.

Monitoring the events is the start of the process. The actual aim of the process is to monitor and then capture the events so that the administrator can analyze the information and act on the analysis. By using the information he or she may adapt the configuration, change the installation, change the application design, and so on. In fact, his or her job may simply involve informing other administrators of the problem for them to resolve—the DBMS administrator, for example.

Monitor and capture

The Windows Event log is an important part of the administrator's toolkit and is used by all the other tools. Windows NT Event logs are kept for each machine. In other words, there is no centralized event log for the entire system, although SNMP can be used to provide this.

We saw in an earlier chapter on security that the Event log is used to record security breaches and violations, but it is also used to record other sorts of event. Each NT workstation or server in fact has three event logs:

▶ a system log

▶ a security log

▶ an application log

The system log is used to record configuration problems, state of services, startup, shutdown, and use of peripherals.

Security events cover successful accesses and failures—cases where access was denied. Security permissions can be set from the appropriate Explorer tool. The audit policy has to be set for each server to specify which actions to audit (objects, users) and which types (success, failure, both).

The application log is used to record application events, which can be for information, warnings, and error messages.

The messages sent to the log all have the type of message, the date, time, source, user, eventid, and computer. Although problems are logged, serious problems are also written to the console.

Diagnosis

Events can be viewed from each Explorer tool or from the Windows NT Event Viewer. Event logs can also be viewed using SNMP links to SMS tools—Netview, etc.

Whereas each Explorer tool displays events only related to that particular tool—MSMQ Explorer, for example, displays events only of type MSMQ—the Event Viewer covers all events but supports sorting, filtering, and searching of events.

Problem resolution

Problem resolution tools are there to help in resolving problems once they have either been identified by the administrator by analysis of the event information, or once they have been identified by the event monitor itself. Thus, for example, the administrator may realize from analysis of the event log that a transaction is caught in a deadly embrace and needs to be terminated manually. In this case, specific functions may be available to help him or her perform this problem resolution task.

Alternatively, the event monitor could, for example, identify that a server process has failed and, using the data, trigger a middleware process to restart the server process automatically.

In the first example, administrator intervention is needed, and the administrator uses the problem resolution tools after he or she has identified a problem exists. In the latter case, the process is entirely automatic, no administrator intervention is needed—all problem resolution is handled automatically.

As we saw, DCOM performs little in the way of automatic problem resolution. There is no automatic fault handling, and those tools there are to support problem resolution are currently somewhat specialized and administrator controlled. The administrator can resolve transactions from the Transaction Server interface, for example, as well as reset the log and start and stop the DTC.

In the future, more facilities are expected in this area. The Zero Administration Initiative, for example, is due to support remote problem diagnosis and resolution.

Performance Monitoring

Performance Monitoring is the capture of quantitative data on the performance of the applications, middleware, and network to analyze the information and take corrective action to improve the configuration and, thus, its performance. The middleware should monitor times (maximum, minimum, average, and median) and volumes (maximum, minimum, average, and median).

Windows NT has a Performance Monitor and Performance Analyzer. The Task Manager also provides a simple graph of processor time taken by each application and can monitor process status.

Transaction Server–With the Transaction Server Performance Monitor, the administrator can monitor performance and view transaction statistics. The statistics collected can be cumulative or current. Current statistics can be such things as the number of active transactions, maximum number of active transactions, and number of in-doubt transactions.

The aggregate figures can cover such things as the number of committed, aborted, forced commit, and forced abort transactions. Other statistics covered include the duration of transactions.

MSMQ–MSMQ Explorer is used to monitor the performance of MSMQ. Queue, session, queue manager, and other objects can be monitored. Also included is a network monitor parser that enables the administrator to monitor messages on the network. Two parsers are included—one compatible with

Windows NT Server Network Monitor and the other compatible with SMS Network Monitor.

In Summary

Microsoft's tools for the administrator are actually vastly better than many of the CORBA ORB tools or tools with RPC products—even DCE, which in its raw form provides command line and very basic administration utilities (although many add-ons from third parties have improved this situation). It also has the advantage of being from a central console covering the entire network—a feature not often provided in MOM products, for example.

But it cannot yet match the sophistication of DTPM products and their administration tools, which already provide centralized administration from a single console and provide unified monitoring, installation, configuration, and problem resolution tools. Perhaps of most importance, however, is that Microsoft's administration tools only cover Windows NT—a really serious deficiency that will make administration on other platforms something of a problem. DTPM products soundly beat DCOM in this respect as all the DTPM tools provide a single common central console for administration with the functionality I have described on all the platforms they support—Unix, Windows (all sorts of Windows) mainframe, AS/400, and so on.

So, on the whole, at the moment DCOM administration can be characterized as being better than many middleware products, but not yet as good as the best products on the market.

19

In Summary

Like all summary chapters in books, this is the one place where you will tend to see what the author really thinks about their subject matter. This chapter is no exception, so if you don't want to be bombarded by my opinions, stop reading here!

Let me start with the good things.

Figure 19.1 →

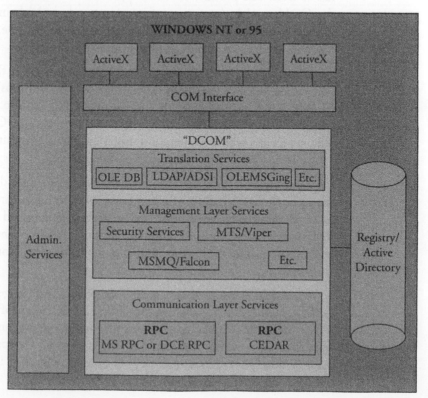

Figure 19.1
Summary of services

The Strengths of DCOM

Visionary–There is no doubt that what Microsoft has produced with DCOM is visionary stuff. They have provided middleware—an infrastructure for building distributed systems—that can be used with components, is accessed using a common interface based on the same component model, and that encompasses a vast range of services.

Integrated–This is an enormously powerful concept. It is worth pointing out that no other middleware products on the market are built in this way with all the services a developer may need to build a distributed system integrated within one product and with one interface to access all the services.

All the other vendors provide a particular type of middleware—DTPM, RPC, MOM product. If you want to use messaging with distributed transaction processing you usually have to use a MOM product with a DTPM. With DCOM you have no need to do this—practically all the services you need are built into DCOM and provided using the same interface.

What this means from the developer's point of view is that he or she only has to learn one product and one approach. After mastering the concepts in the COM model, the notion of interfaces and methods invocation, and the service interfaces that do exist, the developer is well on the way to being able to build most types of application with the one product.

Cheap–And DCOM is cheap—perhaps we should say that DCOM is free with Windows NT, but nothing really comes free. The cost of Windows NT is being adjusted to reflect the increased functionality, so in fact it is being paid for in a different way. But comparatively speaking, DCOM is exceptionally good value when compared to other middleware products.

Good services–Some of the services in DCOM are also particularly well thought out and compare very favorably with other middleware products. I particularly like MSMQ, which is a very well thought through product and uses exceptionally novel ways of achieving guaranteed delivery services, deferred delivery services, polling, pushing, and routing that are highly advanced. Transaction Server also shows considerable promise. The transaction services themselves are very good.

Microsoft–I am now seeing the little phrase "no one gets fired for buying IBM" changed to "no one gets fired for buying Microsoft." What any purchaser wants is a stable base on which to build systems, and a stable product comes from a stable company—a big successful company—with lots of money, massive revenues, and many customers. Microsoft isn't going to disappear (not within many programmers' career lifetimes anyway), and use of any Microsoft products does ensure a relative measure of stability.

The Weaknesses of DCOM

Complex–I have tried to simplify things in this book to help in the understanding of DCOM and to provide you with an idea of what you can do with the services it provides. What I have not done at any stage is expose you to the actual interfaces you'll have to use or the sequence of exchanges needed to perform various tasks.

The point is that DCOM and its interfaces are complex—perhaps unnecessarily so. It may be a function of the fact that object/component-based communication is being used, I'm not sure, but the calls are very low level and also high in number.

I have given you some idea of the complexity. The description on triggers, for example, should have given an inkling that triggering from the programmer's point of view was error prone. You should also come away with the impression that multithreading was not for the fainthearted. Furthermore, you should also have gained a feeling for the complexity of the Directory service interfaces as I explained the need for class factories.

But why is DCOM so complex?

If we take a product like MQSeries (with only four basic commands) or BEAmessageQ (with perhaps only 20–30) and compare them with DCOM (which has literally hundreds of service interfaces), you start to wonder what has gone wrong. All these products use a function-based API, not object-based invocations.

CORBA is actually worse than DCOM. Some CORBA ORBs have over 500 sets of interfaces for service invocation that provide only very basic functionality—nowhere near the functionality of DCOM.

I have yet to decide whether it is a weakness of object technology itself—that is, object technology creates complexity and results in low-level invocation—or whether it is because the DCOM or CORBA developers are themselves used to low-level programming and are unaware for the need to hide the complexity from the average programmer. Perhaps it is both. Certainly a function-based API seems to be able to capture in only one simple call what in an object-based world often takes several invocations.

Does the low level of the interfaces matter?

If low-level interfaces are used or a complex command set, in the first place applications become harder to program and productivity suffers. In other words, it will take longer to build an application based on DCOM than one based on many of the other non-CORBA or -DCOM middleware products.

In the second place, the more commands there are, the easier it is for the programmer to make a mistake. A third, and perhaps less obvious problem, is that by using a low-level set of interfaces, DCOM itself will be difficult for Microsoft to evolve and enhance—programmers will have used services exposed to them rather than hidden from them, so any change to the services will necessitate either considerable work by the programmer or an upgrade path from Microsoft that preserves the old service interfaces. The more interfaces are provided, and the lower level they are, the more opportunity there is for them to be misused too, which means that any upgrade to the interfaces Microsoft applies could have completely unforeseen consequences in your programs because the programmer used them in an unusual way.

One of the major middleware vendors recently said to me that there is only one way to provide reliable, high performance, available middleware—middleware that could be enhanced easily—and that is to hide *everything* from the developer and automate all the services: automatic multitasking, automatic security, automatic failover, automatic restart, automatic Directory services, and automatic error handling. All the programmer should need to do is send a message and get a message. I think he was right.

Legacy system integration difficult– It is clear that Microsoft is having as much difficulty as the other ORB vendors in integrating "legacy" technology (for legacy read not object/component based)—RDBMSs, existing procedural language-based applications, network DBMSs, other operating systems (such as MVS), simple flat files (like VSAM or ISAM), application packages, and so on.

Integration in DCOM has been achieved via a quite complex set of drivers, translators, proxy objects, and gateways. The more "legacy" technology needs to be accessed, the more complex is the overall environment.

In general, it should be clear that the more intermediate software layers are used, the more processing power is needed and the greater becomes the risk of slowing processing, increasing the likelihood of error and increasing the difficulty of finding where errors came from.

Oddly, it is the use of component based technology that is the problem here. The rest of most companies' systems and databases are procedurally based. In fact all development up to now has been procedurally based. Object/component technology turns this approach on its head, but by doing this the object technology inventors create a world that is difficult to marry successfully with all that has gone before.

Component-based technology may be (may being the operative word) a good idea in theory, but it doesn't look so attractive if you then cannot access or use everything you have already developed.

New and possibly unstable–Microsoft's middleware products have taken some time to come to final fruition and are only now beginning to take shape. The potential purchaser needs to be aware that the pieces in this vast puzzle are still not all in place—MSMQ had only just been released at the time of writing this, the Active Directory will not be available until 1998 (or later) and is likely to affect the design of MSMQ, the Zero Administration Initiative with Management Console is also not due until 1998, and so on.

Some of the pieces are also very new and as such will need some time to settle down (like most release 1 software)—particularly Transaction Server. Thus even though the picture does look impressive, it is still some way from being fully complete and it is all in a state of flux.

Don't let this totally put you off, however; this particular weakness will obviously disappear in time. But it should affect when you decide to use DCOM—perhaps waiting until things have settled down a bit.

Not yet enterprise level–DCOM cannot be described as "enterprise-level" middleware. What do I mean by enterprise level? Enterprise middleware can be used by a company across the entire company on all its machines to support applications of many types (transaction processing, query processing, heavy duty, light duty, high volume, or low volume). It is also geared towards high availability, high reliability, and excellent performance. So what does make an enterprise-level product? The services I believe make a middleware product into an enterprise-level product are:

▶ fully automated end-to-end security (all platforms including non-Microsoft)

▶ fully automated multitasking (or multithreading)

▶ fully automatic load balancing

▶ advanced fault handling services such as failover, automatic restart, and recovery

▶ totally automated triggering or no triggering in the case of transaction processing

▶ automated memory management (or none being required)

- ▶ multiplatform remote administration services and setup
- ▶ a replicated publish/subscribe directory service
- ▶ full context bridging (all platforms)
- ▶ a distributed shared memory service
- ▶ a distributed time service
- ▶ fully distributed transaction processing support (on multiple platforms)
- ▶ full message queuing support (on multiple platforms)

Microsoft still has some way to go to catch up with the really heavy-duty DTPMs or DCE, which are the only products on the market currently that can be deemed enterprise level.

Other platform support is weak–I explained in the chapter on other platforms that DCOM was being ported to other platforms by Digital, HP, Silicon Graphics, Software AG, and with some input from Level 8 for MSMQ.

A reminder of the other platforms being supported is shown in Table 19.1.

But Microsoft's entire middleware strategy and services are, not surprisingly, entirely dependent on the user having Windows NT as their strategic platform, and this should not be forgotten.

This is fine if the user wants to go this route, but if the developer has a mix of platforms at the moment—Unix, mainframe, and Windows, with no one platform being strategic—it will limit the architecture of the systems being built and may make design more difficult. The developer loses a great deal of flexibility by having to use the Windows NT platform as the main location of services and focus of development. The emphasis upon Windows NT as the prime platform is inevitable given the tight integration between Windows NT and the middleware services.

This approach is excellent from Microsoft's point of view—they can optimize the performance of DCOM, but it becomes extremely difficult to provide an exact functional match of all the middleware services on other platforms. If Software AG, for example, was to provide an exact copy functionally on the other platforms, it would have to port all DCOM *and* many embedded Windows NT services to Unix and the mainframe—an almost impossible task. The alternative route, and the one they are taking, is to port some services, but provide *access* to Windows NT and some other middleware services from the other platforms. What this means is that many services we might find useful are confined to Windows NT, and this situation is not likely to change.

Table 19.1 *Platform support*

Operating system		DCOM	Who
UNIX	AIX	*Planned*	Software AG
	HP-UX	*Planned*	HP, Software AG
	Solaris	YES	Software AG
	SINIX	*Planned*	Software AG
	Linux	*Planned*	Software AG
	SCO UnixWare	*Planned*	Software AG
	Digital Unix	*Planned*	Digital, Software AG
	IRIX	YES	Silicon Graphics
PC	Windows 95	YES	Microsoft
	Windows NT WS	YES	Microsoft
	Windows NT Svr	YES	Microsoft
	Macintosh	YES	Microsoft
Propty			
	Open MVS	YES	Software AG
	OS/400	*Planned*	Software AG
	OpenVMS	*Planned*	Digital, Software AG

I do find this one of the more limiting—perhaps the most limiting—aspect of DCOM.

Middleware should provide an infrastructure on which to build applications spanning a whole host of platforms. In fact, its very purpose is to ensure that a company's investment in the machines and the applications and databases that run on those machines is not wasted. By using middleware, the company can reuse all the legacy data, access legacy applications, and link together what were previously islands of data and function.

Microsoft almost seem to have provided a middleware product that can only be used for building new applications. What is the point of this?

In the following tables, I have provided a summary of the services provided by DCOM and whether they are provided on other platforms or not. The tables have been divided up into "Communication-level services," "Management-Level services," "Translation-Level services," and "Other services" in line with the diagram I have been using throughout this book.

Table 19.2 *Communication-level services*

Service	Other platforms?	Windows NT
Pack/Unpack	YES	YES
Translate Data formats	Generally yes	YES
Buffer packing	YES	YES
Compression/Decompression	NO	NO
Long message handling	NO	NO
Session management	YES	YES
Network calling	YES	YES
Transmission coordination	YES	YES
Fault handling	YES	YES
Client retries	YES	YES
Client time-out	YES	YES
Server retries	YES	YES
Alternative server search	NO	NO
Automatic server restart	NO	NO
Failover	NO	NO
Triggering	YES	YES
Automated?	NO	NO
Context bridging	NO	YES (TCP/IP, UDP, IPX/SPX, NetBIOS, LU6.2)
Communication options		
Request/reply	YES	YES

Table 19.2 *Communication-level services (Continued)*

Service	Other platforms?	Windows NT
One way	NO	NO
Broadcast/Multicast (Outgoing Interface)	Not clear at the time of writing	YES
Memory Management	Basic YES	YES
Automatic?	NO	NO
Distributed Shared memory	NO	NO
Shared memory single host	NO	YES
Internet version?	NO	NO

Table 19.3 *Management layer services*

Service	Other platforms?	Windows NT
Thread support	YES (but different from Windows NT)	YES
Automatic creation?	NO	With MTS only
Automatic lock handling?	NO	NO
Security	YES (but not same as Windows NT)	
Authentication		
User/password	YES	YES
Digital certificates	Internet only	YES
Smart cards	NO	YES
Authorization	NO (or alternative approach)	YES
Confidentiality		
Public key	YES (Internet)	YES
Secret key	via third parties only	via third parties
Integrity checking	YES	Some
Nonrepudiation	YES (Internet)	YES
Audit	Some on some platforms	YES

Table 19.3   *Management layer services (Continued)*

Service	Other platforms?	Windows NT
Load balancing	NO	NO
Distributed Transaction support	NO	YES
Transaction Buffer Pool	NO	YES
MSMQ (Message queuing)	NO (some client gateways)	YES
Polling/pulling/ notification		YES
Prioritization?		YES
Broadcast/multicast		YES
Guaranteed delivery		Mostly yes
Deferred delivery		YES
Message routing		YES
Static or Dynamic?		Static
Distributed File service	NO	YES
Distributed Time service	NO	NO
Single host time service	NO	YES

Table 19.4   *Translation services*

Service	Other platforms?	Windows NT
OLE DB	NO	YES
OLEMSGing	NO	YES
Structure storage	YES	YES

Table 19.5 *Other services*

Service	Other Platforms?	Windows NT
Administration	NO	
Installation		Part
Configuration		YES
Event monitoring		YES (not central)
Problem resolution		Minor
Performance monitoring		YES
Directory		
Single file	NO	NO
File per machine	Registry	Registry
Replicated file	*Planned*	*Active Directory (planned)*
Publish/subscribe	NO	NO

So Overall?

On the whole, DCOM and all the services it supports is an attractive proposition for any user contemplating using Windows NT as their strategic platform and are happy with the component-based interface. Long term, DCOM will probably emerge to be a major player in the middleware area, but not the only player.

I do feel DCOM is a less attractive proposition for heavy users of Unix and the mainframe or other non-Windows platforms simply because there may not be the same level of support provided on these platforms—look at the DTPM products or DCE; they provide an attractive alternative.

Index

Other Books from Digital Press

Building an Optimizing Compiler by Robert Morgan
1997   300pp   pb   1-55558-179-X

Migrating to Windows NT by Steve Heath
1997   450pp   pb   1-55558-185-4

Oracle8 in Windows NT by Lilian Hobbs
1998   350pp   pb   1-55558-190-0

SQL Server 6.5: Performance Optimization and Tuning by Ken England
1997   250pp   pb   1-55558-180-3

TCP/IP Explained by Philip Miller
1996   450pp   pb   1-55558-166-8

Windows NT/95 for UNIX Professionals by Donald Merusi
1997   200pp   pb   1-55558-181-1

Windows NT Infrastructure Design by Mike Collins
1998   450pp   pb   1-55558-170-6

Windows NT Security Guide by Stewart S. Miller
August 1998   352pp   pb   1-55558-211-7

. . . .

Feel free to visit our web site at: http://www.bh.com/digitalpress

These books are available from all good bookstores or in case of difficulty call:
1-800-366-2665 in the U.S. or +44-1865-310366 in Europe.

E-MAIL MAILING LIST

An e-mail mailing list giving information on latest releases, special promotions, offers and other news relating to Digital Press titles is available. To subscribe, send an e-mail message to majordomo@world.std.com.
Include in message body (not in subject line): subscribe digital-press

Printed and bound by CPI Group (UK) Ltd, Croydon, CR0 4YY

03/10/2024

01040342-0004